ENCOUNTERS WITH ANCIENT EGYPT

# Views of Ancient Egypt since Napoleon Bonaparte:

imperialism, colonialism and modern appropriations

UCL
PRESS
Institute of Archaeology

Encounters with
Ancient
Egypt

## Titles in the series

### Ancient Egypt in Africa
*Edited by David O'Connor and Andrew Reid*

### Ancient Perspectives on Egypt
*Edited by Roger Matthews and Cornelia Roemer*

### Consuming Ancient Egypt
*Edited by Sally MacDonald and Michael Rice*

### Imhotep Today: Egyptianizing architecture
*Edited by Jean-Marcel Humbert and Clifford Price*

### Mysterious Lands
*Edited by David O'Connor and Stephen Quirke*

### 'Never had the like occurred': Egypt's view of its past
*Edited by John Tait*

### Views of Ancient Egypt since Napoleon Bonaparte: imperialism, colonialism and modern appropriations
*Edited by David Jeffreys*

### The Wisdom of Egypt: changing visions through the ages
*Edited by Peter Ucko and Timothy Champion*

OAT
2004

# Views of Ancient Egypt since Napoleon Bonaparte:

## imperialism, colonialism and modern appropriations

Edited by

**David Jeffreys**

**UCL**

**PRESS**

Institute of Archaeology

First published in Great Britain 2003 by UCL Press,
an imprint of Cavendish Publishing Limited, The Glass House,
Wharton Street, London WC1X 9PX, United Kingdom
Telephone: + 44 (0)20 7278 8000   Facsimile: + 44 (0)20 7278 8080
Email: info@uclpress.com
Website: www.uclpress.com

Published in the United States by Cavendish Publishing
c/o International Specialized Book Services,
5824 NE Hassalo Street, Portland,
Oregon 97213-3644, USA

Published in Australia by Cavendish Publishing (Australia) Pty Ltd
45 Beach Street, Coogee, NSW 2034, Australia
Telephone: + 61 (2)9664 0909   Facsimile: + 61 (2)9664 5420

© Institute of Archaeology, University College London   2003

British Library Cataloguing in Publication Data
Jeffreys, D.
Views of ancient Egypt since Napoleon Bonaparte: imperialism,
colonialism and modern appropriations – (Encounters with ancient Egypt)
1 Egypt – Historiography  2 Egypt – History
I Title
932

Library of Congress Cataloguing in Publication Data
Data available

ISBN 1-84472-001-2

1 3 5 7 9 10 8 6 4 2

Designed and typeset by Style Photosetting, Mayfield, East Sussex
Email: style@pavilion.co.uk

Printed and bound in Great Britain

Cover illustration:   'The Great Pyramids of Carlingford Lough, Irelantis', collage by Seán Hillen, 1994. "Carlingsford Lough, where I grew up, neatly marks the border between the North and the Republic of Ireland. I was aware of bridging it visually with the group of pyramids. I've been told since, to my delight, that Giza is Arabic for 'the border'" (© Seán Hillen & Irelantis Ltd: www.irelantis.com).

# Series Editor's Foreword

This series of eight books derives from the proceedings of a conference entitled 'Encounters with Ancient Egypt', held at the Institute of Archaeology, University College London (UCL) in December 2000. Since then, many new chapters have been especially commissioned for publication, and those papers originally provided for the conference and now selected for publication have been extensively revised and rewritten.

There are many noteworthy features of the books. One is the overall attempt to move the study of Ancient Egypt into the mainstream of recent advances in archaeological and anthropological practice and interpretation. This is a natural outcome of London University's Institute of Archaeology, one of the largest archaeology departments in the world, being the academic host. Drawing on the Institute's and other related resources within UCL, the volumes in the series reflect an extraordinary degree of collaboration between the series editor, individual volume editors, contributors and colleagues. The wide range of approaches to the study of the past, pursued in such a vibrant scholarly environment as UCL's, has encouraged the scholars writing in these volumes to consider their disciplinary interests from new perspectives. All the chapters presented here have benefited from wide-ranging discussion between experts from diverse academic disciplines, including art history, papyrology, anthropology, archaeology and Egyptology, and subsequent revision.

Egyptology has been rightly criticized for often being insular; the methodologies and conclusions of the discipline have been seen by others as having developed with little awareness of archaeologies elsewhere. The place and role of Ancient Egypt within African history, for example, has rarely been considered jointly by Egyptologists and Africanists. This collaboration provides a stimulating review of key issues and may well influence future ways of studying Egypt. Until now, questions have rarely been asked about the way Egyptians thought of their own past or about non-Egyptian peoples and places. Nor has the discipline of Egyptology explored, in any depth, the nature of its evidence, or the way contemporary cultures regarded Ancient Egypt. The books in this series address such topics.

Another exceptional feature of this series is the way that the books have been designed to interrelate with, inform and illuminate one another. Thus, the evidence of changing appropriations of Ancient Egypt over time, from the classical period to the modern Afrocentrist movement, features in several volumes. One volume explores the actual sources of knowledge about Ancient Egypt before the advent of 'scientific' archaeology, while another explores knowledge of Ancient Egypt after Napoleon Bonaparte's expeditions and the unearthing of Tutankhamun's tomb. The question asked throughout these volumes, however, is how far fascination and knowledge about Ancient Egypt have been based on sources of evidence rather than extraneous political or commercial concerns and interests.

As a result of this series, the study of Ancient Egypt will be significantly enriched and deepened. The importance of the Egypt of several thousands of years ago reaches far beyond the existence of its architectural monuments and extends to its unique role in the history of all human knowledge. Furthermore, the civilization of Ancient Egypt speaks to us with particular force in our own present and has an abiding place in the modern psyche.

As the first paragraph of this Foreword explains, the final stage of this venture began with the receipt and editing of some extensively revised, and in many cases new, chapters – some 95 in all – to be published simultaneously in eight volumes. What it does not mention is the speed with which the venture has been completed: the current UCL Press was officially launched in April 2003. That this series of books has been published to such a high standard of design, professional accuracy and attractiveness only four months later is incredible.

This alone speaks eloquently for the excellence of the staff of UCL Press – from its senior management to its typesetters and designers. Ruth Phillips (Marketing Director) stands out for her youthful and innovative marketing ideas and implementation of them, but most significant of all, at least from the Institute's perspective, is the contribution of Ruth Massey (Editor), who oversaw and supervized all details of the layout and production of the books, and also brought her critical mind to bear on the writing styles, and even the meaning, of their contents.

Individual chapter authors and academic volume editors, both from within UCL and in other institutions, added this demanding project to otherwise full workloads. Although it is somewhat invidious to single out particular individuals, Professor David O'Connor stands out as co-editor of two volumes and contributor of chapters to three despite his being based overseas. He, together with Professor John Tait – also an editor and multiple chapter author in these books – was one of the first to recognize my vision of the original conference as having the potential to inspire a uniquely important publishing project.

Within UCL's Institute of Archaeology, a long list of dedicated staff, academic, administrative and clerical, took over tasks for the Director and Kelly Vincent, his assistant as they wrestled with the preparation of this series. All of these staff, as well as several members of the student body, really deserve individual mention by name, but space does not allow this. However, the books could not have appeared without the particular support of five individuals: Lisa Daniel, who tirelessly secured copyright for over 500 images; Jo Dullaghan, who turned her hand to anything at any time to help out, from re-typing manuscripts to chasing overdue authors; Andrew Gardner, who tracked down obscure and incomplete references, and who took on the complex job of securing and producing correctly scanned images; Stuart Laidlaw, who not only miraculously produced publishable images of a pair of outdoor cats now in Holland and Jamaica, but in a number of cases created light where submitted images revealed only darkness; and Kelly Vincent, who did all of the above twice over, and more – and who is the main reason that publisher and Institute staff remained on excellent terms throughout.

Finally, a personal note, if I may. Never, ever contemplate producing eight complex, highly illustrated books within a four month period. If you *really must*, then make sure you have the above team behind you. Essentially, ensure that you have a partner such as Jane Hubert, who may well consider you to be mad but never questions the essential worth of the undertaking.

*Peter Ucko*
*Institute of Archaeology*
*University College London*
*27 July 2003*

# Contents

Note: No attempt has been made to impose a standard chronology on authors; all dates before 712 BC are approximate. However, names of places, and royal and private names have been standardized.

# Contributors

**Morris Leonard Bierbrier** was Assistant Keeper in the Department of Egyptian Antiquities at the British Museum from 1975 until his retirement in 2000. His principal publications are *The Tomb-Builders of the Pharaohs* (1982), *Who Was Who in Egyptology* (1995), and *Historical Dictionary of Ancient Egypt* (1999). His received his doctorate from the University of Liverpool.

**Timothy Champion** is Professor in the Department of Archaeology, University of Southampton. His research interests are in later European prehistory, the history of archaeology and the use of the past in contemporary social and political discourse. His recent publications include *Nationalism and Archaeology in Europe* (1996, ed. with Margarita Diaz-Andreu), *England's Coastal Heritage* (1997, ed. with M. Fulford and A. Long), and 'The Appropriation of the Phoenicians in British Imperial Ideology' (*Nations and Nationalism*, 7, 2001). He received his D Phil from the University of Oxford.

**David Dixon** was formerly Lecturer in Egyptology in the Institute of Archaeology, University College London, and Honorary Curator of the Petrie Museum of Egyptian Archaeology. He specializes in the history of the Red Sea area, and 19th century military history of Egypt and the Sudan, on which he has published extensively.

**Fekri A. Hassan** is Petrie Professor of Archaeology at the Institute of Archaeology, University College London. He is the editor of *African Archaeological Review*. His current research interests focus on the cultural dynamics of Ancient Egypt, and the strategies of cultural heritage management. His current fieldwork includes an investigation of the archaeology of Farafra Oasis (with B. Barich) and he is the principal investigator at Kafr Hassan Dawood in the eastern Delta. His recent publications include *Droughts, Food and Culture* (2002), *Alexandria's Greco-Roman Museum* (2002) and *Strategic Approaches to Egyptian Cultural Heritage* (2001). He received his PhD from the Southern Methodist University, Dallas, USA.

**Mary Horbury** received her PhD from the Institute of Archaeology, University College London. Her research was on Egyptian self-definition in the New Kingdom and Coptic Period. She has participated in archaeological fieldwork in Israel (Tel Hazor) and has conducted research in Egypt on the Coptic Period occupation of Luxor. Mary is currently working as a Care Leader for the Orders of St John Care Trust.

**David Jeffreys** is Lecturer in Egyptian Archaeology at the Institute of Archaeology, University College London and is Director of the Egypt Exploration Society's Survey of Memphis. His publications include archaeological reports and discussions of excavation and surveys at Memphis, discussions of the topography of the Memphite area, and archaeological sources for the regional survey. He has made a special study of the work of Joseph Hekekyan, who made geological soundings at a number of sites in Egypt in the early 1850s. He gained his PhD from the University of London.

**Isabel Medina-González** is Restorer-Conservator in the National Coordination of Restoration of Cultural Patrimony, INAH, Mexico City. She is about to complete her

PhD at the Institute of Archaeology, University College London, her research being on the concept of ancient cultures and their representation in 19th century displays.

**José-R. Pérez-Accino** is Lecturer in Egyptology at Birkbeck College, University of London. He has participated in archaeological fieldwork in Egypt (Herakleopolis Magna, Tell Ibrahim Awad) and in Israel (Tel Hazor). He was a member of the organizing committee of the 1998 first conference of Egyptology in Spain, and is co-editor of *Trabajos de Egiptología*. He obtained his doctorate from the Complutense University of Madrid, Spain.

**Jane Rowlandson** has recently been appointed Reader in Ancient History at King's College, University of London. Her doctoral research on land tenure in Roman Egypt, funded by the Social Science Research Council, was published as *Landowners and Tenants in Roman Egypt* (1996). She is editor of *Women and Society in Greek and Roman Egypt: a sourcebook* (1998) and currently holds a Leverhulme Research Fellowship to write a book on *The Culture of Roman Egypt*. She gained her D Phil from the University of Oxford.

**Sandra Arnold Scham** is editor of *Near Eastern Archaeology* and contributing editor to *Archaeology* magazine. She is a research development consultant with the Department of Anthropology at the University of Maryland. She is also co-ordinator of the Wye River People to People project on *Recognizing and Preserving the Common Heritage of Israel and the Palestinian National Authority* and the *Negev Bedouin Identity Project*. Her publications include 'The Archaeology of the Disenfranchised' (*Journal of Archaeological Method and Theory*, June 2001) and 'The Days of the Judges: when men and women were animals and trees were kings' (*Journal of the Study of the Old Testament* 97, March 2002). She obtained her doctorate at the Catholic University of America in Washington DC, USA.

**Covadonga Sevilla Cueva** is Professor of Egyptology and Ancient History, and co-director of the Centro Superior de Estudios de Asiriologia y Egiptologia, at the Autonoma University of Madrid. She has participated in archaeological fieldwork in Egypt (Herakleopolis Magna) and was a member of the organizing committee of the 1998 first conference of Egyptology in Spain. She is co-editor of *Trabajos de Egiptología* and her main interests and publications have focused on the role of the wives of Amun in the Third Intermediate and Late Periods, and the topography, archaeology and history of Egyptian Naucratis (Per Meryt). She gained her doctorate from the Autonoma University of Madrid, Spain.

**Jason Thompson** is Associate Professor of History at the American University in Cairo. His current research is a biography of Edward William Lane. His principal publications and ongoing research include *Sir Gardner Wilkinson and His Circle* (1992), an edition of Lane's previously unpublished *Description of Egypt* (forthcoming), and analyses of various aspects of the western encounter with the ancient and modern Middle East. He obtained his PhD from the University of Chicago.

**David Wengrow** is a Junior Research Fellow at Christ Church, University of Oxford. His research addresses the nature of early social transformations in Egypt and Iraq, and the role of the remote past in the formation of modern political identities. Recent publications include 'The Intellectual Adventure of Henri Frankfort: a missing chapter in the history of archaeological thought' (*American Journal of Archaeology* 103,

1999) and 'Landscapes of Knowledge, Idioms of Power: the African origins of Egyptian civilization reconsidered' (2003, *Ancient Egypt in Africa*, in the *Encounters with Ancient Egypt* series, UCL Press). He received his D Phil from the University of Oxford.

# List of Figures

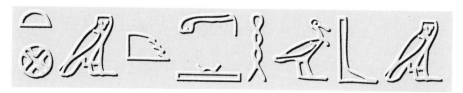

## CHAPTER 1

# INTRODUCTION – TWO HUNDRED YEARS OF ANCIENT EGYPT: MODERN HISTORY AND ANCIENT ARCHAEOLOGY[1]

### David Jeffreys

Few past societies can have exerted a broader or stronger cultural attraction in recent times than that of the Nile Valley. This book explores some of the ways in which that appeal has been translated, at the level of modern nation states as well as that of the individual, into expressions of a collective awareness that take Ancient Egypt, and above all pharaonic Egypt, as a model. It looks not only at the effect of European colonialist mentalities on the way that pharaonic society was explored, portrayed, purveyed and exploited, but also at the adoption of Egypt as a resonant image and a paradigm for more far-flung empires, notably in the New World.

The volume takes as its starting point Bonaparte's expedition to Egypt, between the years 1798 and 1801, which was a watershed event, not only in the development of professional academic Egyptology and in the increasingly important role that Egypt and its culture played in the international politics of the 19th century, but also as the first major imperialist incursion into the Middle East in modern times. Until then, interest in the Egyptian past had been of a largely individual, antiquarian nature, exemplified by Pococke, Norden, Sonnini and other European travellers since the beginning of the Renaissance, who had increased in number and in their intimacy with the country during the 18th century. Bonaparte's supplementary army of *savants* (the Commission) brought an unprecedented weight of scholarly authority to questions of history, geography, identity and the value of traditional classical and medieval sources on Egypt (Ucko and Champion 2003).

Familiarity has perhaps clouded somewhat the extraordinary nature of the French Expedition: not only was it a strategic military undertaking, designed to pre-empt Britain's easy access to its acquired territory farther east and to counter its rising profile in the area itself; it was also an ideological strike, against the political and intellectual oppression by the Mamluk rulers of the great labouring majority of the population, framed in an historical setting that directly recalled and invoked the supposed 'liberation' of Egypt by Alexander of Macedon ca. 330 BC. Napoleon's reasons for launching both a cultural and a military offensive may have been partly to do with personal initiative – he had apparently already become intrigued by pharaonic civilization in the 1880s (Hassan, Chapter 2) – but he was also motivated by the intellectual acquisition of the territory, its contents, including its inhabitants, and its past. The Egyptian campaign, which followed a brief intervention in Italy (similarly intended to be a combination of military, fact-finding and collecting exercises, and an imposition of cultural superiority over a supposedly backward neighbour), was also considered an extension of French revolutionary and republican culture into a primitive but deserving part of the world (see Wengrow, Chapter 12).

Bonaparte may also have been motivated by a sense of the British lead in discussions of pharaonic Egypt up to that time. If not exactly dominating the antiquarian debate, writers in English certainly had a prominent role: John Greaves (1646) as the most scientific and independently-minded authority on the pyramids; Richard Pococke as the author of one of the key texts (his *Description of the East*, 1743–45) on contemporary and Ancient Egypt; and James Bruce (1813) as a pioneer explorer of the Upper Nile in the 1790s.

The result of the Commission's work, the encyclopedic *Description de l'Égypte* (Anderson and Fawzi 1987; Gillispie and Dewachter 1987; Wheatcroft 2003) consists of not only the *Antiquités* volumes of elephant folio plates and accompanying text, but also two other sections, at the time considered equally important: the *État moderne*, a catalogue of the contemporary environment, life and customs; and the *Histoire naturelle*. Significantly, it also produced in a companion *Atlas* volume the first large-scale maps of the Nile Valley, reliable on the whole (Ball 1932), and a body of privileged information, as a preliminary to the acquisition of cultural knowledge, territorial occupation and control of land rights (Godlewska 1995). At the same time a popular account of the Expedition, published with much greater speed by a Commission member, Vivant Denon (1802), captured the public imagination on both sides of the English Channel – British audiences were attracted to this adventure by the successful involvement of their hero Nelson at the naval Battle of the Nile (Abu Qir) in 1798. From the shared European perspective, the French Expedition appeared as one of a series of early military forays by Bonaparte that later encompassed most of Europe itself and provided a grand theatre for world events; it has also often been portrayed as a conferring of the benefits of advanced western civilization on a backward subject, as well as providing the kickstart that such a stagnant, oriental society needed to set it on the road to progress. To many Egyptians, however, it has been symbolic as the first example, since the Crusades, of many unwanted and resented western intrusions into the Arab and Muslim worlds (Dykstra 1998: 115).

The recent bicentennial commemorations of the French Expedition (Bret 1999) with their particular focus on the colourful personalities involved and on the discovery and decipherment of the Rosetta Stone (Parkinson 1999) – again a race to the finish between the French and English scholars Champollion and Young – have if anything tended to obscure the longer and broader perspectives of others' perceptions of Ancient Egypt and its place in the world. The narratives reproduced in such accounts rarely consider the effects of the Expedition, the highly politicized background to the official acquisition of antiquities, and the intrusive and destructive field expeditions that ensued during the early 19th century. In addition, despite its reputation, the publication of the work of the scholarly Commission was not necessarily an unqualified boon to the study of Egypt: the finished result of the *Description* (1809–1828) volumes is rightly regarded as a monumental achievement;

but its weight of antiquarian authority, and the reverence accorded to it at the time and subsequently, have to a certain extent stifled the spirit of inquiry.

Timing is crucial to an appreciation of the French Expedition, its aftermath, and Ancient Egypt's recent role in the modern world. The Egypt recorded in the *Description* (1809–1828) is a world already on the point of disappearing: by the time the publication appeared in full, the emergence of Mohammed Ali as semi-autonomous ruler of Egypt in the early 1800s had set Egypt on a trajectory of economic reform and territorial expansion that changed its character in fundamental ways, from a passive and agricultural community to one reliant on heavy industry and a massive military capability (Fahmy 1998). Egypt's industrial revolution directly impinged on archaeological sites of all periods, many of which were quarried for their limestone for slaking and stripped of their topsoil for fertilizer and saltpeter: in several instances munitions factories were established alongside substantial sites for greater efficiency. A development of equal or greater significance since then has been the sequence of dams at Aswan, which have transformed Egypt's economic infrastructure in stages from one of seasonal flood recession agriculture to perennial irrigation, planting and cropping.

For global strategic reasons the western powers, notably France and Britain, viewed Mohammed Ali's developments with alarm and moved to establish larger numbers of diplomatic personnel within Egypt (Figure 1:1), both to observe and to influence his domestic and foreign policies (Dykstra 1979). In response to their increasing demand, Egyptian artefacts were turned into a kind of currency in the competition between the major players, as is illustrated by Bierbrier (Chapter 3) and Thompson (Chapter 4), from small portables such as amulets and figurines to monumental trophies such as colossal statues and architectural fragments including obelisks (Hassan, Chapter 2). A classic example of the antiquities race was the competition between Henry Salt (Manley and Rée 2001) and Bernardino Drovetti (Ridley 1998), Consuls of Britain and France respectively, both of whom retained and

Figure 1:1   The British Consul in audience with Mohammed Ali Pasha at Alexandria, 16 May 1839. Note in the background: Alexandria harbour and the site of the Pharos. Roberts himself is seated on the sofa, leaning slightly forward (Bourbon 1996: 10–11; Roberts 1849, 3: pl. 1).

deployed large numbers of agents to trawl the country for prestige pieces (Werner 2003). One of the leading agents – for the British – was Giovanni Battista Belzoni, whose exploits brought him at times to open hostility with the rival collectors of Drovetti – who continued to be a proxy for Napoleon's acquisition of antiquities. The Egyptian authorities, while deriding the western obsession with antiquities as items of ownership, colluded in this activity, often using art objects (or the promise of them) to play off the representatives of different nationalities against each other. Although national prestige was certainly served by the financing of these collecting expeditions, it is curious how reluctant some of the fledgling national museums were to benefit from them. Belzoni, Salt, Drovetti and others, in addition to the logistical problems of organizing their expeditions, often had difficulty hawking their collections around the major institutions (Manley and Rée 2001). The chaotic nature of such activities at this time, and the constant process of extraction, confiscation or exchange, and transport, go a long way to explain why so many collections, even those of national and international stature, contain hundreds of exhibits which are virtually without provenance or whose pedigree is at best uncertain. For example, a contorted background history is found in the case of a small block-statue of Nedjem, originally found at Memphis in 1852 by Joseph Hekekyan, which somehow came into the possession of a Boston sea captain, who shipped it home during the American Civil War. It then disappeared into private ownership before being bought by the Boston Museum of Fine Arts in 1929 (Dunham 1935: 150–151) with documentation records only going as far back as the captain's purchase in Alexandria. The Boston Museum of Fine Arts then allowed it to go on permanent loan to the Egyptian collection of Memphis State University, where it has remained on display – until recently listed as "provenance unknown" (Crown 1982: 14)!

At the same time, and entirely in the western Orientalist tradition (cf. Said 1978), the myth developed of two kinds of cultural superiority: that of the west over the east, and by extension that of the ancient east over the modern. In this way the Egypt of remote antiquity was conveniently detached from the Islamic world and, like the etic study of that world, became the preserve of western scholarship: Egyptian nationals (with one or two remarkable exceptions) were excluded from any participation in the teaching or administration of Egyptian archaeology until the early 1900s (Reid 1985; Wood 1998). Even today, as a discipline 'Egyptology' has an unusually precise meaning, being specifically the study of society in the Nile Valley from 3000 BC (the beginning of unitary rule, or the dynastic period) to 330 BC (the arrival of Alexander), or at the latest the first century AD. Many would even narrow it down still further and define the end date as 1000 BC (regarded as the final period of indigenous dynastic rule). Egyptian prehistory (except very late prehistory) is often not considered a proper concern of Egyptology; Islamic archaeology in Egypt is similarly treated as the territory of Arabists, and its administration is the responsibility of an entirely different department of government. Few other regional culture-historical specialisms are so narrowly defined: Sinology, for example, deals with all recoverable periods of Chinese history and culture, including the present, in a discipline that is certainly as intrinsically rich in data as Egyptology.

Egypt's industrial revolution also brought into the country a first generation of foreign technocrats and engineers, who often became absorbed with the physical remains of Egypt's past and applied their own area of expertise to its observation and explanation. Thus began a curious duality in the 19th century study of pharaonic civilization: on the one hand a group of highly specialized practitioners (architects and engineers, geologists and botanists, physicians and surgeons) who treated the study of many aspects of Ancient Egypt with seriousness and as something more than a mere hobby; and on the other the profession of Egyptology – the term dates from the mid-1850s (see Champion, Chapter 8) – with its core of academics usually, but not exclusively, raised in the Classical-textual or Biblical-textual tradition.

The textual emphasis in the history of Ancient Egypt's appropriation is particularly significant. At the time of the French Expedition the original Egyptian language was still effectively a closed book; although Coptic (written using mostly Greek characters) was recognized as a descendant of the ancient language, and some preliminary insights had been gained into the nature of the three indigenous scripts, a full consensus on the decipherment of the hieroglyphic script was not to emerge until the early 1830s. After that the number of expeditions organized to feed the academic demand for new inscriptions grew exponentially, and such enterprises were pursued with little or no reflection on, or regard to, archaeological context (France 1991); interpretations of pharaonic society were increasingly made almost exclusively from written sources, and even today documentary evidence is privileged (Kemp 1984). To complicate matters, the practice of field excavation in Egypt, with its notorious bias towards funerary and monumental municipal sites and away from settlement zones (Bietak 1979a; 1979b; O'Connor 1993: 577–578), and towards the Nile Valley and away from the Delta, has also generated a frame of reference which is at variance with that of many other regional archaeologies.

This emphasis on documentary and representational sources, and the very nature of many of the sources themselves, may be in part responsible for the widely felt belief in an almost revelatory personal access to the Ancient Egyptians. Compared with other contemporary or near-contemporary literate societies, and in addition to its huge, colourful and lively representational record, Egypt presents a greater than usual quantity and range of documents with some human appeal, such as private letters, popular tales, proverbial sayings and teachings, poetry, and even satirical and erotic texts. As Wengrow (Chapter 12) points out, the strength of the phenomenon of 'Egyptomania' is more or less unique: there was, for example, no corresponding 'Babyloniamania', in that other region of the Middle East where there had been study of developments in social behaviour of a comparable scale and date. The perception of Egyptian society as a unique entity has also persisted almost unchallenged to the present: until quite recently few students of pharaonic Egypt seemed prepared to make cross-cultural comparisons with civilizations elsewhere in the region, much less to consider Egypt's achievement on a global scale against those of more remote cultures; Trigger (1984) being, significantly, an anthropological – not an Egyptological – exception (see Manley and Rée 2001). Egyptologists are collectively accused of being concerned with the particular and descriptive rather than the general and explanatory, and of being generally resistant, if not actually hostile, to methodological progress, especially in archaeological theory, taking place in most of the rest of the world (Lustig 1997; Meskell 1999; Weeks 1979). In some recent syntheses of archaeology globally, and even some collective treatments of the Middle East, Egypt features rarely or not at all: for example, in Renfrew and Bahn's introductory manual to archaeology worldwide, which contains several general references to Egypt, only two are concerned with developments within Egyptian archaeology since Petrie's time (1991: 80, 189).

There are, however, heartening signs that this trend may be changing: recent studies of gender, the aged, climate change, and of state formation, wealth and legitimacy in the ancient Near East, all adopt a more or less integrated approach in which Egypt features equally or prominently (Baines and Yoffee 1998; Cameron and Kuhrt 1983; Dalfes *et al.* 1997). Even voices from outside a Near Eastern specialism have suggested that Egypt, with its rich documentary and archaeological resources, might be rehabilitated into a more rewarding worldwide debate, and contribute more substantially through new approaches to cognitive aspects of all past societies (Scarre 1994).

It comes almost as a surprise today that Egyptian archaeology has at any time given any kind of lead in archaeological thought and method. There have been, exceptionally, suggestions and observations from within that have generated discussion outside the narrow boundaries of Egyptology (Hoffman 1984; Hoffman *et al.* 1986; Smith 1969; Trigger 1981, 1984); and as Champion (Chapter 8) observes, Egyptian material at least, in the form of well-preserved human anatomical specimens, provided Elliot Smith with fuel for his ideas – innovative and influential at the time – on theories of hyperdiffusionism in the early 20th century. As Medina-González describes (Chapter 7), it is interesting that even before an academic formulation of diffusionist theory, the discoverers and colonizers of Mesoamerica had already taken Egypt as a prescriptive model and frame of reference for the past cultures encountered there. In general terms the study of Egypt may be said to have had a broader influence on antiquarian thinking elsewhere during the 19th century than in the 20th.

By the end of the 19th century, Flinders Petrie had introduced new methodological advances such as quantitative methods, in the form of seriation, into archaeological analysis, and new non-intrusive recording techniques (x-radiography) for delicate specimens such as mummified remains. Petrie also had an almost visionary approach to archaeological assemblages, collecting for information value rather than financial return, and building the superb teaching and research collection at University College London that bears his name. It is often forgotten too that in the early 1900s pioneering work was done in Egypt on predictive survey techniques such as soil phosphate analysis, long before it was widely applied in Scandinavia (Proudfoot 1976: 110; Russell 1957: 145). Significantly, few of these pioneering methods were appreciated or adopted at the time, and through the 20th century Egyptian archaeology became increasingly out of step with the practice of archaeology elsewhere. There were many who, like Petrie, had begun their archaeological careers in Europe or the United States, but unlike him remained competent and respected practitioners rather than contributing to innovative approaches, and even the Unesco Nubian campaign of the 1950s and 1960s, which involved an unprecedented infusion of international expertise, failed to convey other than incidentally to the mainstream of academic Egyptology any of the current archaeological thinking elsewhere (e.g. processualism).

The early years of the 20th century also saw one of the rare periods in which archaeologists in Egypt paid any attention to settlement archaeology as opposed to funerary and religious sites. Attention had first been paid to settlement sites in Egyptian Nubia during the construction of the first Aswan Dam at the end of the 19th century; a major change came about with the building of a second, far more ambitious Aswan Dam in the 1950s, and the Unesco campaign to record as much as possible of the Nubian sites and monuments that were about to be submerged by the new reservoir. In a replay of the influx of foreign expertise that accompanied Mohammed Ali's economic changes, archaeologists from all over the world became involved in the project, often with little previous experience of traditional Egyptology but being expert in the management of dam-threatened archaeological zones. This infusion of new skills might have been expected to open up the general trend of Egyptian archaeology to more contemporary approaches, but this failed signally to happen to any lasting extent. It is perhaps another curiosity that this injection of new experience and new approaches from all over the world, which had the most telling effect on the complexion of Egyptian archaeology and introduced at least some contemporary issues (e.g. Adams 1984), came only when the last vestiges of a colonial presence in Egypt had formally ended.

There is, then, a seeming paradox between the massive popular appeal of the subject today, and its relative isolation academically. There has been little engagement by Egyptologists in the larger issues that archaeologists are absorbed with elsewhere, but this is in any case unlikely to perturb the large public constituency for whom Egypt simply presents a visual feast and a range of problems of detail that allow scope for individual detective work (notably popular in this respect is the Amarna period). Even at times when Egypt seemed to be central to larger issues of human evolution and development, as in the hyperdiffusionist debate as described by Champion (Chapter 8), Egyptologists were more concerned with the external sources of Egyptian political development than in the possible part that Egypt itself had played in the dissemination of religion, ideas and ideology to other regions including northern Europe.

Mohammed Ali's reign is usually regarded in political terms as a transition from an essentially medieval form of rule (the Ottoman empire and the Mamluks) to a modern dynastic succession: the subsequent rulers through the 19th century, the Khedives, were all his family members, and they presided over the continued industrialization of the country (Hunter 1998; Ibrahim 1998; Toledano 1998). Egypt's economic success was boosted when the European market for its cotton crop increased in value during the American Civil War in the 1860s: the western powers' interests also continued to be inextricably bound up with Egypt, but eventually brought it economic decline as a result of loans, at punitive interest rates, to finance public works and, to some extent, the opulent lifestyle of the rulers; the key construction in strategic terms, the Suez Canal, was a project proposed early in the century, but initially dismissed for (mistaken) technical reasons and financed by France and Britain. The construction of the canal in particular highlighted the logistical importance of the area to Britain, by dramatically cutting the journey time to and from India, and the British preoccupation with the canal zone dates from this time. An even more important programme in national terms was the reshaping of the agricultural infrastructure of the Nile Valley and Delta, begun by Mohammed Ali but only completed with the building and subsequent raising of the Aswan Dam in the

1880s and early 1900s, after the British had occupied Egypt and had come to dominate its economic affairs.

The British naval blockade and bombardment of Alexandria in 1882, in response to Urabi's officer rebellion (Reid 1998), and the establishment of a British military presence that lasted through the 20th century to full Egyptian independence in the 1950s, also had its effect on the demography of foreign residence and influence in Egypt and on the French monopoly of the country's academic machinery. Although the first army commanders and officers to arrive in the country showed little interest in its archaeology, or at most regarded visits to archaeological sites and monuments as merely recreational opportunities, as described by Dixon (Chapter 5), later mandarins such as Cromer were less detached and were ready to further the interests of archaeological compatriots such as Petrie, often clashing with French academic officialdom in the process (Drower 1985: 168–198).

Significantly, a more formal involvement of both French and British archaeologists began at this time. The Institut Français d'Archéologie was opened in 1881 on the eve of the British bombardment; the Egypt Exploration Fund (EEF; later the Egypt Exploration Society, EES), a London-based organization committed to the recording and recovery of archaeological material, was founded shortly afterwards. Although initially launched as a result of individual initiative, most importantly that of Amelia Edwards, a wealthy journalist and traveller, in its funding structure the EES is now the equivalent of the British Schools and Institutes of Archaeology – many of them equally colonial in their origins – in other countries (James 1982). For largely historical reasons, in contrast to many other countries with an Egyptological programme (and in contrast to British policy in many other archaeologically rich areas of Europe and the Middle East), Britain has never established a permanent base in Egypt, with the exception of a small EES office in Cairo in recent years. There was also the British School of Archaeology in Egypt; despite the similarity of its title to that of fully-fledged British archaeological bases elsewhere (Rome, Athens, Jerusalem), it developed from the Egypt Research Account, a small funding venture launched in 1894 by Flinders Petrie to be independent of the EEF, and was never really more than a vehicle for the fieldwork carried out by him in the early 1900s. Bierbrier (Chapter 3) makes the point that Britain's official attitude towards any commitment to a cultural institution in Egypt has been less than wholehearted: while Britain occupied Egypt and controlled its economy there seemed to be no need for such a body, and since Egyptian independence the political will has been lacking.

Petrie and his successors (some of whom were equally at home in British archaeology) for a while spearheaded a new competency in the excavation and recording of archaeological sites and of primary observation, although it was probably as much a preoccupation with the testing or verification of biblical sources that motivated them as an attempt to strike a true evidential balance which is the priority for most settlement archaeologists today. With the exception of Amarna, most town sites to be tackled at this time were in the eastern Delta or on the Sinai land bridge.

Despite Petrie's formidable reputation, it is also worth remembering that his strengths and those of many of his contemporaries were in cemetery archaeology; almost all their settlement excavations were poorly conducted, even by the standards of the times. In some ways Egypt, particularly the Nile Delta, was regarded as an accessory to biblical archaeology, in the same way that, if included at all, it had been the last leg of the traditional route for visits to the Holy Land as part of the Grand Tour from the 18th to the earlier part of the 19th century. This only began to change with mass tourism in the later part of the century, and the targeting of Egypt as a destination in its own right (El Daly 2003a). From the end of Egyptian–Israeli conflict in the 20th century, Egypt has come to far outstrip the Levant as a tourist location; and until very recently this tourist traffic, contributing significantly to the nation's wealth, has been generated almost entirely by the country's archaeology, concentrated on a few major accessible sites in the Cairo region, in Luxor, and Aswan (El Daly 2003a).

The colonial domination of the study and dissemination of Egypt's past continued – unpopular but unchallenged – throughout the 19th century and well into the 20th (Hassan, Chapter 2). The scientific work of the Institut d'Égypte, set up by Napoleon, published monographs and an annual *Bulletin* which carried articles on archaeology, but only rarely were contributions by Egyptians included in comparison with those in other areas of science. Two outstanding exceptions to this pattern were Rif'a Raf'i al-Tahtawi, a high official under Mohammed Ali and his successors, who is well known for being one of the first Egyptian proponents of an official interest in the conservation of antiquities and sites. Far less well known is Joseph Hekekyan, an Armenian engineer born in 1807 in Constantinople and educated in Britain (Heyworth-Dunne 1939: 174), who rapidly became responsible for many aspects of Egypt's industrial development and who was also keenly aware of the need to promote education and training within Egypt: he was a founder member of the Cairo Polytechnic in the 1830s and collaborated with al-Tahtawi over the proposal for a national collection of antiquities. In terms of colonial attitudes Hekekyan's is perhaps the more interesting case: born an 'oriental' but brought up a European, he clearly inhabited a limbo region of social acceptance in between the Turcophone court and the multinational European community in Egypt, but certainly felt more at home in the latter: in fact his outspoken criticism of the shortcomings of court life, and of eastern lethargy and inefficiency in general, was undoubtedly one of the main reasons for his truncated career (Adalian 1980: 130; Mustafa 1968: 68–75).

Hekekyan was retired in the late 1840s and turned to a life of scientific and scholarly inquiry, carrying out, among a number of other projects, a series of geoarchaeological investigations – the earliest in the history of archaeology – in the Cairo area in the early 1850s. What is particularly significant is the reception in Britain of his findings and observations: the results of his work were hugely important, both for the data on the individual sites themselves, and for an understanding of settlement archaeology in Egypt generally, and his field techniques and recording were years, even decades, ahead of archaeological practice anywhere; however the stigma of being a 'local' lay behind the main criticism of the work, which was that Hekekyan's sponsor, Leonard Horner (then President of the London Geological Society, later President of the Royal Society), had not personally conducted and observed the fieldwork. Hekekyan's practical excavations and geological borings were carried out, under Horner's supervision, in the spirit of 19th century rationalism and as the pursuit of a natural science (Jeffreys forthcoming); the other side of his intellectual composition was, however, brought out in a series of almost fantastical musings on ancient chronology and semi-mystical speculation, which unfortunately remained his only published work (Hekekyan 1863).

The exclusion of Egyptians from even the lower echelons of antiquities administration (see Hassan, Chapter 2; Haikal 2003) shows how much at variance archaeological practice was from that of other branches of science and of public life. From the time of Mohammed Ali, promising young Egyptians had been sent to Europe (primarily to the Egyptian School in Paris) to learn vital skills fitting them for positions of responsibility that would lessen Egypt's reliance on imported expertise. Hekekyan himself had been a direct beneficiary of this policy, although his training was in England and under a more personal form of supervision and sponsorship. This form of training, however, concentrated on applied sciences such as hydraulics, engineering and other technical studies, and administration; archaeology only featured as an individual hobby, and if not actively prohibited was certainly not encouraged.

In official archaeology the Service des Antiquités de l'Égypte, conceived and ruled over by Auguste Mariette (Humbert 2003: 53–54), was set up in the late 1850s to oversee fieldwork and publication, but its executive staff were always French or (increasingly after 1882) British officials. The Service, with its Inspectorate, a network of local offices throughout the country, replaced (or rather was a modified form of) the old system of *firman*, or personal permission granted by a local, regional or national authority, with a licensing procedure which approved or rejected applications to work on the basis of their academic merit and put excavators under a contractual obligation to report their findings and to submit important objects for selection by the authorities. Significantly, for over a century the head of the Service was also automatically Director of the National Museum, reflecting the finds-dominated attitude of archaeological officialdom.

The government licensing system, still in use today, had a number of effects on the pattern of archaeological fieldwork in Egypt. Its concession system, under which, once an application is approved, lots are reserved for the applicant until rescinded or relinquished, has led to the creation of archaeological preserves that are often defined along national lines, such as the German concession on Elephantine Island (Aswan) or the Canadian remit to survey the whole of the Dakhla Oasis (Western Desert). The time required to prepare and lodge an application – rarely less than six to nine months – means that any rapid response to sudden or unforeseen threats, such as new building development or flash flooding, is almost out of the question.

During the 20th century little changed in this respect until Egypt gained full independence as a Republic in 1952, and foreign activities were curtailed in 1956 following the Suez crisis: thereafter the Service des Antiquités – later renamed the Egyptian Antiquities Organization, and now the Supreme Council for Antiquities (SCA) – has been entirely staffed by Egyptian nationals. The last surviving European to have held office in the *Service*, J-Ph. Lauer, was still active in the field until his recent death. From 1900 an official publication, the *Annales du Service*, was started, to report archaeological excavations and public works. All fieldwork in Egypt is now undertaken in co-operation with, or under license from, the SCA, although some structures remain from the European colonial period in the form of the larger archaeological Institutes with their own publication programmes. The oldest of these, the Institut Français d'Archéologie Orientale du Caire, founded in 1881, started to issue its own annual *Bulletin* in the same year (1901) as the *Annales* appeared, and for many years its printing press was responsible for producing the *Annales* as well.

The discovery of the tomb of Tutankhamun is of course now legendary for its contribution to archaeology (perhaps overstated) and its hold on the public imagination (see MacDonald and Rice 2003: 4, 21), but it is probably less well known as a turning-point, downwards, in the relations between foreign (often old colonial) enterprise and Egyptian officialdom (Carter 1998). Several factors come into play in this sorry tale: the background politics of Saad Zaghlul's opposition to British rule and his subsequent exile, resulting in uproar and anti-British protest nationwide; Carter's former status as an unpopular and previously disgraced official of the Antiquities Service (James 1992), his subsequent position, at the time of the discovery, as a freelancer in the pay of an English aristocrat (Figure 1:2), and his all-too-obvious lack of patience with bureaucracy; and not least the sensational and highly publicized nature of the find itself. The discovery of the tomb marks the point at which the congenial arrangement of equal shares, between the finder and the government, of the finds from an excavation came to an end – a development that drove Petrie out of Egypt to the Levant (Drower 1985: 355–356; Ucko 1998). From that time onwards government restrictions on fieldwork, and the possibility of export licenses for study material, have grown increasingly strict, to the point today where no archaeological material (including, for example, soil samples) is allowed out of the country.

In contrast to the continuity of procedures for licensing professional fieldwork, the means by which individuals have experienced Egypt, and have had access to the knowledge of Ancient Egypt, has changed dramatically. Even before the later 19th century, when Egypt was opened to mass tourism, there was latitude for private individuals to travel the Nile Valley for themselves and form their own impressions

Figure 1:2   Howard Carter (left) and Lord Carnarvon (right) with the Governor of Qena Province in 1922, the year of the discovery of Tutankhamun's tomb (Reeves 1990: 53a).

of its society, past and present. There was little attempt to provide an accessible, popular account of Ancient Egypt or to refresh existing ideas about it: Gardner Wilkinson's *Manners and Customs of the Ancient Egyptians* (1878), unofficially a companion volume to Lane's ([1836] 1842) masterly work on contemporary Egyptian society, remained the standard account in English to the end of the century. Flinders Petrie, best known for his technical and methodological innovations, is perhaps less well known today as the effective popularizer and communicator of his subject that he was – as much through his apparently inexhaustible capacity for exhibitions and lecture tours as through his books for a lay readership.

The result has been that the purveying of Ancient Egypt has generally taken place in a vacuum of really informed discourse. It was either in the hands of authority figures in the academic profession; or exploited by an occult fringe exemplified by Alastair Crowley (Hornung 2001: 173); or for that matter was open to anyone – spiritualists, theosophists, artists, novelists – to interpret. This extreme relativity and the closeness of easily accepted stereotypes about ancient and contemporary Egypt are particularly clear in, for example, the case of the Romantic Oriental and Egyptianizing movements (Humbert and Price 2003) in art, architecture and interior decoration, in which observed cameos and scenes from the directly experienced Egypt were used to reconstruct vistas of pharaonic life and society (Conner 1983; Curl 1994). In many ways Egypt was the perfect candidate for a Romantic working over, with its appealing and lavish artistic record, its equally colourful contemporary society, the ease of disguise for western visitors and of a comfortable 'native' life for western residents, its remarkable ecological niche, especially the annual inundation, and perhaps above all the proximity of a teeming population to a vast desert with its lure and promise of escape.

This idea of an exclusive appeal of, and an instant access to, Ancient Egypt – and even, at times, of personal identification with its people (Hornung 2001; Montserrat 2000: 130) – reinforced today by media and internet coverage (see Schadla-Hall and Morris 2003) – may help to explain the ease with which Egypt and its artefacts have over the years been commandeered by others as a symbol of past glory and power. Egypt was after all the oldest pristine territorial state (Trigger 1984); however different it may have been from later ancient examples (Assyria, Persia, Rome), let alone modern ones, it seemed to provide a comparative and even justificatory example for the transnational empires of recent centuries. The ideological impetus behind the French Expedition (liberating Egypt from its Ottoman/Mamluk oppressors) and the invented historical context (Bonaparte as a new Alexander) provided not only a template for other existing or incipient empires and political collectives to follow, but also an example of how it might be achieved. Pérez-Accino and Sevilla Cueva (Chapter 6) give the examples of the ready reference to Ancient Egypt in the emergent Iberian culture of the early 1800s, and the attempt to emulate the French Commission by launching collecting campaigns of cultural objects and natural history specimens to less fiercely competitive parts of the Mediterranean basin.

Hassan (Chapter 2) shows that the acquisition of Egyptian monuments has a history stretching back far further than Bonaparte: imperial Rome in particular was an avid importer of Egyptian cults and also of particular kinds of monuments, especially obelisks. It is worth remembering that the Roman emperors also prized Egypt for its premium-grade stones, especially porphyry, and the difficulty of extraction and distances travelled in bringing it to the capital conferred extra prestige (Peacock 1992). As in Egypt itself, obelisks (as well as colossal statuary) were ideal for relocating from one cult- and power-centre to another, Rome, and were even imitated as occasion arose. Whether the sacredness of the original location, and the power of the inscriptions on these monuments, were part of the value to Roman usurpers as they may have been to the Egyptians is unclear (Goedicke 1971: 3–7). The specific religious symbolism of obelisks may have been understood and appreciated by the Romans, or it may not: their importance probably lay in their relative portability, their high profile, and the thermodynamic value embedded in their transport. The embellishments that Roman, Byzantine and ecclesiastical leaders added to obelisks certainly suggest that they took on a new set of symbolic associations in their new setting.

The lack of a satisfactory, inclusive and coherent discursive framework for the study of Ancient Egypt, and the susceptibility of the subject to individual (usually dissenting) marginal views – for example, the "Orion mystery" (Bauval and Gilbert 1994) – may have left it more open to specific appropriations in the present than most other ancient (and not so ancient) societies. The Afrocentrist movement in the United States (Howe 1998) is an interesting case in point, with its politicized convictions prompted by Anta Diop (1974) and given new impetus by Martin Bernal (1987, 1991, 2003). The association of the American black diaspora with ancient Egyptian civilization (see MacDonald 2003; O'Connor and Reid 2003a: 3, 7–8; Scham, Chapter 11) is particularly bound up with the attribution of Greek culture not just to Egyptian inspiration or influence but to an actual Egyptian presence in the Aegean, and the corollary accusation that western academics have conspired to bury or obscure those associations. These have been possible largely because, with their emphasis on the 'special' character of Egypt, they have allowed little popular perception of the full interaction between the Nile Valley and other eastern Mediterranean societies during the Bronze and Iron Ages, or for that matter in Hellenistic and later times (Matthews and Roemer 2003). Such arguments, based on judgments about race (which few scientists would now recognize as any basis for identification), lead directly from traditional (most would agree outmoded) views about an Ancient Egyptian 'race', with its extended idea of the Nile Valley itself being colonized by a Mesopotamian 'Master race'. Interestingly, no movement of any strength similar to that of American Afrocentrism or its self-declared academic discipline of Kemetology has emerged in the UK or western Europe, far less in the eastern black diaspora that diffused throughout the Islamic world from East Africa (Segal 2002).

The reaction of the western/traditional academic community to Bernal and to the Afrocentrist challenge, coming so far largely from a broadly liberal-leaning community of North American classicists and historians, is revealing in itself (O'Connor and Reid 2003b). On the one hand there is a natural reactive refusal to condone what are seen as outdated research methods and slack scholarship, and a resistance to the aggressively political nature and objectives of the Afrocentrist movement, while acknowledging the need to be more open to the possibility of greater cross-cultural influence and more self-aware of the prejudices held by historians themselves (e.g. Lefkowitz 1996; Lefkowitz and Rogers 1996). On the other hand, some have been inclined to try to find common ground, or at least a common vocabulary, and engage in some shared discursive forum with the Afrocentrist position (Roth 1995). There is even some evidence that the debate has caused some academics to rethink their position, for example the Classical historians and archaeologists who might have resisted the idea that Egypt and the Levant could have offered anything other than technical expertise to the culture of Greece and Rome, and those who, like the Hellenophile novelist and poet Lawrence Durrell, identified with, and thought of the Aegean as, the 'right side of the Mediterranean' (see Durrell 1971: 74–75).

At the same time there is a marked ambivalence to the question of how and to what extent Egypt actually provides a cultural legacy for western and other industrial societies. Despite the extent of self-identification with the 'Ancient Egyptians', there still seems to be a considerable Romantic colouring of the exotic about this appropriation. Only rarely is there any attempt to track a concrete line of transmission from the Nile Valley to present society, and some of the more telling actual aspects of an Egyptian legacy (adoption of writing systems, religious communal behaviour) often go completely overlooked. The initial appeal often seems to lie much more in a visceral or aesthetic reaction to Egyptian forms and styles, for which any further explanation seems to be merely rationalization.

The reaction of Egyptians themselves to the Afrocentrist claim – generally speaking one of dismissal – is intriguing, and raises the question of how Egypt views its own pre-Islamic past. The official attitude of Islamic Egyptian governments and society towards pharaonic monuments oscillated between reverence and iconoclasm in medieval times (Haarmann 1980, 1996; El Daly 2003b), and more recently between approval and hostility, depending on the strength of pan-Arabist feeling and its promotion (Hassan 1998; Reid 1985; Wood 1998).

One curious feature of the development of Egyptology within Egypt itself since independence is how little it actually differs from the traditional-colonial model. Comparatively few new insights have been provided, with the exception of comparisons between ancient and contemporary ethnographic phenomena, for example ritual or recreational games (e.g. Brewster 1960; Saad 1937), and the scholarly preoccupations are broadly those of the early to mid-20th century, centring on culture-historical detail, textual criticism and language study. This focus has certainly provided important and interesting new data, but cannot be said to have extended the boundaries of discourse in a way that might have been hoped for. Perhaps most disappointing is the way in which the teaching of archaeology and history in Egypt at secondary and tertiary levels is almost entirely parochial, despite the fact the one of the few attempts to break the mould – by Bruce Trigger (1993) – originally took the form of a series of lectures at the American University in Cairo.

The blame for this lack of a creative sea-change should probably be laid at the door of the very colonial monopolists who kept Egyptians out of the study of their own remote past for so long, and denied or neglected the relevance of ethnological data from modern or medieval Egypt to pharaonic society (Haikal 2003). For example, with the exception of a token acknowledgment that the condition of the Egyptian peasantry had changed little during 5,000 years of settlement in the Nile Valley, and one influential study which attempted such comparisons over the long term (Blackman

1927), there has been no real concerted effort in the Egyptological community to explore this line of inquiry further.

One must of course be cautious about assuming too great a uniformity in the ethnicity and shared cultural experience of Egyptian society now or, for that matter, at any time in the past. Horbury (Chapter 10) examines the reaction of western visitors to Egypt to one particular section of the population, that of the Christians, overwhelmingly belonging to the Church of Egypt or Coptic community. As a significant and influential minority, Copts have been the subject of special interest from the west, not least because their language was, and their culture was perceived as being, directly descended from the language and culture of the pharaonic civilization. The idea of a physical link to the pharaohs was irresistible to visitors and commentators, particularly from Victorian Britain, but what is perhaps most instructive is their disappointment with, and even disdain for, the sample presented to them, especially in the rural hinterland. Few seem to have imagined or accepted that perhaps many aspects of Ancient Egypt, of which they held such a cherished, rose-tinted view, might have been equally squalid, uncomfortable and certainly unfamiliar, or that there might have been an equivalent difference between the character of urban and rural communities that they themselves had observed.

Perhaps the most remarkable feature of the attraction exerted around the globe by Ancient Egypt is its extraordinary geographic range. None of the populated continents is without at least one formal outlet for an interest in Ancient Egypt: most European countries, western and eastern, have a national institution, and many have individual academic- or museum-based projects, some located in Egypt, which are either research- or fieldwork-active. In South America, Argentina, Uruguay and Brazil (Bakos 2003) have learned societies, and a Caribbean Society of Egyptology has recently begun publishing a *Cahier d'Études*. In North America, Canada and in particular the United States both have a long record of Egyptological research (Delamaire 2003; Thomas 1995; Wilson 1964). Australia has several vibrant Egyptological centres although, as with many North American institutions, at least one of these originally grew from, or was based on, interests and sometimes antiquities imported from Britain (Merrillees 1990; Sowada 1994).

These examples are all perhaps understandable in the historical context of modern imperial states and their ideologies; what is less clear is the nature of the appeal in countries that have no long-standing connection with the eastern Mediterranean, North Africa or the Middle East. China and Japan, for example, both have at least one active Egyptological research centre (at Changchun and Waseda Universities respectively). The former Soviet Union became briefly involved in Egypt and its past culture when it contracted to build the Aswan High Dam in the 1950s, but had since been inactive until 2000, when the Russian National Academy of Sciences launched a field programme at Memphis. The Imperial Russian and Soviet experience of Egypt has had a comparatively low profile in the west (Whitehouse 2003): despite the general acknowledgment of the individual brilliance of scholars such as Grdseloff and Rostovtzeff, the particular political orientation of Russian/Soviet Egyptologists should not be overlooked as it offers a fresh perspective on Egyptian history and society, as is shown by Rowlandson (Chapter 9).

In a recent informal survey of Egyptological nations,[2] both those of long standing and those that have only recently emerged, the indications are interesting and point to multiple motivations for establishing or promoting a cultural connection with Egypt. It is suggested, for example, that Japan, since the end of World War II, has encouraged, in its educational and media coverage of Egypt, a direct comparison between Japanese emperors and Egyptian pharaohs (for example, in the arrangements for their burial and funerary cults). In addition, modern Japan and Ancient Egypt invite comparison with one another as both being technologically advanced in their time: the scientific surveying by Japanese archaeologists of the Giza pyramids is cited as a vehicle for this kind of association to be drawn, although perversely this overlooks or sidesteps the reality that Ancient Egypt was perhaps one of the least technologically innovative societies in the eastern Mediterranean arena. China, on the other hand, had contacts with Egypt at the level of individual Chinese merchant- or soldier-travellers from the second century BC, and in the form of returning prisoners of war during the eighth century AD. Trade markets (glass and ceramics) between the two countries were especially strong during the 12th and 13th centuries AD, but ironically a formal and popular interest in Ancient Egypt did not develop in China until the French Expedition and the publication of the *Description* (1809–1828). However, the sense of a cultural bond may have been encouraged by the idea, based largely on a perceived (although very superficial) similarity in their writing systems, that Egypt and China shared a common origin and background. In recent times Chinese Egyptology has been particularly strong, with two major national academic initiatives into China's own imperial past, and its self-awareness as a world civilization, being inspired by the study of Ancient Egypt (see also Mu-Chou Poo 1998; *The Times*, 1 May 2002, for an up-to-date example of 'civilization-building' in the form of a Chinese "Egyptian-style" pyramid).

New World involvement in the study of Egypt follows a different pattern, usually associated with the imperial-colonial aspirations of the founding European nation states. In Brazil (and see also the chapter on Mexican parallels with Egypt by Medina-González, Chapter 7), Pedro Funari sees the particular identification with Ancient Egypt as a product of the relocation of the Portuguese court to Rio de Janeiro (hounded out of Portugal by Bonaparte's armies), and the creation of Brazil as part of a united Portuguese kingdom, during the 1820s. Although its Egyptian collections were again begun in emulation of the other rival imperial powers, it is suggested that a particularly strong bond with Ancient Egypt developed in people's minds due to the patriarchal, hierarchical and hugely inegalitarian nature of Brazilian society, even following its conversion to a Republic at the end of the 19th century. The gulf in status and wealth between rulers and manual workers is directly compared to that assumed to exist between pharaoh and fellahin, major aggrandizing public works being popularly known as 'pharaonic'. In educational terms, Ancient Egypt assumes a more prominent role in secondary school teaching than it does in European countries; and in this case the divorcing of Ancient from Islamic Egypt was also a function of the reaction to the memory of Moorish rule on the Iberian peninsula: the Christian authorities in Brazil were keen to promote the idea of pre-Islamic Egypt as a golden age. A particularly powerful cause of the appropriation of Ancient Egypt in Brazil was the importance among the elite of freemasonry, with its rich stock of allusion and the contrived belief in the direct transmission of occult information from Ancient Egypt itself (see Hamill and Mollier 2003).

In the United States (Thomas 1995; Wilson 1964), as in Europe, academic Egyptology was fired by the findings of the French Expedition and by the decipherment of hieroglyphics, with much of the 19th and early 20th century research being led by attempts to supplement biblical research. As happened elsewhere (see above), the spectacular 1922 discovery of the tomb of Tutankhamun in the Theban Valley of the Kings provided an extra boost to Egyptian studies and especially to a broader public interest in Egypt. Canada and the United States are now active in Egyptological research and fieldwork and both have permanent archaeological institutions in Egypt, although the American Research Center also funds research into Coptic, medieval and contemporary Islamic Egypt. In the public domain it is worth noting that, long before any formal Afrocentrist movement, societies – often secret and based on occult associations with Egypt, paralleling the rise of Kardecism in Brazil – proliferated in the US, especially the southern states, and that Ancient Egypt featured prominently in early discussions on race and racial origins (Dain 1993). Although these were rarely concerned with detailed historical or archaeological issues of evidence, they inculcated a general sentiment of association with Egypt – almost to the exclusion of any other past African society – despite the fact that of all the elements in the black diaspora, the oppressed communities of the New World were perhaps the least connected to Nilotic cultures.

The main absences in such a geography of interest in Ancient Egypt seem to be the areas closest to home, or those which boast as it were rival past cultures: the Indian subcontinent, the Middle East and Africa itself (for African attitudes to Ancient Egypt, see Folorunso 2003; O'Connor and Reid 2003a). This almost seems to reflect the way that debate within Egyptology has largely been conducted in its own geographical vacuum.

In a wide-ranging discussion, Wengrow (Chapter 12) analyses the tension between the patterns of Republican European political thought and rational philosophy, and Europe's absorption with a despotic and exotic east, from the arrival of the French army in Egypt, through the influential work of Frankfort, Childe, Said and others, to the present, post-*Black Athena* climate of debate. Just as specialists in Egypt, the Near East and Classical Greece and Rome are responding to Bernal with either outright rejection or a new willingness to consider his position, they are constrained by the parameters of that debate, whereas archaeologists elsewhere are taking a very different tack and following a non-progressivist path.

In the spirit of self-enquiry that a book like this both stimulates and requires, it is worth asking what the role of the modern archaeologist or historian of Egypt is, or should be, in a postcolonial world. While some foreign archaeologists working in Egypt might unconsciously (or self-consciously) act as if nothing had changed, most of the important differences since independence are unavoidable: the Egyptian government now controls and inspects fieldwork projects, project staff members are subject to security clearance and periodic checks, the official language of communication is Arabic, and many parts of the country are sporadically or permanently out of bounds (the entire south-eastern desert, containing many important and threatened archaeological sites, has now been declared a prohibited zone). Restrictions on fieldwork, notably the lack of access to analytical and laboratory-dating procedures, means that many archaeological techniques taken for granted in most of the rest of the world cannot be applied to material from Egypt. The presence of foreigners in the country in such numbers, busily revealing and recovering, advertising and presuming to interpret its own heritage, is a matter for criticism in parts of the Egyptian media, although this has not noticeably affected official attitudes so far. At the same time a lack of effective planning controls means that archaeological sites and information are disappearing faster than ever, and any attempt at rescue or salvage programmes are at best reactive. A realistic programme for the recovery of archaeological information is, however, now no longer associated with negative criticism of national resources and the way they are used, but is to a great extent informed by similar problems at home. In particular, fieldwork in Egypt is now driven by information recovery and not by any hope of acquiring artefacts. Ironically, this is happening while the illicit market in antiquities is thriving as never before and the disappearance of objects into private ownership has become a serious concern.

This volume deals with the effects of imperialist and colonialist policies and attitudes on the development of the study of Ancient Egypt. It also introduces, describes and discusses some of the ways in which Egypt has been seized upon, not only for its appeal as a colourful and exotic culture, with a superficially attractive ecological setting, but also for the example that it presents, or seems to present, of a powerful polity whose strategic thinking and territorial aggression in the past are in a sense mitigated or made acceptable (unlike those of other comparable, contemporary societies) by that very appeal.

## Notes

1    With apologies to Ian Morris (1994).
2    The survey was carried out for this volume by Koji Mizoguchi (then of the Institute of Archaeology, University College London). Dr Mizoguchi began by canvassing views from practitioners of archaeology in a number of regions worldwide, including western and eastern Europe, the Far East, and South and North America. The responses to his questionnaire varied in the degree of detail they contained, so instead of being included in this volume as a separate chapter, the information is summarized here. Correspondents to this survey were David O'Connor (North America), Pedro Funari (Brazil) and Wang Tao (China); Dr Mizoguchi himself provided the data on Japan.

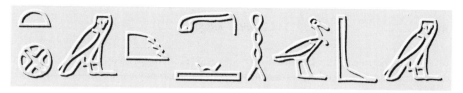

## CHAPTER 2

# IMPERIALIST APPROPRIATIONS OF EGYPTIAN OBELISKS

*Fekri A. Hassan*

## Introduction

The rise of nationalism and industrialization in modern Europe and the imperial hegemony of European nations have radically transformed the world over the last 200 years, precipitating a major divide between rich industrial nations and a majority of the world's nations that are poor and disadvantaged, a divide that has now culminated in the emergence of a new world order dominated by transnational global giants operating from western world cities (and Tokyo).

It is in this changing political climate that an examination of the link between nationalism, colonialism and archaeology may be attempted as a means of elucidating the role archaeology may play, or is playing, in shaping a new global regime (see e.g. Dìaz-Andreu and Champion 1996; Gathercole and Lowenthal 1990; Hassan 1998; Lamberg-Karlovsky 1997, 1998; Meskell 1998).

This chapter provides a case study of the appropriation of archaeological monuments by colonial powers in order to canonize their world hegemony. The premise is that imperial powers aim to legitimate their rule by cannibalizing other civilizations in order to assume a supreme position in the order of the world. Empires embody the notion of the 'end of world': their supremacy is based on re-directing the course of human civilization so that they can be regarded as the end and ultimate destination of history. In inventing an imperialist narrative, imperialists seize and show off the memorials, monuments and mementos of other civilizations either as their very own (through mythologized descent) or as theirs by virtue of conquest. In doing this, living peoples of other civilizations are marginalized and cast aside as the refuse of history, whom history has bypassed in its imperial course. Their history had ended yielding the stage to the 'Empire' (Fannon 1968; Prakash 1995; Said 1993; Wolf 1982; Young 1990).

The development of modern archaeology has been closely intertwined with the expansion of European imperialism in the 19th and the early part of the 20th centuries. The scramble to dominate other countries of the world, most successfully by Britain and France, has been associated with diligent work by missionaries, explorers, botanists and archaeologists.

In this chapter I examine the history of appropriating obelisks and the probable rationale for such undertakings in order to develop a historically grounded opinion on how archaeological heritage ought to be managed in a globalized world.

Smith (1986) argues that the past is used to appeal for precedent, especially at times of rapid change or major ruptures, as in the rise of nationalism or the establishment of a new political regime, when the past acquires a special relevance. As new imperial, political and economic forces shape a new world order using new technologies of power and control, archaeologists should examine the political manipulation of the past by the media, the internet, tourism, and transnational corporations. Case studies such as this one should not be regarded as cautionary tales or a critique of modernity, but as a source of insight on the configuration and operational strategies and tactics of empire building.

This chapter concerns specifically the removal of Egyptian obelisks to the cities of Europe (and subsequently the USA), commencing with the transport of obelisks by Roman emperors. Successive appropriations of Egyptian obelisks are treated within the context of the historical transformation of imperial power by which obelisks were invested with ideological garbs that ranged from Christianity to Nationalism. However, regardless of this overt manifestation of imperialist ideology, obelisks remained a symbol of cultural hegemony and dominance. With each historical transformation the obelisk accumulated cultural capital (Figure 2:1), adding to its status as an icon of imperial power.

## Imperialism, colonialism and dispossession: a historical preamble

I must have been a few years old when my father showed me the Qasr el-Nil army barracks where the Hilton Hotel and the building of the Arab League now stand in Cairo. These were the barracks of the British occupying forces. Britain was an empire with possessions in Egypt, India, Iraq, and many other countries beyond my limited geographical knowledge. As I have since discovered, in Britain and in Europe 'Empire' and 'imperialism' were (and still are for some) proud words. In Egypt, my first exposure to politics was through the pages of *Al-Ithneen wa'l-Douniya*, a weekly Egyptian magazine, where 'empire' had different connotations. Reporters of the resistance movement in the (Suez) Canal Zone spoke of *Al-Ihtilal Al-Britani* (British occupation) from the Arabic verb, *Ihtalla*, to occupy or colonize. For the Egyptians, the term meant that Britain, with its military apparatus and diplomatic manoeuvres, was effectively a major force in steering Egyptian state politics, economy and social affairs, with no consensual legitimization for such control by the Egyptians.

The British occupation of Egypt was actively resisted both by the religious scholars – heirs of a long tradition of Islamic learning – and the French-educated lawyers and professionals, who represented the vanguard of modern Egypt by the 1850s. On 16 October 1954, after 72 years of British occupation, Egyptian officers led by Gamal Abdel-Nasser succeeded in dislodging the forces of occupation (with a negotiated agreement by which the British withdrew their troops from the Suez Canal Zone), securing full independence from British control. Under Nasser the favoured

Figure 2:1 Historical transformations of contexts of obelisks invest the obelisk with accumulated cultural capital. This obelisk, originally erected by Ramesses II in Heliopolis (with three of its sides inscribed by Seti I and the fourth by Ramesses II), was taken by Emperor Augustus in 10 BC and erected in the Circus Maximus in Rome, Italy. It was subsequently re-erected by Pope Sixtus V in 1589 in Piazza del Popolo, Rome, Italy. See Figure 2:16 (© Suzie Maeder).

Arabic term for colonialism was *Al-Isti'mar*, a term for 'colonialism', in opposition to *Al-Istiqlal*, 'independence', and *Al-Tahrir*, 'liberation'.

Colonialism for the Egyptians was not about the establishment of British colonial settlements in Egypt. Colonialism in Egypt was viewed as an act of dispossessing the Egyptians of their own independence and sovereignty. It was perceived in terms of bondage and dependence, a form of subjugation and virtual enslavement. This was a source of humiliation and degradation for Egyptians. In Arabic, the word for 'liberation', *Al-Tahrir*, belongs to a vocabulary that includes *Hur* ('free') as opposed to *Abd* ('slave'). The act of dispossessing the Egyptians of their freedom was clearly manifest in the active intervention of the forces of occupation to control Egyptian affairs.

Before Egypt was occupied by the British in 1882, the appointment of European (French and British) controllers to manage Egypt's finances in 1879 was a prelude to the use of military force to dictate the terms of colonial rule. These terms were for the economic benefit of Britain and France to the detriment of Egypt, which was maintained as a cotton farm (Stavrianos 1981: 224). Industrialization, begun in Egypt by Mohammed Ali in the first decades of the 19th century, was fiercely resisted, and eventually undermined, by the European powers. The ambitious educational programme initiated at that time to provide Egypt with engineers, inventors and doctors was also countermanded. The British Foreign Minister, Lord Palmerston, in 1837 accepted the position that Egypt must not become a manufacturing country. Hence, Mohammed Ali became an anathema to Palmerston, whom he castigated as an ignorant barbarian. Palmerston went further to remark, "I look upon his boasted civilization of Egypt as the arrantest humbug" (in Stavrianos 1981: 217–218).

That a Minister of Foreign Affairs would use in his political discourse terms of cultural reference (a practice that continues today in international political discourse) is symptomatic of the rhetoric of colonialists who aimed to legitimate their colonial rule by appointing themselves as the rightful overseers of civilization, setting themselves apart from 'barbarians'. Their 'mission to civilize' in the name of *their* God and *their* Country subverted the universalizing mission of the Enlightenment, degrading it to the bogus claims of European politicians and financiers whose aim was world domination rather than the rule of justice and equality.

The European colonial project rested on the economic exploitation of other countries by force and the threat of force, but more importantly by dispossessing other countries of their claim to 'civilization' and by presenting themselves as the custodians of world cultural heritage (see Bernal 1994: 126). The rhetorical strategy adopted by European powers was matched by the use of the materiality of the past to buttress their hegemonic pretensions. National museums, instead of housing collections of national archaeological relics, were established as showcases of imperial possessions. Curiously, the British Museum, for example, is not a museum of British artefacts. Crammed with 'treasures' from Egypt, Iran, Iraq, India, and many other countries of the world's great civilizations, it developed into a temple of British cultural imperialism at a time when Great Britain was an empire with immense global power.

Of course, the role of materiality and the appropriation of the archaeological heritage and 'treasures' of other civilizations have a much longer history than that of

modern European colonialism. The changing, and often chequered, history of relations between Egypt and neighbouring cultures and peoples, in both ancient and modern times, is well documented (Jeffreys Chapter 1, this volume; Matthews and Roemer 2003; O'Connor and Quirke 2003). What has received much less attention is the role that obelisks played within such events. At one level at least, obelisks serve as icons of power, glory, triumph and prominence – they were almost archetypal (see Rice and MacDonald 2003), cropping up in various successive cultural contexts – ultimately inspired by historically-grounded signification and perhaps a convergence to what appears like a universal symbolism of monumental superstructures. This appears to be the case, even when parodied in the form of small desktop decorative items made of bright coloured stones, which are believed to be endowed with mystical powers. The historical legacy of the obelisk and its probable universal symbolism may also lie behind the decision by Mussolini to erect an obelisk immortalizing himself and his fascist empire (Figure 2:2), or the new Faisaliyah obelisk (complete with a capstone) (Figure 2:3) towering over Riyadh in Saudi Arabia, commemorating King Feisal, the founder of the modern Saudi state (www.rense.com/general19/occ.htm). Similarly, the supremacy of our electronic technological age has been heralded by a new monument of light, the Obelisk of Light' (Figure 2:4), which was erected on 31 December 1999 to stand throughout the Jubilee of 2000 in the Piazza Cinquecento in Rome (where an Egyptian obelisk with a star symbolizing Italy once stood, with the names of Italian soldiers who were killed in the attempt to colonize Ethiopia; see below). The base of the 'shimmering Obelisk of Light' is wrapped in 3M Optical Lighting Film and there are three large real-time displays which provide up-to-date information on the status of nuclear disarmaments. Italian Senator and President of the Disarmament Archive, Luigi Anderlini, noted that "the 'Obelisk of Light' is a powerful symbol of Peace" (www.3m.com).

## Obelisks and colonial rule

In 1798, Napoleon Bonaparte invaded Egypt. His aim was to secure Egypt as a power base for his world empire. Egypt was important because it controlled the way to India, a country prized by the British as the jewel in their crown. It was also important because of its rich agricultural resources (Jeffreys Chapter 1, this volume). But, perhaps more important in the struggle for world hegemony, Egypt was the land of a legendary ancient civilization: a civilization that was admired by the Greeks; a civilization that captured the imagination of Alexander (the Great) and dazzled Roman emperors and senators (Ucko and Champion 2003; Matthews and Roemer 2003). Its obelisks adorned many parts of Rome, the capital of an ancient empire adopted by western Europe as its own cultural birthplace. The publication of the *Description de l'Égypte* (1809–1828), as one of the greatest legacies of the Napoleon Bonaparte campaigns, marks the modern phase of Egyptological learning. Bonaparte's interest in the pharaonic past was already kindled before he embarked on his Egyptian campaign. By 1803, he was gone from Egypt, but Champollion was there to seek permission from Mohammed Ali, who had become *de facto* ruler of Egypt after the defeat of the French in 1799 (Marsot 1985), to study the monuments of Egypt. The Albanian-born ruler, who came to Egypt as a supply officer in the Turkish army and aspired to create his own empire, acceded to Champollion's request on the condition

Figure 2:2   Modern obelisk erected by Mussolini in the Foro Italiano, Rome, Italy. 16.76 m, Carrara marble (© Francesco Trifiló).

Figure 2:3   The Faisaliyah obelisk-like structure in Riyadh, Saudi Arabia (© Majeed Khan).

Figure 2:4   The 'Obelisk of Light' erected in Rome for the Jubilee of 2000, Italy (designed by P. Bodega and G. Ceppi; © Alberto Novelli).

that he provide him with a translation of the Alexandrian obelisks, known then as 'Cleopatra's needles' (see Hamill and Mollier 2003: 213; Figures 2:5, 2:6).

At that time, obelisks, the monumental wonders of Ancient Egypt, were a cardinal feature of Rome, the eternal city that was once the capital of the Roman Empire. Britain, France, Germany and other European nations, who were actively forging their nationalistic identities by the end of the 19th century and early decades of the 20th, were keen on appropriating the icons of the imperial past as their own emblems of power and imperial status. Obelisks are physically prominent. Whether standing in the ruins of temples or the centre of European cities, obelisks attract attention by their polish, their decoration and, above all, their lofty height (Habachi 1984: xiii). They were among the first skyscrapers: their height could reach more than 30 m (e.g. Tuthmosis III's 'Laterano' obelisk (Figure 2:7), or the obelisk of Hatshepsut in Karnak (Figure 2:8)).

## Obelisks: the Egyptian legacy

The obelisk is an upright monolith with a square cross-section tapering upward. Its top is carved in the shape of a pyramid (a pyramidion). Known to the Egyptians as *Tekhenu*, the Greeks referred to them as "spits" (*Obeliskos*) while the Arabs called them "needles" (*Messalah*). Obelisks have often been dedicated to sun gods, as Atum (setting sun) and Ra (rising sun). The oldest presumed association was with the *ben* or *benben* stones, resembling the pyramidion in the form of the rays of the sun and the mount of creation. These stones are associated with Heliopolis, the Egyptian solar cult centre. Iconographic and textual evidence for obelisks dates back to the fifth Dynasty and the sixth Dynasty, when the sun cult became a manifest royal preoccupation. The *benben* and the obelisks were also associated with the *Benu*-bird, the 'phoenix', for the Greeks. Obelisks were often dedicated to the god of writing and wisdom, Thoth (Habachi 1984: 3–14), depicted as an ibis or a baboon. Hermes, in post-pharaonic times, was an adaptation of Thoth (Hornung 2001: 48), providing a link between obelisks and the Hermetic tradition (see Haycock 2003).

The obelisk was undoubtedly of great religious significance in Ancient Egypt, as revealed by inscriptions dedicating the obelisks to various divine forms of the sun god (including the sacred bull of Mnevis, the living soul of Ra). Used in funerary contexts in the pyramids of the kings of the fifth Dynasty, obelisks were also used as funerary stelae, inscribed with the name and titles of the deceased, from the fifth Dynasty onwards (see Habachi 1984: 44).

The remarkable discovery by Mattawa Balboush of the remains of the earliest known use of a royal obelisk, inscribed with the name of King Teti (Figure 2:9; Habachi 1984: 41–42) proves that obelisks were erected as royal monuments by the middle of the third millennium BC. Kings of the Middle Kingdom erected obelisks in Heliopolis, where only one, erected by Sesostris I (1971–1926 BC), is still standing (Figure 2:10).

Tuthmosis I (1504–1492 BC), the third king of the New Kingdom, set Egypt on the course of empire building and erected a pair of large obelisks in Karnak. The one still standing of this pair is 19.5 m tall (Figure 2:11). His daughter Hatshepsut erected two

Figure 2:5   Obelisk of Tuthmosis III from Heliopolis (one of the so-called 'Cleopatra's Needles') in London, England. 20.88 m, red granite (© Suzie Maeder).

Figure 2:6   Obelisk of Tuthmosis III from Heliopolis (one of the so-called 'Cleopatra's Needles' ca. 1890) in Central Park, New York, USA. 21.21 m, 193 tonnes, red granite (© Adolf Wittman, Museum of the City of New York).

Figure 2:7 Obelisk of
Tuthmosis III from
Karnak, now in Piazza
S. Giovanni, Laterano,
Rome, Italy. 32.18 m,
37 m with base, 455
tonnes, red granite
(© Suzie Maeder).

Figure 2:8   Obelisk of Hatshepsut in Karnak (right), Luxor. Obelisk of Tuthmosis I (left) (postcard, 1900–1915, courtesy of Fathi Saleh, National Centre for Documentation of Cultural and Natural Heritage, Cairo, Egypt).

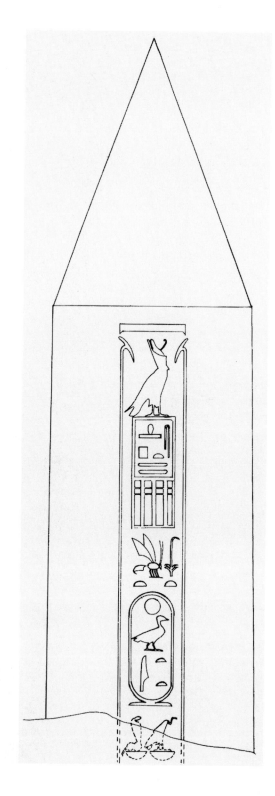

Figure 2:9    Inscribed obelisk of King
Teti (after Habachi 1984: fig. 16).

Figure 2:10   Obelisk
of Sesostris I in
Heliopolis, Cairo,
Egypt (© Fekri Hassan).

10   KARNAK — Obelisk and Great Hypostyle Hall. — LL

Figure 2:11    Obelisk of Tuthmosis I in Karnak, Luxor, Egypt. 19.5 m (postcard, 1900–1915, courtesy of Fathi Saleh, National Centre for Documentation of Cultural and Natural Heritage, Cairo, Egypt).

pairs of obelisks in Karnak – one of them is still standing. The inscription on this obelisk testifies to its dedication to the creator god, her 'father' Amun, in an apparent assertion of the legitimacy of her rule. On the fallen obelisk, the inscription speaks of the dominion granted by Amun-Ra to her over her neighbours (Habachi 1984: 66):

> I am his excellent [heir] beloved of His Majesty (Amun-Ra) who placed the kingship of Egypt, the deserts and all foreign lands under my sandals. My southern border is at the region of Punt ... My eastern border at the marshes of Asia ... my western border at the edge of the horizon.

In her red quartzite shrine in Karnak, inscriptions refer to Hatshepsut's construction of a pair of obelisks (Figure 2:12).

Tuthmosis III, who succeeded Hatshepsut, began to launch a long series of military campaigns in south-west Asia, and erected numerous (at least seven) obelisks in Karnak (five) and Heliopolis (two). Four of these obelisks are now abroad, in Rome, London, New York and Istanbul (formerly Constantinople). The latter obelisk (Figure 2:13) features an inscription (Figure 2:14) that identifies Tuthmosis III as "a king who conquers all the lands, long of life and lord of Jubilees" (Habachi 1984: 9).

The association of grand obelisks with military exploits and imperial power is also manifest in the obelisks erected by Ramesses II, including those now in Piazza del

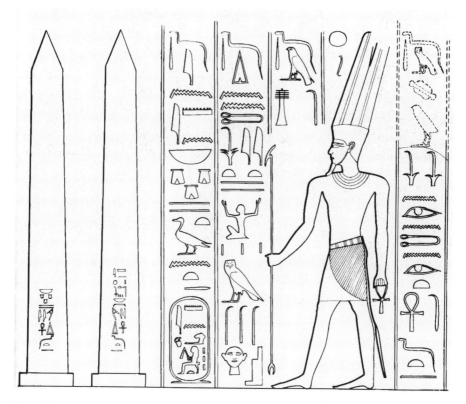

Figure 2:12   Block from Hatshepsut's red quartzite shrine, Karnak, Egypt, showing her dedicating two large obelisks to Amun-Ra (Luxor Museum; after Habachi 1984: fig. 26).

Figure 2:13  Obelisk of Tuthmosis III from Karnak, now in Istanbul, Turkey. Originally ca. 30 m, 400 tonnes, red granite (© Okasha El Daly).

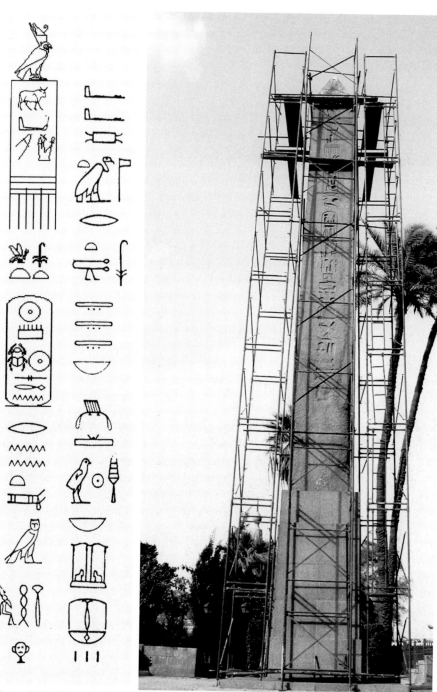

Figure 2:14   Hieroglyphic inscriptions on the obelisk of Tuthmosis III in Istanbul, Turkey. See Figure 2:13.

Figure 2:15   Ramesses II obelisk from Tanis, located since 1958 in Gezira Gardens, Cairo, Egypt. 13.5+ m (© Ahmed el-Bindari).

Popolo, Piazza della Rotunda, Viale delle Terme, Villa Celimontana in Rome, the Boboli Gardens in Florence, and in the Place de la Concorde, Paris. One of his obelisks (Figure 2:15), now in Cairo (the Gezira obelisk), proclaims Ramesses' military might and hegemonic rule (Habachi 1984: 94):

> (west face) The King, the son of Ptah who is pleased with victory, who makes great mounds of corpses of (Bedouin);

> (south face) The one who seizes all lands with valour and victory, who establishes the Land [of Egypt] again as it was at the First Occasion;

> (east face) A Monthu [god of war] among kings, who attacks hundreds of thousands, the strong one like Seth when he enters the fray;

> (north face) The king who smites every land and plunders this land?

## Obelisks: an august legacy

The ancient Egyptian empire crumbled as Persia and Greece became the main contenders in empire building. Defeated by the Persians first in 525 BC, and again in 343 BC, Egypt fell to Alexander the Macedonian in 332 BC, to be ruled by the Ptolemies after Alexander's premature death. By 30 BC, Egypt had become a province of the Roman Empire. Roman emperors, with their predilection for public display, removed obelisks from Egypt to be erected in Rome as a mark of their imperial power and possession of Egypt and its ancient past. The symbolic significance of obelisks that

Figure 2:16   General view of the obelisk of Ramesses II in Piazza del Popolo, Rome, Italy. See also Figures 2:1, 2:17 (© Suzie Maeder).

once glorified an Egyptian pharaoh "who conquers all the lands" was now passed to the rulers of the new world empire, the Romans.

Amongst many such activities, Augustus, in ca. 10 BC, placed an obelisk belonging to Ramesses II (now in front of S. Maria del Popolo) (Figures 2:1, 2:16, 2:17) in the centre of the Circus Maximus in Rome to commemorate his conquest and annexation of Egypt. He also transported another obelisk, originally belonging to Psammetichos II, from Heliopolis to be erected in the Campus Martius (since 1751 located in Montecitorio, thanks to Benedict XIV), where it was used as a monumental sundial (Figure 2:18). The site itself was the centre for the ritual of deification, and an imperial personification of Rome holding an obelisk (Figure 2:19) was carved to represent the Campus Martius. Two obelisks that were once in front of the mausoleum of Augustus are now in the Piazza dell'Esquilino (Figure 2:20), re-erected there by Pope Sixtus V in 1587, and in the Piazza del Quirinale (Figure 2:21), re-erected by Pope Pius VI in 1781.

In 37 AD, Caligula brought an obelisk (Figure 2:22) erected by Augustus in Alexandria to Rome, now in the Piazza di San Pietro (Curran 2003: 105, 116, Figure 5:6). Domitian erected an obelisk at the Temple of Isis in Rome, now located in Piazza Navona (Figure 2:23). An obelisk attributed to Hadrian (second century AD) was erected first outside Porta Maggiore at Circus Varianus, and then moved in 1822 by Pope Pius VII to its current location in the Monte Pincio Gardens, Rome (Figure 2:24; see Grafton 2003: 128).

## The obelisk and the cross

After a lapse of 150 years, obelisks made a comeback within Christianity when Constantine (274–337 AD) attempted to erect an obelisk, originally belonging to Tuthmosis III, in his new capital, Constantinople. However, the obelisk (Figure 2:13), which was taken from its location in Karnak to Alexandria on the orders of Constantine in preparation for its transport to Constantinople, was not in fact erected in the emerging centre of Christendom until the reign of Thodosius I (346–396).

For centuries, the obelisks in Rome were neglected. Indeed, more than a millennium passed before Pope Sixtus V began to resurrect obelisks, and re-present them under the banner of Christianity. Only one obelisk remained standing in the Vatican Circus – the obelisk originally erected by Augustus in Alexandria (Grafton 1993: 118) (Figure 2:22).

Pope Sixtus V was instrumental in re-erecting fallen obelisks in order to proclaim the power of the Catholic Church and to glorify its triumph over pagan civilizations. In his own colourful words, he stated (quoted by Tompkins 1981: 31):

> ... to quench the detestable memories of idolatry ... and exalt the mysteries of the Catholic Religion ...

This Pope's achievements included the ordering of the re-erection of four more obelisks in the span of two years: at Montecitorio (Figure 2:18) in 1587, Piazza dell'Esquilino (Figure 2:20) in 1587, Laterano (Piazza S. Giovanni) (Figure 2:7) in 1588, and Piazza del Popolo (Figure 2:1) in 1589 (see Curran 2003: 124). As it turned out, the

Figure 2:17    Obelisk of Ramesses II in Piazza del Popolo, Rome, Italy. 23.30 m, 238 tonnes, red granite. See also Figures 2:1, 2:16 (© Suzie Maeder).

Figure 2:18   Obelisk of Psammetichos II first erected in Campus Martius, now located in Montecitorio, Rome, Italy. 21.79 m (29 m from base of globe), 230 tonnes, red granite. See also Figure 2:19 (© Suzie Maeder).

Figure 2:19    Representation of Rome holding the Campus Martius obelisk, Rome, Italy. See also Figure 2:18 (© Mary Ann Sullivan).

Figure 2:20    Uninscribed obelisk in Piazza dell'Esquilino, Rome, Italy. 14.75 m (© Suzie Maeder).

Figure 2:21   Uninscribed obelisk in Piazza del Quirinale, Rome, Italy. 14.64 m, 43 tonnes
(© Suzie Maeder).

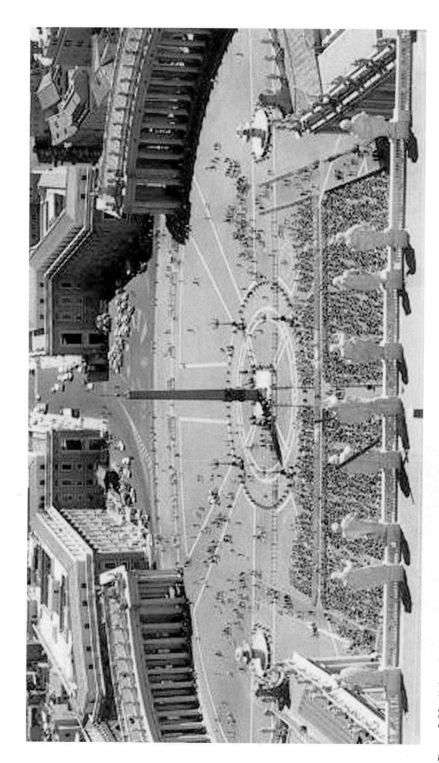

Figure 2:22 Uninscribed obelisk of Augustus, re-erected by Pope Sixtus V in 1586, in Piazza di San Pietro, Rome, Italy. 25.37 m (source: www.uweb.ucsb.edu).

Figure 2:23   Obelisk now in Piazza Navona, Rome, originally quarried from Aswan by order of Domitian, and hieroglyphs inscribed in Rome, Italy. 16.54 m. See also Figures 2:25, 2:26 (© Suzie Maeder).

Figure 2:24    Obelisk with two columns of hieroglyphic text, in Piazalle del Monte Pincio, Rome, Italy. 9.75 m (© Suzie Maeder).

Montecitorio obelisk (Figure 2:18) was considered to be too fragile to erect at that time. However, it was restored and erected in 1792 by Pope Pius VI. When it was found in what was once the Circus Maximus, the Laterano obelisk (Figure 2:7) was buried 5 m below the surface of vineyards and gardens (Tompkins 1981: 41). The search for it, using a 6 m pointed rod, could be claimed to be one of the first 'remote sensing' applications in archaeology.

In 1662, Pope Innocent X re-erected an obelisk that once stood between the Serapeum and the Temple of Isis in ancient Rome. Unlike other obelisks, this one was not originally made by Egyptians, but was quarried on the orders of Emperor Domitian (51–95 AD) from the granite quarries in the Aswan area. His name in hieroglyphic script was carved on the obelisk. Innocent X decided to erect it next to the building in Piazza Navona where he lived when he was a cardinal. Gianlorenzo Bernini had conceived of placing this obelisk above a fountain (Figure 2:25), not only linking the obelisk with water – symbol of life – but also including in his design of the fountain the Nile, the Ganges, the Danube and the Plate (Curran 2003: 128, 131), representing respectively Africa, Asia, Europe and America (Wengrow Chapter 12, this volume). This obelisk thus symbolized the dominion over the world appropriated by the Pope.

During the 17th century, great wealthy families were forming a new class of princely nobility. It is telling that the Piazza Navona obelisk was crowned with a dove, the heraldic symbol of Pope Innocent X's Pamphili family (Figure 2:26). Not surprising, from this perspective, was the transfer of an obelisk in the 17th century (originally erected by Ramesses II at Heliopolis) that once stood in the Temple of Isis in Rome to the Roman Villa of the Medici, the noble family of Florence, who became

Figure 2:25   Fountain by Gianlorenzo Bernini under the obelisk in Piazza Navona, Rome, Italy. See also Figures 2:23, 2:26 (© Bruno Cancellieri).

Figure 2:26   A dove, the heraldic symbol of Pope Innocent X's Pamphili family, on top of the obelisk in Piazza Navona, Rome, Italy. See also Figures 2:23, 2:25 (© Suzie Maeder).

its rulers from 1434 to 1737. This obelisk was moved to its current location in the Boboli Gardens in Florence in 1720 (Figure 2:27).

As early as 1582, collector Ciriaco Mattei managed to acquire, as a gift from the Roman authorities, an obelisk that was perhaps first placed at the Isis temple but, when it fell, was used as an entrance step for the covenant of S. Maria in Aracoeli. This rather short (2.68 m) obelisk adorned his private Villa Celimontana (Figure 2:28). Later, another collector, Sir William John Bankes, arranged for an obelisk (originally erected by Ptolemy IX in 116–81 BC at Philae) to be transported by Belzoni during 1815–1821 to England, to become, on its pedestal, the centrepiece of his estate in Dorset in 1830 (Figure 2:29; Usick 2002: 60).

Obelisks were also used in Italy outside Rome to adorn the new Renaissance centres. Urbino received its 'Egyptian' red granite obelisk from Rome in 1737 (Figure 2:30). This obelisk, from Sais, belonging to pharaoh Apries (ca. 90 AD), was discovered broken in the 18th century and was later donated by a cardinal to Urbino. It is one of a pair of obelisks now in Piazza di S. Maria sopra Minerva (Figure 2:34).

In Rome at about the same time (1711), an obelisk from Heliopolis of Ramesses II was re-erected by Clemens XI on top of a fountain in front of the Pantheon (Piazza della Rotunda) (Figure 2:31; Curran 2003: 117, Figure 5:7). In 1789, a curious obelisk with three columns of hieroglyphs on each face was erected by Pius VI overlooking the Spanish Steps at S. Trinità dei Monti (Figure 2:32).

In 1822, an obelisk commissioned by Hadrian in memory of his beloved friend Antinous was placed by Pius VII in the Piazalle del Monte Pincio (Figure 2:24). Champollion deciphered the name on the obelisk as Anteins, 'proving' that it was carved in the memory of Antinous (Tompkins 1981; and see below).

## Obelisks, nationalism and colonialism

In 1885, the newly established Italian government seized Rome. The Pope shut himself up in the Vatican and declared that he was a prisoner. He remained there even when the tension between church and state had relaxed. When Pius XI (1857–1939) became Pope in 1922, *rapprochement* between church and state led to a treaty signed with the Italian dictator Mussolini in 1929. The Pope was given St Peter's basilica, along with 108.7 acres. The obelisk that presumably was the last witness to the martyrdom of St Peter was now a witness to the transformation of power from Christendom to the modern nationalist state.

By 1883, a Ramesses II obelisk, originally from Heliopolis, had been discovered during the course of systematic archaeological excavations in Rome, the capital of a united Italy. In 1887, the Italians captured Massawa, Ethiopia's Red Sea pearl, after Emperor Yohannes of Ethiopia had ambushed 548 Italians, of whom only about 100 survived. As a national memorial to the soldiers who died in this failed colonial campaign, the Heliopolis obelisk was erected, with the names of the dead soldiers inscribed on its pedestal. King, queen and nobility attended the dedication of the obelisk. In 1924 it was removed to a garden south of the Viale delle Terme (Figure 2:33).

Figure 2:27 Obelisk of Ramesses II in the Boboli Gardens, Florence, Italy. 4.87 m, red granite (© Gloria Rosati).

Figure 2:28   Ramesses II
obelisk originally from
Heliopolis, erected near S.
Maria in Aracoeli, Rome, Italy,
and subsequently used to
decorate Ciriaco Mattei's
private villa. 2.65 m (source:
www.romeartlover.it/
obelisks.html).

In 1935–1936, Mussolini invaded Ethiopia. As a trophy, the Italians removed to Rome an Axumite obelisk (erected at Piazza di Porta Capena) and a bronze sculpture representing the Lion of Judah, the emblem of Ethiopian monarchy. In Rome, they placed the 'Lion of Judah' at the foot of the Viale delle Terme obelisk. The installation was unveiled in a public ceremony on 9 May 1937 (Habachi 1984; Iversen 1968).

Obelisks, at that moment in history when Italy was consolidating its power as a unified nation-state in a world of colonial expansion, were being used – as they had been used before by Roman emperors and popes – to proclaim the establishment of a new order.

Mussolini, in fact, erected an obelisk bearing the words "Mussolini Dux", proclaiming his hoped-for 'Fascist Empire' (www.informa.it). This obelisk (Figure 2:2), which stands in the Foro Italiano, carved from a single block of Carrara marble, is 16.76 m tall, the only modern monumental obelisk carved from a solid block of stone.

## Obelisks, hieroglyphs, and the power of knowledge

In 1665, Dominican friars were laying the foundation for a new wall around the gardens of their church when they unearthed an obelisk. The obelisk stood originally at Sais, in the Nile Delta. Pope Alexander VII, who was alerted to the discovery, commissioned Athanasius Kircher (1602–1680) to complete the clearance of the obelisk and its erection. In 1667, the obelisk was raised in front of the Church of S. Maria sopra Minerva to rest on Bernini's (or, rather, Ercola Ferrata's) sculpted elephant (Figure 2:34; Curran 2003: 131, Figure 5:11; D'Onofrio 1967). Kircher, a Jesuit priest, was fascinated and intrigued by the glyphs inscribed on Egyptian obelisks (Curran 2003: 124–129; Iversen 1993; Kircher 1650, 1652–1654, 1666), being convinced that the temples of Egypt incorporated the cosmology of the ancients and the knowledge of physics. He also believed that the hieroglyphs were "a sacred instrument bequeathed by the gods to the Egyptians ... enabling them to express their wisdom and the secrets of esoteric knowledge in symbolic pictures, the meaning of

Figure 2:29   Obelisk of Ptolemy IX on the lawn of Kingston Lacy, Dorset, England. 6.7 m, ca. 6 tonnes, red granite (© Okasha El Daly).

Figure 2:30 Apries' obelisk originally from Sais, then located in Rome, and subsequently donated to Urbino, Italy (source: www.bibleufo.com).

Figure 2:31   Obelisk of Ramesses II in Piazza della Rotunda, Rome, Italy. 6.34 m (© Suzie Maeder).

Figure 2:32 Obelisk of Trinità dei Monti, Rome, Italy. 13.91–14.10 m, red granite. See also Figure 2:37 (© Suzie Maeder).

Figure 2:33  Obelisk of Ramesses II in Viale delle Terme, Rome, Italy. 6.34/9.25 m, red granite (© Suzie Maeder).

Figure 2:34  Obelisk of Apries standing on a statue of an elephant, Piazza di S. Maria sopra Minerva, Rome. 5.47 m, red granite (© Suzie Maeder).

which was directly revealed to initiates by divine inspiration" (Tompkins 1981: 94). With the consent of Pope Alexander VII, Kircher added the following inscription to the Piazza Minerva obelisk base:

> O you who here see transported by an elephant, the strongest of animals, the hieroglyphs of the wise Egyptians, heed this monument: to sustain solid wisdom, a robust mind is needed.

> (Quoted in Tompkins 1981: 100)

The recognition that Ancient Egypt was not just a dreadful pagan civilization, but was a source of powerful knowledge, was an aspect of the Hermetic traditions (Haycock 2003) that can be traced to the Neoplatonic school in Alexandria (Tompkins 1981: 56–59), which was kept alive by secretive societies like the Sufis, who passed their knowledge to the Templars, and eventually to the Rosicrucians and Freemasons (Hamill and Mollier 2003; Hornung 2001: 48–54, 83–91, 116–127). This metaphysical tradition fuelled an interest in hieroglyphs; for example, Pierio Valeriano (d. 1558) included in his comprehensive treatment of 'Hieroglyphica' an obelisk that was believed to bear the inscription (Figure 2:35) from the temple of Neith at Sais, mentioned by Plutarch (Hornung 2001: 88, 89, fig. 18; Tait 2003). Kircher felt secure enough in his decipherment of the meaning of the hieroglyphs that he even drafted his own hieroglyphic inscriptions on an obelisk in honour of Emperor Ferdinand III (Hornung 2001: 101, fig. 21; Figure 2:36). Poor copies of Egyptian inscriptions and invented 'Romanized' hieroglyphs, as on the Trinità dei Monti obelisk (Figure 2:37), mark a stage in the preoccupation with hieroglyphs as an integral element of the obelisk in their Roman context. Whatever the detail of the particular 'reading'/'decipherment', inscriptions on obelisks were presumed to be proclamations of the wisdom of Ancient Egypt, thus transforming the appropriation of obelisks into an appropriation of another civilization's wisdom, rather than merely the evidence for material achievements. Power itself had shifted to the power of knowledge. It was as if, where the Bible was no longer the source of useful knowledge, symbols of other kinds of knowledge were sought to legitimate a new order. Obelisks once more possessed the aura of historical validation and were, additionally, enigmatic inscriptions that promised the secrets of all knowledge.

Napoleon Bonaparte's foray into Egypt was indeed short, but his officers found the Rosetta Stone, which provided the key for deciphering the hieroglyphs. Underscoring the contest between the two major colonial powers, France and Britain, the Rosetta Stone was one of a number of artefacts seized by the British following the defeat of the French troops and their surrender (Bierbrier Chapter 3, this volume). That a contest for legitimacy based on the acquisition of knowledge was a major element in the conflict between the French and the British is made clear by the forceful proclamations of the French *savant* Étienne Geoffrey Saint-Hilaire (quoted in Tompkins 1981: 157) when he learned that the British planned to keep all the antiquities collected by the French as spoils of war:

> You are taking from us our collections, our drawings, our copies of hieroglyphs; but who will give you the key to all of that? Without us this material is a dead language that neither you nor your scientists can understand ...

Jean-François Champollion cracked the code of the hieroglyphic signs not only by using the Rosetta Stone, but also by examining obelisk inscriptions: a cartouche from

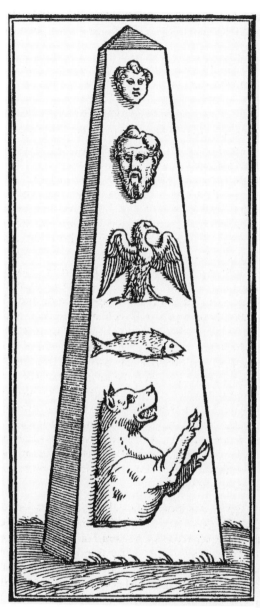

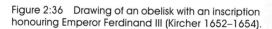

Figure 2:35   Drawing of an obelisk with simulated
hieroglyphs (Valeriano in Hornung 2001: fig. 18).

Figure 2:36   Drawing of an obelisk with an inscription
honouring Emperor Ferdinand III (Kircher 1652–1654).

Figure 2:37  Romanized hieroglyphs on the obelisk of Trinità dei Monti, Rome, Italy. See also Figure 2:32 (© Suzie Maeder).

a Karnak obelisk gave Champollion 'Alksdr' for 'Alexander'. The obelisks in Rome gave him the names of 'Antinoüs', 'Lucilius', 'Vespasian', 'Titus', 'Sextus', 'Africanus', 'Tiberius', 'Domitian', 'Nirva', as well as titles such as 'Caesar'. King Louis XVIII (1755–1824), himself passionately interested in Ancient Egypt, assigned to Champollion the task of studying Egyptian collections looted in Egypt by the French Consul Bernardino Drovetti, and bought by the King of Sardinia for his museum in Turin. Champollion also became the curator of a special Egyptian collection at the Louvre, which included the antiquities that had been acquired from the king of Sardinia.

## Obelisks and colonial rivalry

In 1814, Louis XVIII asked Mohammed Ali to grant him an obelisk for his capital, no doubt as a form of celebration for the re-establishment of kingship in France. Seeking favour with the French to gain their support against Turkey and to help him in modernizing Egypt, Ali offered the French the still standing obelisk of Tuthmosis III at Alexandria, but he was coaxed into offering the fallen one to the British (Bourbon 1996: 30–31). As the French prepared to transport the obelisk, the British succeeded in also persuading Mohammed Ali to assign them the pair of obelisks standing in front of the Luxor temple (Figure 2:38). Under pressure, Ali offered the British the magnificent obelisk of Hatshepsut in Karnak, ceding the pair of Luxor obelisks to the French, who would also keep the standing Alexandria obelisk. The British accepted. However, on consideration the French realized that they could not transport three obelisks and opted, following Champollion's advice, to transport first the most beautiful of them all, the one west of the entrance to the Luxor Temple (Bourbon 1996: 136, 157; Habachi 1984: 152–158).

When Lebas, the engineer appointed to direct transport operations, thanked him for securing the obelisk for France, Mohammed Ali (quoted in Tompkins 1981: 238) replied:

> I give her [France] the relic of an old civilization, it is in exchange for the new civilization of which she had spread the seeds in the Orient. Let the Obelisk be a tie between our two countries.

On 25 October 1836, the obelisk was erected in the Place de la Concorde, Paris (Figure 2:39).

The Middle East was chiefly the battleground for the British and the French (for the case of Spain, see Pérez-Accino and Sevilla Cueva Chapter 6, this volume). The British dealt a blow to the colonial plans of France overseas, when they destroyed Bonaparte's navy in 1799 in the Battle of Abu Qir. The statue of the triumphant Admiral Nelson, who defeated Napoleon's navy at one of London's main squares, Trafalgar, is emblematic of the British national pride as manifest in its ability to defeat its European rivals. In Egypt, the Earl of Cavan, who was in charge of a British regiment in Egypt, hoped to commemorate the defeat of the French army on land in 1801 by the removal of the fallen obelisk belonging to Tuthmosis III from Alexandria to London. The obelisk of this king "who conquers all the lands" was now to celebrate the victory of one imperial power, Britain, over France. By appropriating the Egyptian

Figure 2:38   Remaining obelisk of Ramesses II in Luxor Temple (© Francis Frith, ca. 1822).

Figure 2:39 Luxor obelisk of Ramesses II in Place de la Concorde, Paris, France. 22.83 m (© Fekri Hassan).

obelisk and erecting it in London, Britain signalled its inheritance of world power. London would thus become virtually a 'New Rome' (Habachi 1984: 165–170).

Cavan left Egypt before taking possession of the Alexandria obelisk. But in 1820, Mohammed Ali conceded to a request by Samuel Briggs, former British Pro-Consul in Alexandria, to remove the obelisk to London. Nevertheless, the British government did not take action, perhaps because the eminent Egyptologist Sir John Gardner Wilkinson considered the obelisk to be in such bad condition as to be unworthy of removal (Bierbrier Chapter 3, this volume). It took the Crystal Palace Company, though unsuccessfully, on the occasion of the Great Exhibition of 1851 (Hamill and Mollier 2003: 213; Werner 2003: 95–100), to take charge of bringing the obelisk to London. An Egyptian obelisk was thus to glorify not only Britain's political and military power, but also its position at the centre stage of economic world affairs. However, the transportation of the obelisk was delayed for various reasons until James Alexander (1803–1885), a British Army officer, determined "to do my utmost to have it transported to London, to grace the metropolis with a monument similar to those of Rome, Paris and Constantinople" (quoted in Habachi 1984: 170). On 13 September 1878, the obelisk was erected on the Victoria Embankment (Bourbon 1996: 30–31; Iversen 1972; Noakes 1962) (Figure 2:5). The Union Jack and the Egyptian flags were run up on the flagstaff that topped the obelisk; the crowds cheered the queen and the Khedive of Egypt, Ismail (1830–1895). Later, Britain and France forced the Khedive to abdicate in order to take full control of Egyptian finances and to manage the Suez Canal. In 1956, following the nationalization of the Canal by Nasser, Britain and France, in alliance with Israel, invaded Egypt to re-establish control and take possession of the Suez Canal (Mansfield 1969). The Suez crisis resulted in the withdrawal of the occupying force and brought about the resignation of Eden, the British Prime Minister, signalling the end of the British Empire and the transition to a new international phase dominated by the USA.

## Obelisks and the empire of commerce

In 1881, three years after the installation of one of the Tuthmosis Alexandria obelisks on the Victoria Embankment in London, and one year before the British occupation of Egypt, a reporter for the *New York Herald* wrote:

> ... it would be absurd for the people of any great city to hope to be happy without an Egyptian obelisk. Rome has had them this great while and so has Constantinople. Paris has one. London has one. If New York was without one, all those great cities might point the finger of scorn at us and intimate that we could never rise to any real moral grandeur until we had our obelisk.
>
> (D'Alton 1993: 11)

On 22 January 1881, the obelisk was installed in New York's Central Park, in view of the Metropolitan Museum (see Figure 2:6). Tickets were sold to the huge crowds who came to the formal presentation of the gift to New York from the government of Egypt. The principal address, by Henry G. Stebbins, the first President of the museum, encouraged the wealthy citizens of New York to enlarge the museum and to fill it with all those treasures which so greatly increase the attraction of the metropolis.

Pictures of the obelisk on the occasion of its erection were used in New York to sell medicines against haemorrhage and inflammation, using the pun on the word 'needle' (for obelisk) to advertise "the greatest thread and needle in the world" (Figure 2:40). Once the paramount symbol of military and religious power, the obelisk became for enterprising New Yorkers a means to gain commercial profits.

## Independence and decolonization

After 1954, the year when the Egyptians expelled the British (see above) and at a time when Egypt was not yet gripped with the political aim of aligning itself with Arab countries to enhance its political weight in the postcolonial order (Hassan 1998), Cairo was surprisingly lacking an obelisk. Today, Cairo boasts two obelisks, both from Tanis, where they were erected by Ramesses II. One of them now proclaims the pharaonic heritage of Egypt and hints at its ancient glory to tourists as they make their way from the airport to the city (Figure 2:41) (Abd Alrazek *et al*. 1994: 4). On their way out of town they may glimpse the colossal statue of Ramesses II, originally from Meit Rehina (Memphis), which has been placed in another hub of transportation – the railway station, which is now known as Ramesses Square. This icon of pharaonic Egypt appears to be aimed at Egyptians arriving from the countryside. Cairo's other obelisk is located on the Gezira Embankment (Figure 2:15), overlooking the Nile Hilton Hotel (the first American hotel built after the 1952 revolution), and the building of the Arab League on the east bank replacing the barracks of the occupying British troops. The context of the Gezira Obelisk, with the lingering traces of a British colonial past and the burgeoning tourist hotels and restaurants, hints at an Egypt well past the struggle against colonialism witnessed by my father, and even my memory of the same spot where I used to come with my schoolmates to take advantage of the Gezira Gardens, once the privileged grounds of the British.

Although standing more than 13.5 m high on an elevated pedestal, the Gezira Obelisk is barely noticeable, hidden by tall palm trees. Egypt's struggle to gain independence, which involved highlighting its ancient glory (Hassan 1998), has been compromised by the colonial appropriation of that past, creating a paradoxical encounter between Egyptians and the legacy of their own country. It has also been problematized by a move to engage Egypt in world politics as an "Arab" nation, and by the pressure exerted by some radicals to undermine Egyptian nationalism in favour of an Islamic identity. The obelisk, for now, is a thing of the past.

## The imperial power of knowledge

What is remarkable is that, in parallel with all its historical transformations, the obelisk managed to maintain its power not as an icon of military conquests and imperial glory, but as a key to secret knowledge. The association of the obelisk with Thoth, god of writing and wisdom, appears to have lingered in the memory of humankind well after the hieroglyphic inscriptions could be deciphered. It was apparently the persistence of a distant, faded and confounded memory of an association between inscriptions on obelisks and ancient Egyptian wisdom that led to underground movements and secret societies such as Freemasonry. It is telling that a small obelisk

Figure 2:40   Advertisement for thread on the occasion of erecting the Tuthmosis III obelisk in New York (after D'Alton 1993: 46).

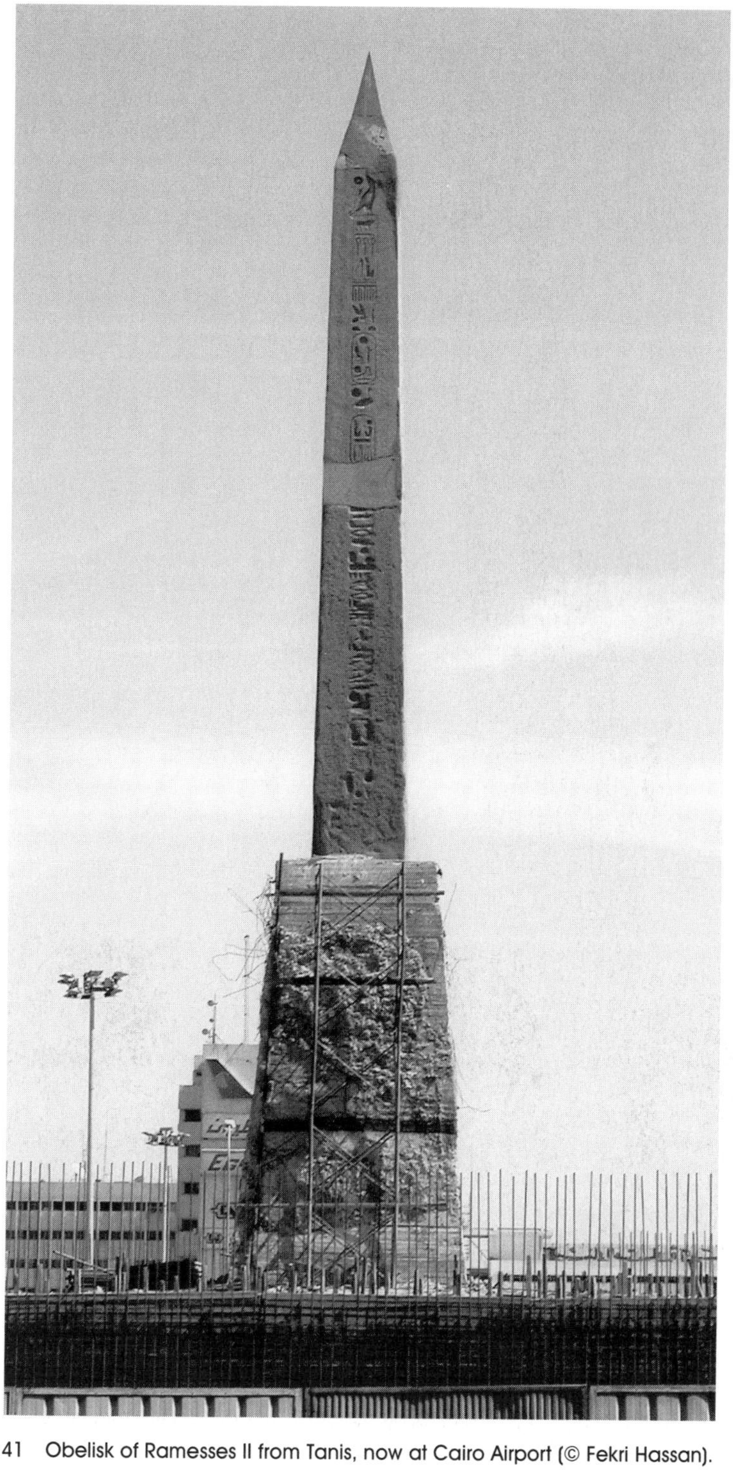

Figure 2:41 Obelisk of Ramesses II from Tanis, now at Cairo Airport (© Fekri Hassan).

stands over George Washington's grave at Mount Vernon (Fazzini and McKercher 2003: 137–138), recalling his Masonic connections rooted in the belief of the Hermetic knowledge of Ancient Egypt.

## Epilogue

Whatever its origins, the obelisk became in Ancient Egypt an icon of cosmic power and creation. The great obelisks were metaphors in stone of the greatness of the king who dedicated them to the gods, and at the same time a validation of the king's divine descent. Towering obelisks were erected by New Kingdom pharaohs to declare their dominion over foreign lands.

Later, Roman emperors appropriated obelisks to proclaim their own imperial might and invested them with a new layer of power. Pope Sixtus V, and a few other Popes after him, invested this age-old stone pillar with yet another coating of power; the power of almighty God as the cross mounted the obelisk.

By the 18th century, the appropriation of obelisks became tantamount to a statement about possession of history and the world. It seemed as if not to have an Egyptian obelisk was a national disgrace during the colonial struggle for world dominance between France and Britain. Within the same colonial, nationalist epoch, Mussolini erected his own obelisk to commemorate an empire that was not to be.

On the other side of the ocean, the Washington Monument (built 1848–1884) (Fazzini and McKercher 2003: Figure 8:2), a hollow, obelisk-shaped structure looming 170 m high, is one of the more prominent features of the capital of the USA, which has since become a global superpower. New Yorkers had their obelisk, which signalled the USA's entry in the race for world power.

### Acknowledgments

I am most grateful to Suzie Maeder for permission to use her photographs for many of the Figures in this chapter. I also thank Okasha El Daly and Ahmed el-Bindari for other illustrations.

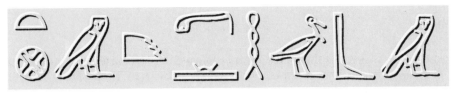

## CHAPTER 3

# ART AND ANTIQUITIES FOR GOVERNMENT'S SAKE

*Morris L. Bierbrier*

A common feature of human behaviour is the way in which those in power and authority attempt to legitimize, advertise and glorify their position with pomp and display, and commemorate their rule through art and architecture. In ancient and, occasionally, in modern times, this desire was also coupled with an imperative to honour and magnify the prestige of the god or gods who were thought to have brought the ruler to the height of his or (rarely) her fame. From Ancient Egypt, little survives of the court display which was designed to overawe subjects and foreigners, but rather more of the architecture, both temple and funerary, and the associated sculpture which filled these monuments.

Most rulers have sought to commission impressive monuments, but this was not always possible, for reasons of time, politics or lack of resources; an enterprising ruler might then recycle the monuments of his predecessors, either by simply usurping them or by moving them to new locations and contexts. It was of course less heinous to strip a city than a major temple, but once a temple had fallen into disuse it also could become a quarry for prestige objects. Thus the famous city of Piramesse, once the newly-founded capital of Ramesses II, was looted as a source of art and architecture for the new capital of Tanis during the twenty-second Dynasty (Kitchen 1973).

The transfer of monuments was not slowed but rather increased during the Hellenistic period in Egypt. The non-classical nature of many of the art works did not deter either the Ptolemaic kings or the Roman emperors from making use of them: Alexandria, for example, was decorated with many monuments from the ancient and sacred city of Heliopolis, which was plundered for that purpose (Empéreur 1998). The Romans in turn despoiled Alexandria, removing both Egyptian and Greek pieces as well as helping themselves to similar objects from other sites. The most notable feature was the interest of the Roman emperors in Egyptian obelisks which were used to decorate Rome and, later, Constantinople (Iversen 1968–1972; see also Hassan Chapter 2, this volume).

Such actions ceased with the fall of the Roman Empire and the advent, in the seventh century AD, of Islamic rule in Egypt, whose new rulers sought to dazzle and display by various means, but certainly not normally with pagan symbols (Haarmann 1980). At the same time in Europe the medieval courts and leading ecclesiastical figures commissioned the construction of cathedrals, monasteries and churches, and amassed collections of holy relics and strange imported animals, but the instinct to impress remained undiluted. The rise of monarchical states increased this tendency, with the political aim of giving the monarch and his court a powerful image. This could be done with the construction of ever more sumptuous palaces culminating in Versailles, but also by patronizing artists and attracting collections of artwork, although for now these included few items from remote antiquity.

Royal national collections of art were built up in the 16th and 17th centuries, and the actions of the monarchs were emulated by their chief nobles. One such ardent royal collector was King Charles I of England, who built up the royal collection with massive purchases (Miller 1972); by contrast his view of court display was opposed by his puritan enemies, who eventually triumphed and who had an extremely limited view of art for government's sake – one of their first acts after the execution of the king was to sell off his art collection and destroy the crown jewels. Thus an ambivalent approach to the government's role in supporting the arts and collecting both art and antiquities was introduced into British government thinking and has persisted in different guises. When the idea of a British Museum was first mooted, the government sought to distance itself from the proposal by refusing to finance it, and instead organized a lottery to raise the necessary funds. Inevitably the government would be drawn into direct financing of this institution, but its support has always been uncertain and well short of its needs. No such problem occurred in 18th century France, where the royal collection remained intact, emphasizing France's leading international role politically, militarily and culturally.

Such ideas were too deeply imbued to be swept away by the French Revolution. Indeed, the Revolution strengthened the idea of France as the centre of world thinking and culture, through the nationalization of the royal collection which now became the people's collection. The leading French politicians and generals of revolutionary France were not insurgent peasants, but were of well-read middle-class or even noble origin. They rapidly grasped the idea of emphasizing French power not only by encouraging the growth of a multitude of sympathetic regimes in neighbouring states, which were then beholden to France, but also by helping themselves to the artwork of these states, which, once displayed in Paris, would conspicuously declare France's superiority and power. Indeed, during the French campaign in Italy (1796) a Special Commission of Science and Art in Italy was set up to acquire loot for France. The two most important members of the Commission were Gaston Monge (1746–1818) and Claude-Louis Berthollet (1749–1822) who later joined the Egyptian Expedition. It is unlikely that their views had changed in three years. What was good for the state was also good for the individual generals, who kept some of the art for themselves both for display and for pecuniary advantage.

Napoleon Bonaparte, a minor nobleman and leading general of the period, was a fervent exponent and indeed instigator of the acquisition of foreign art for the prestige of both the government and himself, helping himself to art collections during his Italian campaign. Thus, when his Egyptian campaign was being planned, the acquisition of antiquities was certainly on the agenda (Asprey 2000; Herold 1963). As is well known, the Egyptian Expedition was organized to include a large number of *savants* and technicians whose task was to examine and detail the geography, natural conditions, ethnography and antiquities of the newly-conquered French possession. Napoleon and his leading scholars had read in advance the works of earlier travellers such as Sonnini de Manoncourt and did not arrive in Egypt unprepared. Following his initial victory in 1798, Napoleon installed his scholars in a special residence in Cairo where they founded their Institut d'Égypte. Scholarly investigations were mounted; papers were prepared; and antiquities were collected for eventual transport to France. In the event, the collection of artwork was curtailed due to the hostility of the population, and transport of any items to France was impossible due to the blockade of Alexandria and the destruction of the French fleet by Nelson. As an obvious symbol of French rule, the Institut later became a target for anti-French protesters but was saved from damage. Of necessity, much of the research work was carried out by educated military officers and engineers rather than the scholars, most of whom were unable or unwilling to venture too far from the relative safety of Cairo and Alexandria. Vivant Denon (1747–1825) was a noted exception: he accompanied the troops to the south (Ghali 1986). The scholars were regarded with mild contempt by the soldiers, but they did have an influence on the behaviour of the military in regard to antiquities. The soldiers – officers and men – became well aware of the interest and value of antiquities, both to the scholars and to their Commander-in-Chief, and so any possible acts of vandalism were avoided (contrary to popular opinion, the French did not damage the nose of the Sphinx, which had already been recorded in its damaged condition by early travellers in the mid-18th century).

Because of the heightened awareness of the value of antiquities, the soldiers excavating the fort at Rosetta, and finding in its foundations a trilingual stone inscription, did not discard it but were careful to save it for scrutiny. The exact circumstances of the discovery remain obscure: Lieutenant Pierre Bouchard (1771–1822) is usually credited with saving the stone, although he appears to have been in overall charge of the repairs to the fort and may have become involved only when the discovery was brought to his attention by ordinary soldiers, so he may not have actually been on the spot when it was found. Certainly he acted quickly to preserve the piece and expedite its removal to Cairo and the scholars' camp. Interestingly enough, the Rosetta Stone was not in the end considered the property of the French state but rather that of General Jacques Menou, the Governor of the city at the time of the stone's discovery (Solé and Valbelle 1999).

The vulnerability of the French research programme increased once Napoleon fled from Egypt in 1799. He took with him several of the leading French scholars such as Denon, Monge and Berthollet, enraging and depressing those who had been left behind. As the British and Turkish forces advanced, the scholars and their collections were evacuated to Alexandria. Embarkation of at least one major object, the sarcophagus of Nectanebo, had already taken place, and others were due to be put on French ships when Alexandria surrendered to the British-Turkish forces on 30 March 1801. Article 16 of the capitulation specified that all antiquities collected by the French should be considered as public property and subject to the disposal of the generals of the combined army. The British were first inclined to interpret this clause very strictly and confiscate all drawings and antiquities from the scholars, but, after frenzied protests and threats of destruction on the part of the scholars, the British relented and the scholars were allowed to keep their papers and small portable antiquities.

The list of confiscated objects, which runs to only 15 items, demonstrates how difficult it had been for the French to amass a collection of major Egyptian antiquities

Figure 3:1 French surveyors measuring a colossal fist, now in the British Museum (EA9), at Memphis, 1799 (*Description* 1809–1828, v. 5: pl. 3).

during their rule in Egypt from 1798 to 1801 (Bierbrier 1999). In view of the major collections that were later put together early in the 19th century, it is obvious that the French had little or no time for excavation, and only objects lying ready to hand on the surface, or re-used by being built into public structures, had been acquired. Indeed, like the Rosetta Stone, very few of the objects were the property of the French government, but rather that of French generals and merchants, almost with the status of 'spoils of war', although such declarations might also have been made in the hope (in which they failed) that Article 16 could be circumvented. The French government only claimed the sarcophagi of Nectanebo and Henta, the statue of Roy, and some statues of the lioness deity Sakhmet. Four French generals were named as owners of five major pieces – a sarcophagus (the late General Lanusse), two classical statues (General Friant), a colossal fist from Memphis (General Dugua) (Figures 3:1, 3:2), and, most importantly, the Rosetta Stone (General Menou, then the French Commander-in-Chief). It is not entirely clear what the generals intended to do with their property – which, with the exception of the Nectanebo sarcophagus, were more valuable than the French government's share. Perhaps they intended to sell them back to the government for a profit, which was almost certainly the fate of seven items listed as belonging to private citizens Hamelin and Liveron: these two seem to have acquired an interesting collection, including two obelisks of Nectanebo and a ram's head from Upper Egypt. If these private individuals had managed to acquire objects from Upper Egypt – then a dangerous area for foreigners – one wonders why the scholars themselves, with their military protection, were so lax in their collecting activities.

The fate of the surrendered objects was quickly decided. The Ottoman Turks, the recognized rulers of Egypt, had no interest in antiquities and ceded them to the British, perhaps surprised that this was all the British demanded for their help in liberating Egypt from the French and returning it to Turkish control. It would appear that the British wanted the objects not so much for any display emphasizing British cultural prestige, but rather as trophies representing British defeat of the French: since

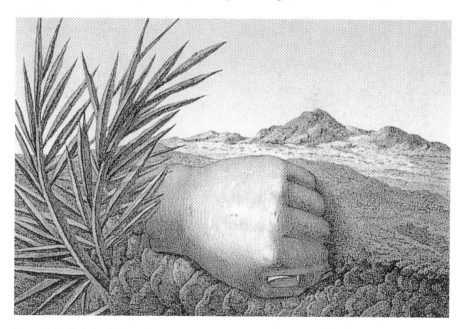

Figure 3:2   Details of the colossal fist in Figure 3:1 (*Description* 1809–1828, v. 5: pl. 4).

the French had wanted them, the British must have them. Some of the officers, and travelling scholars such as Edward Clarke who happened to be present, were certainly aware of the possible academic importance of the Rosetta Stone, the prize piece, which was treated differently and more respectfully than the other objects and dispatched on a ship of its own. The British also picked up a few objects as souvenirs, some of which were added to the French group. It is perhaps indicative of the British attitude that the antiquities were not immediately presented to some academic institution but directly to King George III. He was not interested in the gift and promptly handed the objects over to the British Museum, as he had done with another group of Egyptian objects which he had been given in 1766.

Interest in the antiquities of Egypt was revived after the end of the Napoleonic wars: Egypt now possessed a stable government under Mohammed Ali, and also a strategic importance as the new modernizing power in a Middle East faced with the decline of its nominal Turkish overlord. This stability allowed a limited form of tourism by the most adventurous Europeans, who were not averse to pocketing the odd antiquity or two as souvenirs. The Egyptian government's attitude to its ancient relics was clear: it had absolutely no interest in them. Mohammed Ali and his advisers subscribed to the point of view that pagan remains and indeed pagan history were best ignored, as true history could only begin with the Islamic conquest (although they do not appear to have shown any greater interest in medieval Islamic remains). The destruction of archaeological sites at this time was done not for reasons of religious fundamentalism, but for entirely practical purposes such as the extraction of building materials (limestone for slaking) or the armaments industry (saltpetre for the production of gunpowder). Otherwise the authorities were generally indifferent to them; and as the Europeans expressed a puzzling interest in these antiquities, they were welcome to them since they were thereby indebted, at no perceived cost, to Mohammed Ali and his government.

Substantial excavation and collection of antiquities only began when the foreign Consuls sensed advantages to themselves, and had the resources to organize expeditions and manpower for the purpose. The lead was taken by the French Consul Bernardino Drovetti (1776–1852), followed by his British counterpart Henry Salt (1780–1827) (Manley and Rée 2001; Ridley 1998). Their example was followed by others, such as the Swedish Consul Giovanni Anastasi (1780–1860). Drovetti was an educated military man, but it seems that his desire to amass antiquities was due more to the temporary prestige such a collection brought him in European eyes, and more importantly the potential commercial profits on its sale which would augment his pension. On the other hand, Henry Salt had a more academic interest in the subject of Ancient Egypt, and initially collected objects with a view to displaying them in the British Museum – after payment of his costs. As it turned out, the British Museum refused to pay what he considered reasonable amounts, and, after a furious row, he resolved to sell any future collections to the most profitable source. Thus, curiously, the French Consul's collection ended up in his native region of Turin, and the British Consul's second collection went to Paris, where the appreciation of the display of antiquities for government's sake was practised more generously and more ruthlessly.

Both Consuls have been accused of looting and despoiling Egyptian sites without proper excavation techniques, which is certainly true but needs to be seen in its historical context – few antiquarians were practising any real methodical excavation at this time. However, as indicated above, the Egyptian government certainly had no objection to the work, and gave the necessary *firmans*, or permissions. What the foreign Consuls accomplished was the creation of a market and value for antiquities among the Egyptian populace which undoubtedly saved many objects and sites from total destruction. The side-product of this was the revival of tomb robbery, an ancient Egyptian 'pastime', but one that could only be tackled when an interest in saving Egypt's cultural heritage became a declared aim of the Egyptian government.

The Consuls and their collections began the process that would culminate in the Egyptian Museum and the Egyptian Antiquities Service in the second half of the century, but Egypt in the early 1800s was regarded as a source of antiquities for European (and later American) national museums whose displays would reflect the prestige of the home state, not of Egypt. In the 1840s, for example, Karl Richard Lepsius was sent to gather objects for the new Prussian museum. This expedition, one of the best equipped ever, provided site plans and stratigraphic section drawings, and was unusual in its emphasis on recording as well as collecting. Like the French Expedition, the Prussian one resulted in another gigantic publication, the *Denkmaeler aus Aegypten und Nubien*, running to 12 folio volumes, with a manuscript text that was only published later. The French government, in an eerie replay of Roman imperial pretensions, sought an obelisk to decorate its capital and succeeded in 1831. Britain behaved differently: when offered an obelisk of its own, the British government prevaricated on grounds of cost and left it to private enterprise. Even then, the obelisk acquired in 1877 was allotted an unimpressive location in London on the Thames Embankment (Hassan Chapter 2, this volume: Figure 2:5), and not, as in Paris, in the centre of one of the city's main squares. An offer of the statue of Ramesses II at Memphis to the British was similarly delayed for reasons of expense, and the statue remains in Egypt to this day.

In conclusion, Egypt has been viewed as a source of art and antiquities with which foreign governments could decorate their capitals and fill their museums to demonstrate their power and cultural importance. This tradition extends back to Ancient Egypt itself, when there was no reluctance to move monuments about for the ruler's prestige. Some modern governments adopted a robust approach to this phenomenon and took or purchased whatever they could get hold of, while the British never fully adopted the principle of art and antiquities for the government's (and, in more politically correct times, the people's) sake. Significantly, these different approaches in the past still colour the treatment of the respective national cultural organizations in Egypt to this day. The French maintain a palatial Institut which not only accommodates the administrative and research staff but also hosts visiting French scholars, and runs dozens of archaeological and conservation programmes. Britain, which has never had a permanent base in Egypt, runs its national effort (the Egypt Exploration Society) from London and from a tiny office in the Consular compound in Cairo.

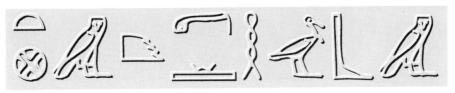

## CHAPTER 4

# "PURVEYOR-GENERAL TO THE HIEROGLYPHICS": SIR WILLIAM GELL AND THE DEVELOPMENT OF EGYPTOLOGY

*Jason Thompson*

Writing about Sir William Gell in one of the first volumes of the *Journal of Egyptian Archaeology*, H. R. H. Hall (1915a: 78–79) noted that "Gell acted for a time as a sort of Egyptological clearing-house. He gathered ideas from all sides, and communicated everybody's discoveries to everybody else with the best of intentions and often, no doubt, the best of results". Gell's Egyptological clearing-house role has become much clearer since Hall's time, especially in light of new material, including Gell's Egyptian notebooks and his letters to his protegé Sir Gardner Wilkinson. These show that Gell, who never travelled to Egypt and published no Egyptological work, nevertheless helped sustain and combine the varying lines of inquiry that eventually led to the establishment of the discipline of Egyptology.

Sir William Gell (1777–1836) was one of the great classical scholars of his day (Clay 1976; Dawson *et al.* 1995; Stephen and Lee 1963). After studying at Cambridge, he travelled extensively in the eastern Mediterranean, at one time leading a notable research expedition for the Society of Dilettanti. The products of these wanderings were *The Topography of Troy* (1804), *The Geography and Antiquities of Ithaca* (1807), and *The Itinerary of Greece* (1810). His method was to compare on-site observations with classical literary sources. This work was of fundamental importance, for it gave a solid background to a literature and history that had hitherto been set against a largely imaginary landscape. After a brief period of service to Princess Caroline in 1814 while she travelled around Europe and the Mediterranean, he settled in Italy where he published such works as *Le mura di Roma* (Gell and Nibby 1820) and *The Topography of Rome and its Vicinity* (1834). During his later years he established his principal residence at Naples, devoting himself to studying the remains of Pompeii and producing his best-known work, *Pompeiana* (1817–1819). Known as 'Classic' Gell to his many friends and admirers, his scholarship embodied the highest standards of topographical antiquarianism.

To understand the peculiar nature of Gell's influence upon the development of Egyptology, it is necessary to realize that besides being a scholar, he also was an intellectual intermediary. His small, book-lined house, to which he was increasingly confined by ill health, drew almost every British traveller with a scholarly bent who passed through Naples. One acquaintance wrote:

> His house is the rendezvous of all the distinguished travellers who visit it, where maps, books, and his invaluable advice, are at the service of all who come recommended to his notice. The extent and versatility of his information are truly surprising; and his memory is so tenacious, that the knowledge of any subject once acquired is never forgotten.

(Clay 1979: 50)

He knew how to make people relax and impart their knowledge to him, which he gathered not only for his own use but also for sharing, without pedantry or superiority. (See also Bury 1908: 57; Madden 1855, 1: 331.) His greatest joy was to bring together the right people and ideas. "I glory in communicating all the new discoveries," he wrote to Thomas Young (Leitch 1855, 3: 407).

Despite the breadth of his classical work, Gell's imagination ranged yet further, for he was especially interested in Egypt, having participated in the excitement and speculation that abounded in the aftermath of Napoleon's Egyptian expedition. He eagerly read Vivant Denon's *Voyages dans la Basse et la Haute Égypte* and the *Description de l'Égypte* that began to appear in 1809, displaying some of the best work of Napoleon's scholars in Egypt. Furthermore, Gell, an erudite man and avid book collector, was well acquainted with the Egyptian material in the Hermetic and Neoplatonist writings, as well as virtually every other Egyptological work, ancient and modern. He became interested in the mystery of the hieroglyphs and conducted an extensive correspondence with his friend, the Scottish polymath Thomas Young, who was devoting a portion of his considerable, though widely dispersed, energies to hieroglyphic translation (Wood and Oldham 1954). It was Young who caught the first, if incomplete, glimpse of the phonetic nature of Egyptian hieroglyphs, the discovery of which was later to be credited to Champollion. Gell's Egyptian connections increased in 1815 when an acquaintance, Henry Salt, was appointed British Consul-General in Egypt (Halls 1834; Bosworth 1974; Manly and Rée 2001). Although Gell took a deprecating view of Salt, the new Consul-General's presence on the ground enabled him to provide exciting information to Gell. From his perspective, Gell could see that great things were about to happen in Egyptian scholarship, and he wanted to participate in them as fully as possible. He was therefore especially attentive to the several young travellers and scholars who called upon him as they passed through Italy on their way to Egypt.

Without a doubt, the traveller that he influenced the most and with the greatest result was John Gardner (later Sir Gardner) Wilkinson (Dawson *et al.* 1995; Stephen and Lee 1963; Thompson 1992). When Wilkinson first called upon Gell he was a young, light-hearted traveller, eager to see the sights, intending to go to Egypt merely as the last leg of his Grand Tour. But Gell saw possibilities in him; he noticed the younger man's enthusiasm for antiquities, love of classical learning, and facility with pen and sketch pad. One day Gell said to him, "You seem to be much interested in these matters. Why do you not take up some branch of antiquarian research, and instead of going to Egypt as a mere wandering traveller, why not turn your attention to its antiquities?" (Lady Wilkinson's biographical MS). Wilkinson replied that he would gladly do so, but had insufficient knowledge. His education, though it included some good experience at Harrow School, had been completed by largely idle years at Oxford, and it left much to be desired. Gell offered to teach him everything then known about Egypt. Wilkinson accepted and spent the late summer and early autumn of 1821 studying under Gell, who provided an Egyptological course of instruction as thorough as one could have hoped for in those days.

Wilkinson's appearance was a great opportunity for Gell, whose thoughts were especially filled with Egypt at that moment. "I have determined upon going to Egypt as soon as circumstances permit," he had written to Young a few months earlier, but events prevented the trip (Gell to Thomas Young, May 1821; Madden 1855, 2: 492). If he could not go himself, then the next best thing was to experience it vicariously through Wilkinson, once Wilkinson was properly prepared to appreciate and report what he saw. Because of Gell's instruction, when Wilkinson left for Egypt, as Gell justifiably boasted later, he was better prepared to study its past than anyone who had travelled there since antiquity. Wilkinson soon afterward mentioned his debt in his first effort at publication: "For whatever I have done or ever shall do in hieroglyphics, I am entirely indebted to the kindness of Sir W. Gell, whose assistance and useful instructions, though I fully appreciated, I do not know how to acknowledge" (Wilkinson's MS 'Journey in Nubia'). Gell afterwards referred to Wilkinson as "My friend and pupil in Ægyptiaca" (Leitch 1855, 3: 224–226).

Once Wilkinson was in Egypt, he and Gell maintained contact by a regular, mutually beneficial correspondence. Gell kept Wilkinson fully informed about Egyptological advances in Europe and often advised him on where to go and what to look for:

> Abydus was so famous a burying place that I have little doubt a great deal might be done by excavating the sands which have filled it up. At Sais why has nobody found the North and South &c. &c. porticoes of the temple with the names of the Kings who built them and those of Memphis which names would be made certain by Herodotus and Diodorus. I hear of surprising discoveries high up the Nile with two Meroes and a nation armed in mail.
>
> (Gell to Wilkinson, July 1822)

Later he passed along suggestions from Champollion about what should be sought. Almost until the moment that Wilkinson left Egypt in 1833, Gell kept sending suggestions and posing new questions.

Gell, for his part, savoured the information that Wilkinson sent him. This, combined with his correspondence with Young, Salt, Champollion and others, probably made him the most knowledgeable outside observer of the progress of Egyptological research in the world at that time. From such sources he compiled personal notebooks of his own Egyptological speculations, attempts at hieroglyphic transliterations, speculations on orders of kings, and so forth. These, and the lengthy discourses in his letters to Wilkinson, show a high degree of application. Wilkinson's letters also provided material for conversation, the medium in which Gell excelled. One of his close friends wrote in her diary, "Gell brought us some extremely interesting letters from his enterprising and learned friend, Mr Wilkinson, the Egyptian traveller, to whom he is much attached" (Clay 1979: 110).

Wilkinson also began sending Gell numerous sketches of antiquities, many of which were extraordinary. For example, Wilkinson was probably the first to examine the northern tombs at Tell el-Amarna whose founder, Akhenaten, was unknown to Gell and Wilkinson. Wilkinson sent Gell a copy of the famous mural depicting the sun bestowing *ankhs*, the symbol of life, upon Akhenaten and his wife Nefertiti. Completely baffled by the artistic style, Wilkinson ventured the guess that it might be Persian. Gell, after copying Wilkinson's sketch into one of his notebooks, was likewise perplexed. The appearance of Akhenaten's and Nefertiti's distended bodies caused him to interpret the scene as "a sacrifice by these two pregnant females" (Gell Notebook).

What especially impressed Gell about Wilkinson's copies was their accuracy. For some time he had correctly suspected that many of the details in the engravings in the French *Description de l'Égypte* were, as he put it, "quite imaginary" and that they were unsuitable for use as Egyptological evidence. But Wilkinson's copies were clearly more objective, a quality that Gell noted in a letter to Thomas Young:

> I think you will find them [the hieroglyphs] quite well drawn for the purpose; and that the hand of a man like Wilkinson now long practiced in hieroglyphs is more likely to give the real character of the objects, than if they were drawn all over again to make the birds and beasts more like the animals they are intended for.
>
> (Leitch 1855, 3: 374)

Young was indeed impressed when he saw them, and he wrote to Gell, "Wilkinson's copies appear to be as accurately copied as they are beautifully executed" (in Leitch 1855, 3: 461). Gell was, however, too well informed to accept Wilkinson's data uncritically. When Wilkinson wrote that he believed he was the first to notice the deification of towns (Hall 1915b: 157), Gell commented in his notebook, "All towns deified which Wilks is the first to notice (not so as Cham$^n$ has long said it)".

Gell realized that Wilkinson was accumulating a large amount of material that deserved to be published; frequently he encouraged Wilkinson to return and attend to it. Wilkinson could not yet bear to leave Egypt, however, and attempted the difficult task of publishing from afar. Gell tried to help by repeatedly writing to Young to ask him to intercede with publishers and scholarly societies: "I long to see his things in print and to send some of them to him – they are worth all the hieroglyphics in the French work" (in Leitch 1855, 3: 395–396). Young, whose attention had by then moved away from Egyptology, was annoyed at these demands upon his time, but eventually arranged for the Royal Society of Literature to publish a portion of Wilkinson's sketches. When this was done, he wrote to Gell to inform him of the fact, adding that he had six author's copies for Wilkinson. Gell's reply is revealing:

> I will write to Wilkinson and tell him of the six copies you have in store for him. I cannot help thinking that as I am (although not one of the triumvirate) purveyor-general to the hieroglyphics, I might have had one copy also, for without me the things would never have come to light, my talent at betraying literary secrets being the only thing I value myself upon in the way of hieroglyphics, and if you read Wilkinson's notes he tells you that without me he should never have attended to them.
>
> (Leitch 1855, 3: 408)

(The triumvirate referred to consisted of Young, Champollion and Gustavus Seyffarth.) Gell, an insatiable book collector, was always anxious to add another volume to his library, but in this instance he also wanted recognition for his role as intermediary of ideas.

Other British travellers influenced by Gell were James Burton and Robert Hay, who spent considerable time with him in the early 1820s (Dawson *et al.* 1995; Stephen and Lee 1963; Tillett 1984). These two men compiled a vast quantity of notes, sketches and other material in Egypt. Though little of this appeared in print, it has been valuable to the many Egyptologists and orientalists who have consulted it in the Department of Manuscripts at the British Library (Add. MSS 29812–60, 31054 for Hay, and 25613–75 for Burton). Also to be seen at Gell's house were those whose interest was more journalistic than antiquarian, such as the travel writers R. R. Madden (1829) and Edward Hogg (1835). He received them, encouraged them, and told them what to look for when they reached the Nile. Usually he supplied them with letters of introduction and wrote ahead to acquaintances already on the Nile to request assistance for the new arrivals.

Gell's broader Egyptological contacts included such people as Baron Christian von Bunsen and the tragically misdirected Gustavus Seyffarth. Baron von Bunsen (1791–1860), Prussian diplomat and oriental scholar, was the author of *Aegyptens Stelle in der Weltgeschichte*, which was published in English as *Egypt's Place in Universal History* in 1844–1857. Gustavus Seyffarth (1796–1885), though a scholar of great industry and ingenuity, diminished the value of his contributions by steadfastly refusing to accept Champollion's conclusions. Though neither Bunsen nor Seyffarth made many original contributions to Egyptology, Gell's dealings with them served to heighten his understanding of the state of the art. Closer to home his friend Edward Dodwell was making a large collection of Egyptian antiquities as well as some sketches, now in the British Library (Leitch 1855, 3: 212–214). Gell's colleague in classical studies, Antonio Nibby, also worked at Egyptology, although he never accepted Champollion's work, causing Gell to call him "a mule in disposition" (Leitch 1855, 3: 230–234). Of more immediate importance were Gell's other correspondents in Egypt, including Robert Hay and James Burton, whose manuscript notes indicate that they both sent material to Gell. This was supplemented by visits of returning travellers from Egypt such as Lord Prudhoe and Major Orlando Felix, who stopped to see him in 1829 (Hall 1915b: 137). Gell's correspondence with Wilkinson also indicates an acquaintance and correspondence with the artist and architect Frederick Catherwood (1799–1855) who worked extensively in Egypt, often with Hay, and is best remembered now for his work in Central America (Medina-González Chapter 7, this volume). Typical of a traveller returning from Egypt whom Gell might meet and debrief is Edward J. Cooper. The dedication to Cooper's *Views in Egypt and Nubia* (1824) reads, "and to Sir William Gell, from whose valuable society, after my return, I derived both information and pleasure".

Then, too, there was Henry Salt, but Gell seems to have always regarded him with some condescension. He was especially harsh in his judgment of an ill-advised publication in which Salt attempted to preserve a place as a pioneer of hieroglyphic studies (Salt 1825). In his comments to Young and others, Gell attacked Salt's book without mercy: "As for Salt's claims to originality, they were fit to be set up in the region of Humbugia ..." (Leitch 1855, 3: 392). He continued in the same vein in his notebooks, where he wrote, "Mr Salt's alphabet [was] almost all published many years before by Young and Champollion. He had not seen the books as he informs us but I had sent the whole contents to Wilkinson in Egypt when first published and written to Mr Salt himself to tell him not to publish as it was all done before". Yet the extent of Gell's disdain for Salt is difficult to comprehend, for Salt nevertheless performed many services to Egyptology. As a collector, he obtained many important artefacts for the British Museum and other institutions (McNaught 1978); his copies of monuments are important Egyptological sources (Bosworth 1974; Bierbrier 1983; Malek and Smith 1983); and he assisted many British scholars and travellers in Egypt.

Gell was naturally excited when Jean-François Champollion published his famous 'Lettre à M. Dacier' in 1822. Gell was, in fact, one of the few who could appreciate Champollion's accomplishment. When many doubted Champollion's phonetic method, Gell knew it was essentially correct, for by using it he was able to read some cartouches (which he called "shields") of Roman imperial names and titles that had previously been unintelligible to him. He was, however, furious that the Frenchman had taken all the credit for himself and given none to Thomas Young. Gell had read Champollion's 'De l'écriture hiératique des anciens Egyptiens' of 1821 in which he had maintained that the hieroglyphs were signs of things, not sounds. Noting Champollion's efforts to withdraw the publication from booksellers and friends, Gell concluded that he was trying to suppress it in order to conceal both his error and his debt to Thomas Young who already had published his opinion that at least some of the hieroglyphs were phonetic (Gell Notebook). In his correspondence with Young, Gell often expressed his annoyance at what he considered Champollion's lack of candour.

Nevertheless, Gell understood the importance of Champollion's work and sent some of the most pertinent findings to Wilkinson in Egypt. Equipped with Champollion's insights, Wilkinson began to make important new discoveries of his own (for an assessment of Wilkinson's work at this stage see Hall 1915b: 134–135). In a subsequent instalment, Gell sent Wilkinson more of Champollion's findings, adding that they:

> superseded the old school of Young who remains the founder while Champollion has finished all the columns and friezes of the hieroglyphical edifice. He has turned all the cats Lions zigzags owls &c. into letters and when you understand coptic you have nothing left but to go on and read on a Theban wall all the newspaper advertisements for places of those days. I cannot give you a dissertation on it but the thing is quite settled so you may put implicit confidence in what I tell you so I must now begin with such letters as you may be supposed not to know ...

After listing a hieroglyphic alphabet with its English phonetic equivalents, Gell concluded, "Thus you have got as far as hieroglyphics go to read everything. It is very odd that Young's groups are often right but the parts have changed places ..." (Gell to Wilkinson, August 1824). In 1825 Gell met Champollion when the latter came to Italy (Hartleben 1909). Perhaps contrary to Gell's expectations, they found each other's company quite agreeable and soon were exchanging information. Gell gave Champollion copies of Wilkinson's work, thereby providing the Frenchman with much more accurate transcriptions from Egypt than he had hitherto seen, though Gell's residual distrust of Champollion prompted him to stipulate that Wilkinson be given credit (Gell to Wilkinson, July and November 1825). This was the only communication channel between Wilkinson and Champollion, for the two men never met or corresponded, though Wilkinson did later exchange some letters with Champollion's brother, Jacques Joseph Champollion-Figeac. He also supplied Champollion with some of James Burton's manuscript material. Champollion, for his part, was generous in showing Gell his own work, so much so that Gell wrote to Young, "I beg to state that so far from hiding his new discoveries, the said Champollion has given me so many things not published, that, if I were so inclined, I could pretend I were the inventor of as much again as he is" (Leitch 1855, 3: 421). During Champollion's visit, he and Gell made several sketching expeditions together, including one to Benevento where they made drawings of Domitian's obelisk and translated the hieroglyphic inscriptions on it (Gell Notebook; see also Hartleben 1906; Lacouture 1988). By 1828 Gell was writing of Champollion in these terms: "He is a great friend of mine, certainly one of the most marked men of the time, and agreeable in many ways and lively in Society" (Gell to Lady Blessington, June 1828).

As Gell came to see Champollion's accomplishment in broader perspective, his opinion of his young friend steadily rose. The matter of primacy in identifying the phonetic nature of the hieroglyphs was but a small portion of the picture. He realized that Champollion, in his later work, had made great progress toward translating the language of the ancient Egyptians. Not long after Champollion's death in 1832, Gell replied to a letter from Wilkinson,

> I am delighted with what you say of Champollion and ... had occasion to observe how very much more imperfect everything must have been left if only the discoveries of Dr Young had existed, for I have set down Young's translations in 1814 and 16 and certainly they are quite vague compared to what one knows after Champollion in the year 1821 and after.

(Gell to Wilkinson, November 1834)

Gell continued to dream of going to Egypt himself, but something always prevented him. In June 1823 he wrote to Wilkinson:

> I am much better in health and much inclined to take a trip to the pyramids and if I go on improving shall be more so next year indeed I think I shall accomplish it. If you do what I so strongly recommend return into Italy to put your acquisitions in order and then go out again I would most certainly do so and I think I am now well enough for boats and jack asses though not for prancing steeds.

"Nothing is wanting but a safe ship," he wrote in his next letter to Wilkinson (March 1824). His plans were, however, foiled by the deteriorating international situation associated with the Greek War of Independence. Then, in the summer of 1827, he was again writing to Wilkinson to say that he was indeed coming to Egypt in company with Champollion, who was preparing his Egyptian expedition. Wilkinson replied, "I was gratefully surprised to find by your letter that you are coming out at last; and hope to be here at Thebes to welcome you and lionize you among the lists of Kings and other curiosities" (Hall 1915b: 146). But this visit also failed to come to pass, for reasons that Gell explained to Young:

> I believe my trip to Palestine is, as you say, in a bad way, and the trip to Amon's habitation little better, for Champollion, who was to have had a frigate or sloop in September, will not be ready till November, as he is making his museum at Paris, and

November is a bad time either by sea or land. I thought I was going with him, and know nothing now to the contrary except lameness and poverty, which you will say are my sufficient reasons.

(Leitch 1855, 3: 410)

Gell was destined to know Egypt only from afar through books and letters from friends like Wilkinson.

Gell's physical condition worsened during the 1830s and finally brought about his death in 1836. During his last years, however, he continued his interest in Egyptology and in Wilkinson, whom he now considered the best remaining hope, Champollion and Young both having died, Young in 1829 and Champollion in 1832. When Wilkinson finally left Egypt in 1833, Gell prepared the way for his return to London by writing to the Secretary of the Dilettanti Society there, informing him of the importance of Wilkinson's work and requesting him to introduce Wilkinson into literary society (Clay 1976: 130–131). Hearing that Wilkinson was writing his comprehensive work, *Manners and Customs of the Ancient Egyptians*, Gell wrote to encourage him, saying, "it would be quite a treasure if you could ever publish it, and nobody but you has the knowledge necessary" (Gell to Wilkinson, September 1834). Later, musing upon the maturity of his former "student in Ægyptiaca", Gell wrote to Wilkinson in a self-deprecating vein:

You talk of coming here in the Spring. It would be a real satisfaction after so many years to me. I unluckily have had my wits at grass ever since while you have been improving and you will probably detect my dullness and ignorance at the first fire though you went away with the impression that I was a great man – among little boys – some 12 or 14 years ago.

(Gell to Wilkinson, November 1834)

As it happened, however, Gell lived neither to see the appearance of Wilkinson's book nor to see Wilkinson again. When Wilkinson published *Manners and Customs of the Ancient Egyptians* shortly after Gell's death, he inserted this memorial:

In him the literary world has sustained a great loss: but friendship and gratitude combine to increase my sorrow; and I can never forget that, for all the satisfaction I have derived from the prosecution of researches to which he first directed my attention – however unimportant their results – I am indebted to his kindness and instruction. To many has he lent his powerful assistance in those studies, whose advancement his 'classic' talents so ably promoted: no distinction of nation ever prevented his generous mind from aiding others in investigating subjects of which he possessed such an extensive knowledge, and no deficiency of good feeling and liberality checked his exertions, or damped his zeal, in furthering the object of those who followed the same pursuits.

(Wilkinson 1836: ix–x)

*Manners and Customs of the Ancient Egyptians* became the most influential book about Ancient Egypt to appear in English during the 19th century. Strangely, Wilkinson never published another work to equal it, even though that book only began to tap the rich material he had gathered in Egypt. Having received much of his initial vision from Gell, that vision may have faded once Gell was gone. The same can be suggested about Robert Hay and James Burton. Both were heavily influenced by Gell when they began their work, and each gathered an enormous amount of material, but without his guidance they could not imagine how to use it.

At first glance Gell's contribution may seem small compared to that of some of the 19th-century giants of Egyptology, but it was nevertheless significant. While his understanding of Ancient Egypt was insufficient to sustain original research of his own, his inquiring mind ranged across the entire field of ancient Egyptian scholarship as it existed in his day. Even more important was the way he taught, inspired, assessed and facilitated scholarly interchange. Without Gell, Wilkinson's accomplishment, the full potential of which is yet to be realized, would have been impossible. There was no one else who could have transmitted information between scholars like Young, Wilkinson and Champollion the way Gell did, or who could have so effectively prepared the way for publications that would have languished, if not for him. These manifold functions later became the province of the Egyptological establishment, but in the days before its development, Gell performed them all personally, justifying his claim to be Purveyor-General to the Hieroglyphics.

## Note

The references to private correspondence and journals cited in this chapter derive from the following sources: Bodleian Library Department of Western Manuscripts, Oxford; British Library Department of Manuscripts, Additional (Add.) MSS; Derbyshire County Record Office, Matlock; Griffith Institute Archives, Ashmolean Museum, Oxford; National Library of Scotland Department of Manuscripts, Edinburgh.

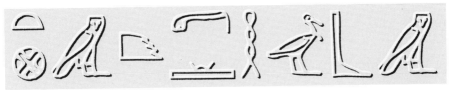

# CHAPTER 5

## SOME EGYPTOLOGICAL SIDELIGHTS ON THE EGYPTIAN WAR OF 1882

*David M. Dixon*

The bilingual inscription which provided Champollion with the key to the decipherment of Egyptian hieroglyphs was discovered at Rosetta in 1799 by a French military officer, during the relatively brief period of Bonaparte's occupation of Egypt (1798–1801) (Bierbrier Chapter 3, this volume). It could therefore be said that the discipline of Egyptology originated amid the turmoil of war and its aftermath; and for a century or so the armies of both France and England (though mainly the latter) were, in varying degrees and in different ways, involved from time to time in Egyptological activities.

At the very end of the 18th century, at least one English Minister had appreciated the strategic importance of Egypt from the standpoint of English imperial possessions. In a memorandum to the then Foreign Secretary, Lord Grenville, the Minister of War (Dundas) wrote: "The possession of Egypt by any independent Power would be a fatal circumstance to the interests of this country" (Dundas in Marlowe 1965: 15). As one recent historian commented, "This is probably the first explicit and official statement of the policy which has governed British relations with Egypt for the last 150 years, and it is interesting to note this expression of opinion by a British Minister seventy years before the Suez Canal was constructed [opened 1869] and at a time when the overland and transit traffic through Egypt was almost at a standstill"(Marlowe 1965: 15–16).

In the decades following the death of Mohammed Ali in 1849, the major European powers watched with increasing concern the gradually deteriorating political and financial situation in Egypt (Hassan Chapter 2, this volume). Fears grew that foreign, i.e. European, lives and capital (particularly the latter) were coming under threat, for "there is no nervousness comparable to the anxiety of an investor" (Elgood 1924). By the mid-1870s it had become clear to some English politicians that intervention might become necessary, and soldiers – individuals and small groups – were sent to Egypt to reconnoitre the land. Often they went thinly disguised as wild-fowl shooters, naturalists, and antiquarians.

Matters finally came to a head in 1882. Following disturbances in Alexandria and other centres, which resulted in the deaths of more than 50 Europeans in Alexandria alone, an English fleet under Sir Beauchamp Seymour bombarded that city on 11 July

1882; and following mob violence in which areas of Alexandria were sacked and burnt, naval brigades and troops were landed to restore order.

A large expeditionary force under Sir Garnet Wolseley later landed at Port Said and proceeded to Ismailiya, advancing towards the Nile Valley along the line of the Sweet Water Canal. Following a number of engagements with Egyptian forces, culminating in the battle of Tell el-Kebir (12 September 1882), the army advanced on and occupied Cairo. This campaign inaugurated nearly three-quarters of a century of English occupation, the extent of which gradually lessened over the years until Egypt was finally freed of foreign forces in 1956.

Unlike the invading French force in 1798 (Bierbrier Chapter 3, this volume), or even the English expedition to Abyssinia in 1867–1868, the 1882 expedition to Egypt was not accompanied by any scientific mission or group of scholars. The ancient history and antiquities of Egypt were not uppermost in the mind of the English government; indeed, they had no place there at all. Interest in, and concern for, such matters was left to the individual private initiative of a number of officers in the occupying army.

Wolseley, as Commander-in-Chief, brought to Egypt the same lack of interest in antiquity that he had displayed in 1878 when he had been High Commissioner in Cyprus. Then, he had made it clear to an enthusiastic young Lieutenant Kitchener that he was not concerned with the needs of scholars and archaeologists, but only with immediate practical military and administrative requirements (Magnus 1958).

However, after the close of the 1882 campaign a bizarre event took place. Sir Garnet laid on a huge picnic for his senior officers and some high civilian officials (Butler 1911) and, despite his lack of interest in the Egyptian past, the venue chosen for the event was Saqqarah, probably at the suggestion of John Mason Cook of the famous travel firm, who had been instructed to organize the outing. At any rate, on the day a large body of officers, including Wolseley and his senior generals, boarded a river-steamer and, riding the Nile flood, journeyed upstream to Bedrashein, the tourist port for Memphis and the Memphite necropolis. There they disembarked; under the palms were assembled, not carriages or horses, but over 100 donkeys, which conveyed the company to the necropolis of Saqqarah. The first half of the day was devoted to 'doing' tombs, including that of Ti. Then they "dived down through the sand of the desert into that vast rock warren of the Serapeum" (Butler 1911: 264). One senior officer was mightily impressed by the huge polished sarcophagi. "How," he wondered, "*did* these old people get all the seventy solid single-stoned tons of granite or porphyry into huge side-niches … ?" (Butler 1911: 264). But it was the technology that impressed him, not the motives behind it. "Greater even than the wonder was the prodigious foolishness of the whole thing. All for dead bulls!" (Butler 1911: 264).

Eventually, drenched in sweat and stifled with the heat, candle-smoke and smell of bats in "this subterranean bull warren", the company emerged into the desert air and soon fell upon the splendid repast that Cook had prepared. Then "more tombs, more pyramids, more stone carvings, more hieroglyphs, more sarcophagi" until, back at last on the donkeys, the great concourse streamed back to the riverbank. And thus the company reached the steamer at Bedrashein "satiated with sarcophagi" and "with a thirst for tea such as only the dust of six thousand years of mummy powder could give us" (Butler 1911: 264).

The Commander-in-Chief's profound lack of interest in Ancient Egypt was, however, more than compensated for by the enthusiasm of others. The army that went to Egypt in 1882 included a surprising number of officers who had considerable interest in, and in some cases prior knowledge and experience of, Egypt and the surrounding areas. Lieutenant-Colonel Sir Charles William Wilson (Watson 1909), KCMG, CB, FRS, RE (later Major-General Sir Charles, KCB, 1836–1905) was by 1882 a distinguished figure in the field of biblical archaeology. He had considerable practical experience of archaeological survey and recording in Asia Minor, Palestine and Sinai, where he had been in charge of the Ordnance Survey of the peninsula from 1868 to 1869. Particular attention had been paid to the Egyptian remains, including the mining settlement at Wadi Maghara, and the Egyptian and Sinaitic inscriptions. Wilson had been a leading figure in the formation of the Palestine Exploration Fund in 1865 and remained a lifelong supporter, becoming Chairman in 1901.

Major (later Colonel Sir Charles Moore) Watson (Lane-Poole 1919), RE (1841–1916) had, as a Lieutenant, served in the Sudan under Charles George Gordon in 1874–1875 during Gordon's first period as Governor of Equatoria. He had been engaged in the survey of the Blue Nile but had been invalided home through illness. After the battle of Tell el-Kebir, it was Watson, at the head of a small force, who led the advance on Cairo and received the surrender of the Citadel (14 September 1882). He continued to serve in Egypt until 1886 when he became Governor-General of the Red Sea Littoral, a post he held until 1891. Like his close friend Sir Charles Wilson, he was a keen student of biblical archaeology and he also was Chairman of the Palestine Exploration Fund from 1905 until his death in 1916. Watson's interest in Egyptian history and metrology led him to undertake a study of the Great Pyramid, which he published in 1903.

In 1882 Lieutenant Horatio Herbert Kitchener (Magnus 1958), RE (later Field-Marshal Lord Kitchener, 1850–1916) was 32 years old, but he was already an experienced archaeologist and a keen student of the ancient world. He was fluent in Arabic and Turkish and had a sound knowledge of biblical Hebrew. He had been responsible, with Lieutenant Claude Conder RE, for the Survey of Palestine in 1874–1877 and had served under Wilson in Anatolia as a Military Vice-Consul. He had also conducted cartographical and archaeological work in Cyprus. In 1881 the Trustees of the British Museum had invited him to undertake the supervision of excavations in Mesopotamia, but he had been obliged to decline the offer. In July 1882 Kitchener, desperate for service in Egypt, sailed from Cyprus to Alexandria, technically on 'sick leave' which it had been supposed he would spend in Cyprus. Although he went ashore, with Major A. B. Tulloch, and, in disguise, undertook intelligence work prior to the bombardment of Alexandria, he was obliged, filled with frustration, to watch the action from the deck of Sir Beauchamp Seymour's flagship. Technically he was absent without leave from his post in Cyprus though he strenuously maintained for the rest of his life that this was not so.

Kitchener could undoubtedly have made a considerable career for himself in Near Eastern archaeology had he chosen to pursue that path; he never lost his interest in the ancient Near East and in the Nile Valley in particular, and in later years, when he had risen to very senior rank, he was always very helpful to Egyptologists working both in Egypt and the Sudan, and did much to further their work.

Among the officers who served in the campaign were two more newcomers to Egypt who soon fell under the spell of its ancient culture and in later years, as senior generals, became avid collectors of antiquities as well as encouraging and supporting Egyptological work. Major Francis Grenfell (n.d.) (later Field-Marshal Lord Grenfell, 1841–1925) served in 1882 as Assistant Adjutant-General on Wolseley's Headquarters staff and was present at the battle of Tell el-Kebir. His younger kinsman, Lieutenant John Grenfell Maxwell (Arthur 1932) (later General Sir John, 1859–1929) was also at Tell el-Kebir. In later years both men became President of the Egypt Exploration Society (Grenfell 1916–1919; Maxwell 1925–1929).

Prior to the outbreak of hostilities, concern had been felt for the safety of the collection of Egyptian antiquities housed in the museum at Bulaq (Delamaire 2003). In his Journal dated April 1882, the American traveller and collector Charles Edwin Wilbour recorded that Arabi Pasha and another Minister were to see the museum. Wilbour speculated that the purpose of the visit was to estimate how much the contents would raise if sold (Capart 1936b). Such speculation may not have been entirely groundless; it was certainly curious that Colonel Arabi, who was not known to have evinced any interest in Egyptology, should, in the midst of the growing political crisis, suddenly have visited the Bulaq museum. On the evening of the very day Wolseley's army entered Cairo, Sir Charles Wilson made it his business (as he later told Eduard Naville) to ride to Bulaq where he was relieved to find that no damage had occurred to the museum (Watson 1909).

Cameras had been used in the army on active service in the Abyssinian War of 1867–1868, and in the Survey of Sinai in 1868–1869 and by Captain W. de W. Abney, RE, FRS in Upper Egypt (Thebes) in 1874. They were, however, large and cumbersome at this time; and until the advent of the small hand-held camera, the ability to make accurate drawings and sketches was a necessary part of an officer's training, particularly in the specialist branches such as the Royal Artillery and Royal Engineers. Painting and sketching were, in any case, part of the accomplishments of a well-educated gentleman.

Among the officers were a number of talented artists. Indeed, Major Francis Grenfell had studied at the Slade School of Art in London. Abilities of course varied, but to all alike, the ancient monuments offered irresistible subjects. Lieutenant (later Colonel) Benjamin Donisthorpe Donne (Harfield 1986) of the Royal Sussex Regiment had already served in the West Indies, Malta and Cyprus and had undertaken the Grand Tour, enthusiastically painting wherever he went. His regiment arrived at Lake Timsah on 12 September 1882, but was a few hours too late for the battle of Tell el-Kebir. On the 29th they joined the 4th Brigade at Cairo. After the great victory parade through the city on 30 September, Donne lost no time in pursuing his painting and Egyptological interests. He was, in fact, later honoured by the French Academy for his services to Egyptology.

He was, of course, not present at Wolseley's *fantasia* at Saqqarah; as a mere subaltern he would not have been eligible. But the event was evidently much talked about and Donne determined to follow in his seniors' footsteps.

In his Journal for 28 October, he records that with a fellow subaltern of his regiment, he:

> went up the River by steamer ... to visit Saqqarah. After landing at Badrasheim, we mounted donkeys and rode off to the Great Step Pyramid of Sakkara, after which we visited [the] Serapeum and other highly interesting tombs of the very earliest dynasties. We passed over the sight of Memphis on our return.
>
> (Harfield 1986: 110)

On 7 November the Colonel took the regiment on a route march to the Virgin's Tree and Heliopolis, and Donne gives a description and potted history of the site. Christmas Day 1882 was wet and cold, but Donne "spent the afternoon very profitably ... at the Boulak Museum of Egyptology" (Harfield 1986: 110). On 21 January 1883 Donne obtained three weeks' leave – he had only been in Egypt just over four months – which he spent in Upper Egypt, visiting all the major sites and busily painting. His subjects included the temples of Karnak and Luxor, the Ramesseum, Edfu, and Kom Ombo.

Captain (later Lieutenant-Colonel) William McCheane of the Royal Marine Light Infantry was a committed Christian and keen Bible student who was greatly interested in such matters as the Israelite sojourn in, and Exodus from, Egypt, and the natural history of the Bible. Although only a short distance from the Holy Land, he was never able to get there. However, whenever there was an opportunity he would withdraw by himself with his Bible, plant specimens and paints; and in Egypt (and partly in retirement later at Clifton, near Bristol) he produced some very beautiful watercolours of biblical flowers and fruits, many of which were also found in Egypt (Chancellor 1982).

So much for the officers; but it would be a mistake to assume too readily that the other ranks were all totally indifferent to Ancient Egypt, as is clear from the diary entries of one Private George Teigh, dating from the latter part of the Second Sudan War (1896–1899) (Meredith 1998). Also, examples have survived of day-passes issued to other ranks to enable them to be absent from their quarters in or near Cairo in order to visit the pyramids. Nevertheless, there does not appear, as far as can be judged from the limited evidence available, to have been any marked enthusiasm for Ancient Egypt among the ranks generally. Many troops were encamped in the neighbourhood of Giza, and for them having their photographs taken against the background of the pyramids and the sphinx seems to have been the limit of their interest. The main staple of many an off-duty ranker seems to have been the two Bs: booze and (judging from men's Medical Records) brothels, and both posed serious problems of health, discipline and efficiency.

By the time the American Charles Edwin Wilbour ventured to return to Egypt after the war was over, Alexandria was still largely in ruins (December 1882). The Hôtel de l'Europe, where he had hoped to stay, was no more. "That with what seems half the town, is a mass of ruins ... In the streets which *have* been cleared the rubbish covers the sidewalks and seems to fill the blocks solid up to about twenty feet high" (Capart 1936b: 179).

In Cairo, Shepheard's Hotel was largely occupied by senior English officers and their staff. "There are fathers and brothers and sisters and mothers of wounded and sick soldiers." Disease (typhoid) was filling the cemetery. "The *Place des Consuls*, the *Grand Place*, is at night aroar with [military] bands and soldiery; it is lined on both sides with beer and spirit booths from end to end. The main business of the British Patrol is to arrest drunken soldiery ..." (Capart 1936a: 179). Many officers, particularly the younger ones, were kept on the 'straight and narrow' by the endeavours of older and wiser colleagues, such as Major Harry Williams, RE. He organized and conducted uplifting tours of the Bulaq museum and the main Islamic monuments, and gave lectures on the history and civilization of Egypt (on which he was well informed). In later years many gratefully acknowledged that they had benefited.

Towards the end of 1882, the Colonel of one Highland regiment, in order to keep his men occupied and out of mischief, marched them out from Cairo, where they were quartered, to Giza to visit the pyramids. The exercise does not seem to have produced any budding Egyptologists. The only remotely 'Egyptological' activity that occurred was a race that was organized to see who could reach the summit of the Great Pyramid first. At a given signal, five or six hundred Highlanders, in their kilts and scarlet tunics, swarmed up the monument. From a window of the nearby Mena House Hotel the spectacle was watched by three astonished French ladies. Remarkably, there seem to have been no casualties among the soldiers; at least none are mentioned.

It is worth noting that there are remarkably few graffiti, of any kind, carved on the Great Pyramid which can with confidence be attributed to troops of the English army serving in Egypt between 1882 and the end of the century. The same is true of earlier French graffiti, though admittedly Bonaparte's army was in Egypt for a much shorter period. This absence of graffiti can hardly have been due to any 'decree' or order forbidding 'vandalism', nor, particularly towards the latter part of the century, to illiteracy.

At the conclusion of a successful military campaign come the victor's rewards, including decorations and medals and, hopefully, promotion or the prospect thereof. Egypt 1882 was no exception; indeed, considering that the entire campaign was over in little more than four weeks, many officers received what can only be described as a medals bonanza. By no means exceptional was Lieutenant-Colonel H. Steward of the 3rd Dragoon Guards: between 8 September and 2 November 1882 he was mentioned in dispatches no fewer than three times, and received the CB, the 3rd Class of the Order of Osmanich, the Egypt Medal with Clasp 'Tell-el-Kebir', and the Khedivial Bronze Star (Figure 5:1); and was also appointed an ADC to the queen – not a bad haul for a month or so's work! (Maurice 1887: 183). Even mere majors and captains did very well.

The campaign medal issued by the English government was a silver medal, 36 mm in diameter, with or without battle clasp(s) as appropriate. It was issued to all sailors and soldiers, and many categories of civilians, who had served in Egypt or Egyptian waters between certain specified dates. It is interesting that it was to Ancient Egypt that the designer of the medal looked for inspiration. The obverse designed by Wyon bore, as usual, the head of Queen Victoria, the reverse (Figure 5:1) just the name 'Egypt' and below it a figure of a sphinx on a pedestal, and in the exergue the date '1882' (*The Medal Yearbook*: medal no. 131).

The reverse of the Egypt Medal was designed by J. Pinches of the well-known family firm of medallists. It is, however, interesting to speculate whether Sir Garnet Wolseley might have had any influence on the design, since the sphinx had been the *only* ancient Egyptian monument that had made any impression at all on him. This was by no means the first time that pharaonic Egypt had influenced English medal design. The medal struck (in gold, silver and bronze) by the Highland Society of London in 1801 and intended for presentation to Sir Ralph Abercombie and his sons, and the Honourable East India Company's medal for Egypt, 1801, also bore common Egyptian motifs: pyramids, obelisks, etc. as well as palm trees and the occasional crocodile, still a feared though rare denizen of the Nile in Upper Egypt until the end of the 19th century (*The Medal Yearbook*: medal nos.

Figure 5:1    The Egypt medal (1882–1889) (reverse) (*The Medal Yearbook*, medal no. 131).

81, 83). More surprising is the prominence accorded to Ancient Egypt on another medal issued for the war of 1882, namely the Bronze Star, made in Birmingham and awarded by the Khedive Tewfik Mohamed to all those entitled to the English medal. There is little to indicate that this was an award from a Muslim ruler, apart from the AH date in Arabic (corresponding to AD 1882) on the obverse and the Crescent and Star in the suspension. The design consists of a representation of the sphinx and pyramids of Giza above which is the name 'Egypt'. The reverse bears simply the Khedivial monogram TM – in Roman letters – surmounted by a crown (*The Medal Yearbook*: medal no. 132).

Following Wolseley's defeat of Arabi Pasha, the Khedive – the puppet first of Turkey and then of England – was reinstated and gradually public order and security were restored throughout the country. The decades that followed undoubtedly witnessed great improvements in administration, health, communications and agriculture, and in the lot of the common people under the quasi-colonial regime presided over by the autocratic Sir Evelyn Baring (later Lord Cromer), the virtual ruler of Egypt from 1883 until 1907 (Cromer 1908).

However, Egypt paid, involuntarily, a heavy price for these material gains; nevertheless it is an ill wind which blows no man to good, and there were individuals and bodies that benefited from the New Order. One of them was the discipline of Egyptology, particularly English Egyptology in the shape of the Egypt Exploration Fund. On 27 March 1882 the first meeting of the provisional committee of the Fund took place, with Sir Erasmus Wilson in the Chair. Proposals had been discussed for excavation in Egypt, but these had to be put into abeyance owing to the disturbed state of that country, and the subsequent outbreak of hostilities rendered work there impossible. Tell el-Kebir, however, and its aftermath changed the situation almost overnight and Egyptologically events moved swiftly. On 3 January 1883, barely three and a half months after the battle, Eduard Naville, on behalf of the Egypt Exploration Fund, commenced excavations at Tell el-Maskhuta, in the Wadi Tumilat, which he identified as the site of the biblical Pithom (Naville 1903). Only three months earlier the site had lain in the path of Sir Garnet Wolseley's invading army. From that date, the Egypt Exploration Fund – later Society – and the British Museum, have continued to work, with intervals of varying length, in the Delta until the present day.

## CHAPTER 6

# FORGERS, SCHOLARS AND INTERNATIONAL PRESTIGE: ANCIENT EGYPT AND SPAIN

### José-R. Pérez-Accino and Covadonga Sevilla Cueva
### (French translated by Daniel Antoine and Lawrence Stewart Owens)

## Introductory background

During the 19th century, Spain was a minor force in the community of nations. Internal political problems and the grave situation of Spanish colonies overseas occupied the attention of the monarchy and government. According to Morales Lezcano (1992: 14), there was a diminution in Spain's international standing between the Old Regime crises (1820) and the start of World War I (1914). This situation prevented Spain from developing a general policy on the Orient, as had been established in other western countries.

From the 15th century onwards north-west Africa had represented an essential expansion zone for Spain, which it used to protect its commercial routes to America and the Far East. This resulted in the construction of a line of fortifications, which played the role of a physical – and psychological – barrier between Muslims and Christians. Even though its foreign policy was focused on its overseas interests and on north-west Africa, Spain avidly followed events in the Near East (Morales Lezcano 1992: 59ff), and was particularly interested in the Ottoman Empire's slow collapse under the combined pressure of Britain, Russia, Austro-Hungary and France. In fact, from the reign of Charles III in the 18th century, the Spanish government had tried to maintain its trade agreements with the Great Turk.

During the 19th century, Spain swayed internal public opinion and international favour by claiming that her north African interventions were an assertion and reinforcement of her vested interests. There were also geopolitical reasons: since the 15th century, Morocco had been Spain's most important southern neighbour. However, in the second half of the 19th century, France had expansionist ambitions that stretched from Algeria to western Africa. Spain could not let France settle so close to the Straits of Gibraltar and her colonies at Ceuta and Melilla, and it entered a period of conflict, clashing with other countries also interested in the region, encountering problems with local populations and, finally, seeing the emergence of increasingly hostile public opinion.

For Spain, 'Orientalism' became 'Africanism' and, more precisely, 'Moroccanism'. Indeed, it was mostly in Morocco – as well as in parts of Guinea – that Spain consolidated her African presence. Morocco thus became a major source of inspiration for artists, writers and journalists, amongst others. Africanist dialogue was made up of a mixture of nostalgia and power. In their works, the political, military and religious bodies defended the importance of Spain's intervention in north-west Africa. As in other European countries, they used cultural imperialism to justify their action. Spain was, however, exceptional in maintaining an Oriental and Muslim legate *in situ*: the Andalusian legate. Whilst for most European cultures the Islamic world represented the 'other' in a negative sense, Spanish thought and culture incorporated certain elements of Islam. This defined Spanish Africanism, the cultural characteristics of which could be perceived in literature, painting, music and, in the 20th century, some cinematographic productions.

## Spanish imperialism

As has been seen, during the 19th and early 20th centuries, Spain's participation in both European colonial imperialism and the Orientalist cultural movement was very modest. Spain's overseas interests were focused on its American colonies, the Philippines and – closer to its own territory – Guinea and Morocco.

Expeditionary reports from Ottoman lands commissioned by the State at the beginning of the 19th century have been preserved. These were recorded as travel logs and provide a good insight into the economic, political and cultural situation of the 'Sublime Porte'. The most representative examples include Joseph Solano Ortíz de Rozas (1793), who was, as Royal Armada frigate Captain, responsible for the historical part of the navigational log on his 1778 voyage to Constantinople. In it he refers to another voyage he had made to Constantinople in 1786, and another journey he subsequently made to Naples and Liverno in 1789. Some other authors wrote about the Orient; for example, Domingo Badía (Abbasi [1814] 1943) (alias Ali Bey) – a Spanish spy – who was sent to the Near East by the Head of the Godoy government. Caballero y Morgay's (1828) work differs from others in its apparent complete lack of understanding of the problem, probably due to the fact that he was the only one of the authors who had never himself travelled to the Orient.

Due to internal political problems, Spain was unable adequately to contribute diplomatically, politically, militarily or economically to the Turkish situation. The texts from that period reveal that, particularly during the second half of the 19th century, the ruling elite and the intelligentsia did not feel directly involved with what was happening in Turkey. The most important exception was Emilio Castelar, a Spanish politician and great ideologist, who was obsessed with issues relating to the Orient, and who saw the situation as being catastrophic (Morales Lezcano 1992: 70). Documents from the Ministry of State also show that Spain had adopted a neutral position, although the government also sent senior commanders to the battle zones in order to learn modern warfare techniques (for example, a contingent from the Spanish army participated in the Crimean War).

Shortly after the inauguration of the Suez Canal, Spain organized several expeditions towards the Red Sea in the hope of finding adequate locations for new colonies. However, this operation was doomed to failure (e.g. Víctor Abargues del Sostén, a government envoy in 1877–1879; Pedro Carrera, who explored the Red Sea in 1883 in order to locate a port which might be used by Spain (Reparaz 1907: 165)). The opening up of the area also stimulated the imagination of Spanish writers and travellers, who produced several interesting works both before and after the opening of the Suez Canal. One was written by Andrés Espala (1870), and was based upon his travels in the Orient in 1859; another by Arturo Baldasano y Topete was published in 1870, in the same year as Bardón y Gómez. Many other such works were produced by people representing scientific and cultural societies (García-Romeral Pérez 1995; and see the Sociedad para la exploración de África and La Sociedad Geográfica de Madrid, whose publications were the main source of communication for scientific expeditions), or by a range of individuals including members of the clergy, casual visitors and local residents, who would occasionally record some of their observations.

## Spain and Egypt

### Egyptology

In the 1800s in Spain, Egypt was considered to be a geographically distant place. Consequently, there was little Spanish Egyptology during the 19th century and the first half of the 20th century. Indeed, there does not appear to have been any real interest in Ancient Egypt prior to the discovery of the tomb of Tutankhamun. With a few exceptions, therefore, most of Spanish society was unaware of advances in Egyptology, basing their limited knowledge of the pharaonic periods on clichés extracted from the Bible and the works of Classical writers. Spain's perception of Egypt as exotic at the beginning of the 20th century is reflected through a musical (Sevilla Cueva 2003).

The first person in Spain to be concerned with the study of Ancient Egypt was an unknown scholar, Eduard Toda i Güell, who arrived in Egypt in 1884 as the Spanish Consul in Cairo. In addition to his diplomatic responsibilities, he engaged in Egyptological research and was involved in an important archaeological excavation. He was also the first Spaniard to create a collection of Egyptian artefacts, which he later sold to Madrid's Museo Arqueológico Nacional and to the Museo Victor Balaguer in the town of Vilanova i la Geltrú. He frequented Egyptological circles and was a great friend of Gaston Maspero, the Director of the Egyptian Antiquities Service. Toda became interested in ancient Egyptian culture and began to learn Egyptian. He also travelled in Upper Egypt and participated in several archaeological projects. In 1886, Maspero offered him the opportunity to excavate the intact, recently discovered tomb of Sennedjem at Deir el-Medina. In spite of his relative inexperience, his excavation, cataloguing and survey appear to have been of a high standard. Using a team of seven men, he also spent three days taking photographs of the objects and tomb architecture. Toda published his results (Toda 1886, 1887, 1920) and went on to hold diplomatic positions in Macao, Hong Kong, Shanghai and Paris, before finally returning to Spain in 1918. Toda was Spain's only Egyptologist during this period. Although he sowed the seeds of Spanish Egyptology, his endeavours were not followed up until much later. Furthermore, it is only very recently that the value of his work has been appreciated (Montero Blanco 1986).

## The 'Arapiles'

The voyage of the war frigate 'Arapiles' reflects Spain's low level of interest in – and involvement with – Egypt, both ancient and modern. The whole episode reveals how Egypt was regarded. King Amédée I of Savoy sent an expedition to the Orient in June 1871. Its objectives were defined to ensure:

> that our flag flies in some of the seas of Greece, Turkey and the Orient, where our armies once dominated ... that our officers and naval forces visit the monuments and, principally, the relics that relate to our history ... [that we establish] an understanding of culture and progress in the states that are visited, their commercial needs and the easiest ways to satisfy these and, in general, all that relates to a preliminary study that may be used as basis for the future enlargement of our trade networks.
>
> (Alvaro Bazán Naval Archives (A.N.A.B.) Leg. 1176/59; and see Pascual González 2001: 31)

The Minister of Fomento intended to take advantage of the expedition to enrich the collections of the Museo Arqueológico Nacional, and he managed to include a Scientific Commission – made up of only three scholars – within it, to study monuments and purchase artefacts (Rada y Delgado 1876). The President/Head of the Commission was Juan de Dios de la Rada y Delgado (1876–1882) (see below).

Although this expedition was obviously an attempt to recreate the great French Mediterranean expeditions, the absence of funds almost turned the voyage into a fiasco. The trip took 86 days to visit a number of ports in the eastern Mediterranean, and the Scientific Commission had to borrow money from the captain of the frigate, who subsequently had problems in obtaining coal supplies and feeding the passengers and crew. Conditions rapidly deteriorated, and upon arrival at each port desperate telegrams were sent requesting more money. The expedition was perpetually on the brink of collapse.

After their eventual arrival at Alexandria, the Scientific Commission was only able to visit Cairo and the pyramids, and was unable to buy any Egyptian artefacts as its money had run out. No oriental or Egyptian artefacts ever arrived in Madrid.

The voyage of the 'Arapiles' (Pascual González 2001) was the only Spanish cultural and archaeological expedition in the Near East. The way in which it foundered clearly demonstrates the precariousness of Spain's position in the Near East compared to other European powers.

In spite of this, Rada y Delgado's account of the voyage provides a glimpse of a picturesque and exotic atmosphere similar to that employed in the European Orientalist literary tradition. His writing resembles a medieval travelogue, in which pilgrims – such as Egeria – provided accounts of their visits to the Holy Land, quoted passages of the Bible and described their participation in liturgical rites. Rada y Delgado both studied and described monuments, landscapes, people and customs, as well as his own religious experiences. Curiosity and reflection led him as much to admiration as to criticism. His writings suggest that certain aspects of Near Eastern culture were somewhat primitive and – even though Egypt is only briefly mentioned – his book offers an almost complete account of the state of the Ottoman Empire.

## Rada y Delgado and the falsification of the discovery of 'Iberian culture'

As has been shown above, Spanish travellers or scholars with an interest in the Orient were rare, and the government was not disposed to offer adequate support to commercial or scientific expeditions. In Spanish academia, ancient history mainly focused upon the world of Classical Greece and Italy. It was only through the efforts of individuals that small contributions were made to Near Eastern studies, particularly with regard to Egypt. When nationalism gained more influence, research was directed towards Spain's own pre-Roman origins. It was then that the interest of certain scholars moved away from the peninsula; for example, Rada y Delgado (see above), who had (meanwhile) become the Director of Madrid's Museo Arqueológico Nacional, attempted to establish a link between the archaeology of the 'Iberian culture' and that of the pharaonic world of Egypt.

## The case of Cerro de los Santos

Following tree-cutting operations in 1830 at the Spanish site known as Cerro de los Santos (Montealegre del Castillo, Albacete), architectural and sculptural remains came to light (Fernández de Avilés 1949). These remains were re-used in the construction of an embankment (Engel 1892), which was later broken up, distributing the material from the site over a large area. It took some time for these finds to arouse any interest: in 1860 Aguado y Alarcón described and sketched several large statues which he was unable to remove because of their large size. His notes and drawings were sent to the Real Academia de la Historia in Madrid as a report – the first official mention of this archaeological site – but they were unfortunately lost.

The fact that these were the very first discoveries of what later would be classified as 'Iberian culture' explains how, in the absence of any other parallels, they were ascribed various curious origins. In 1862 Amador de los Ríos proposed a Visigothic origin for the (subsequently discovered) small temple that held the statues, and in 1865 he described another statue as "of remarkable Egyptian style".

Increasing local awareness of the site, and the lack of any effective official action, led to robbing and uncontrolled excavation by people hoping to sell the finds. Among these was Vicente Juan Amat, a watchmaker in the neighbouring town of Yecla (province of Murcia). He sold statues from the site and eventually, in 1870, the owner of the estate on which the site was located granted him special permission to dig. The large number of statues which Amat acquired, and renewed interest in the site from the Padres Escolapios (priests who were running a school in the town), resulted in Amat's permit being withdrawn, leaving the Padres Escolapios to explore the site by themselves. From 1871 Amat included numerous pieces – which he himself had made – among the statues which he sold to individuals and institutions. Some of these reflected an inventive mind, including figures of fantastic animals. Amat also embellished genuine statues, adding invented alphabetical inscriptions or interesting features such as jewels, clothing and cosmic symbols. These appear to have made his products even more desirable and from 1872 onwards he managed to sell several groups of statues to the Museo Arqueológico Nacional in Madrid. Amat died in a 'lunatic asylum', unable to clarify which of the statues were fakes, thus leaving scholars to try to establish typological criteria to distinguish fakes from originals.

From their first appearance, Amat's fantastic pieces had cast international doubts on the entire collection of more than 400 objects. The first criticism came from Hübner (1876) who rejected the inscriptions on the pieces. Some casts had been sent to the International Exhibition in Vienna (1873) and these were classified as "Modern Curiosities from Spain" (Mélida 1903–1905), thus discrediting the whole collection. The debate concerning the authenticity of the statues continued: on closer examination it emerged that only a small part of the collection should be regarded as fakes. Huebner concluded that it was only the inscribed pieces which were not genuine (Huebner 1888), and Cartailhac (1886) assigned them, if genuine, a protohistoric date, but concluded that they remained anomalous in all respects.

Reconsideration of the collection reached a crucial point in 1890 with the discovery of the now well-known statue, the Dama de Elche. European opinion now began to accept the existence of a developed pre-Roman culture on Iberian soil. Heuzey (1890) studied Iberian art, considering it to show Phoenician, Greek and Roman influences, and other researchers accepted his view. By the turn of the century the protohistoric antiquity of the Iberian Peninsula had been accepted internationally. From now on the major academic effort was devoted to establishing a typology of the statues and to constructing an inventory of the genuine examples.

The Padres Escolapios at Yecla had played an important early role in the discovery of the site (López 1993a, b). In his first excavations Amat had invited Father Lasalde to inspect the site, and the priest even offered Amat some indications as to where to dig. As a result, Lasalde (1871) published an article in which he supported an Egyptian origin for the temple on the hill. He believed that the clothing and the expressions on the faces of the sculptures were evidence of a priestly class similar to that of the Nile Valley civilization. He concluded that:

> if the Egyptians had not colonized southern Spain, the people who did had been rocked in the same cradle and had drunk from the very same fountains as the most illustrious nation of antiquity ... in this way, our civilization is as ancient as the most ancient in the world.
>
> (Lasalde 1871: 12)

Other priests, driven by curiosity and willing to help their colleague, joined him in the exploration of the site, publishing a report the same year. Their aim was to make the site known to scholars and historians, "driven by the passionate aim to see our history illustrated by the scholars from Spain to whom we appeal" (Lasalde *et al.* 1871). For these authors, the remains of a culture older than the Romans and Carthaginians constituted the proof needed to write the history of ancient Spanish civilization. The discovery of the sculptures was inseparable from a pride "burning in our national spirit as we can see the proof of the advanced way of life of the early inhabitants", allowing them to claim "that there was a people in Spain among the first historically known nations, [thus there being] no reason to envy the most celebrated of the primitive world" (Lasalde *et al.* 1871: 23).

Rada y Delgado was another key figure in the history of the site, and the development of international rejection of its antiquity. In 1875 he was appointed member of the Real Academia de la Historia, and delivered an inaugural speech (Rada y Delgado 1875) in which he firmly supported the oriental character and Egyptian features of the temple and its statues. In Rada y Delgado's view the temple was of a hybrid Greek-Egyptian origin, as a solar observatory for Egyptian priests practising Chaldaean magic. His publication included the first engravings and images of the sculptures, but his exotic interpretation of the material contributed to international suspicion of the whole collection.

As seen above, Rada y Delgado had arrived in Spain in late 1871 off the frigate 'Arapiles'. On his return, he must have worked on the Cerro de los Santos material, but his speech at the Real Academia was filled with references to the most outlandish assertions stemming from Amat's imagination. Since 1871 the Museo Arqueológico Nacional had sent several expeditions to the site in order to buy sculptures, mainly from Amat himself, and it had acquired groups of statues irrespective of their likely authenticity (Savirón 1875). Some of them can be immediately rejected, not only the ones inscribed with invented alphabets, but also those labelled 'Egyptian-style' (due to their supposed source of inspiration). Ruiz Bremón's view is that neither the 'Egyptian-style' figures nor the ones inspired from Classical mythology deserve to be accepted as genuine (Ruiz Bremón 1989: 138). A close examination of the 'Egyptian-style' pieces reveals that they are the most homogeneous group among the fakes. Mixed together with a large number of both genuine and faked figures of different kinds, the 'Egyptian-style' ones can be investigated according to their date of purchase by the Museo Arqueológico Nacional, their similarity to genuine Egyptian examples, and to their frequency within the group of fakes.

Despite Rada y Delgado's assessment, the first group includes pieces with no apparent similarity to Egyptian models. All of these examples were acquired by the museum in 1872 (Figure 6:1). The second group is different, for their Egyptian derivatives are clear (Figure 6:2). These pieces were acquired by the museum in 1875 and they must have been made after 1872 (the date of the former purchase). They are clearly modelled on Egyptian statues located in European collections. These pieces include hieroglyphic signs inspired by genuine examples, although the number of signs used is very limited and the inscriptions are repetitive. It would seem that the author of the forgeries, probably Amat himself, was aware of genuine Egyptian examples. The third small group of statues arrived in the museum in 1885. One piece is of 'Egyptian-style' and resembles the former group in every respect.

The forger's level of competence clearly changed between 1872 and 1875, and the actual number of 'Egyptian-style' fakes also increased. The group of fakes that arrived in 1875 is contemporary with Rada y Delgado's *Discurso*, which supported the Egyptian origin for the whole corpus. Between 1872 and 1875 Rada y Delgado himself was studying the material from Cerro de los Santos – while the forger was working to produce materials which would seem to confirm Rada y Delgado's and Lasalde's ideas. Once Rada y Delgado's interpretations were internationally discredited, the production of fakes decreased and 'Egyptian-style' examples virtually disappeared.

Figure 6:1    Some pieces which arrived in the Museo Arqueológico Nacional in Madrid in 1872:
the 'baboon', the 'obelisk' and the 'sphinx' (Rada y Delgado 1875: pls. XVII, XVIII).

Figure 6:2   Pieces, some with fake hieroglyphic signs, received by the Museo Arqueológico Nacional in Madrid in 1875 (Rada y Delgado 1875: pls. I, XIII).

It would be dangerous to point directly to any of the proponents of the Egyptian theory for the origin of the temple as the authors of this whole tale of deception. In Lasalde's case, he discussed the question of an Egyptian origin before any of the 'Egyptian-style' statues had been produced. In Rada y Delgado's case, the arrival of the 1875 group confirmed his ideas. Subsequently, Rada y Delgado enjoyed a distinguished career not only as Director of the Museo Arqueológico Nacional but, when he died in 1901, he was also in charge of the Museo de Reproducciones Artísticas (also located in Madrid). It is possible that the forger of the statues was well aware of Rada y Delgado's theories, and provided him with material with which to be able to prove them. The discredit which fell on the collection after the publication of Rada y Delgado's *Discurso* may have been responsible for the abandonment of the 'Egyptian-style' material, which had been such a success with the museum until then.

## Conclusions

The political and cultural situation in Spain at this time offers a context for the whole affair. Rada y Delgado had arrived from a trip around the Mediterranean in which he had been visiting and describing oriental sites and monuments. He had collected and acquired objects for the newly created Museo Arqueológico Nacional. The aim was to form a collection of the same eminence as those of other European nations. For Lasalde and Rada y Delgado, recovering the Spanish past was to have been the reaffirmation of the country's present. The political struggles in Spain during the 1860s resulted in the Union Liberal government following a policy of international intervention designed to enhance its prestige. It was against this background that the first wars in Morocco commenced in 1860, leading to the partition of Morocco between France and Spain in 1906. During these years France served as the model for the Spanish government of international political behaviour, motivating Spain to intervene in Indochina (1860) and in Mexico (1862), concluding with a costly naval war in the Pacific against Chile and Peru (1866). After 1868 (when Queen Isabel II was dethroned by the army) there was a firm commitment by Spain to an international presence, albeit with very limited means and objectives. The election by parliament of a new king in Spain was the immediate cause of the Franco-Prussian war of 1870, motivated by Napoleon III's opposition to the candidature of Prince Leopold von Hohenzollern to the Spanish throne. In this context Rada y Delgado and Lasalde were trying to establish, in the discovery of a peninsular antiquity, a place for Spain in the Mediterranean and international arenas.

The opposition abroad to Rada y Delgado's and Lasalde's theories can also be explained as a reflection of contemporary international rivalries. In 1872 – the year of the arrival of the 'Arapiles' in Spain and the first purchase of fakes by the Museo Arqueológico Nacional – Clermont-Ganneau, the French Consul in Jerusalem, pieced together and translated the ninth century BC stela of Mesha, king of Moab, the first archaeological document appearing to corroborate the Old Testament. Clermont-Ganneau later unmasked as fakes a large group of so-called Moabite pottery inscribed with a false Moabite alphabet, forged by Bedouin and already purchased in large numbers by the Berlin Museum. International prestige was at stake: the exhibition of the stela of Mesha at the Louvre, Paris in 1873 was unanimously perceived as a scientific triumph over the Prussians, shortly after the military defeat of France in 1871 (Shepherd 1987: 210; Silberman 1990: 111). In this context, it is perhaps not surprising that the German-speaking academic community (represented by Hübner and the Vienna International Exhibition) was so resistant to the proposal of yet another discovery with oriental links, and again supposedly featuring an archaic alphabet.

The whole episode described above of the discovery of 'Iberian culture' took place while Spain was seeking to establish its international credentials. The forging of the statues was a naive attempt to present Spanish antiquity as being of equal merit to any Oriental one – alongside Egypt or the then recently discovered ancient Troy. At that time, the official Spanish attitude hardened against any overseas criticism, doubt or veiled sarcasm, marking its politicized attitude towards its past. Issues of prestige and identity seem to have been at stake throughout the episode, reflecting a desperate desire by Spain to secure a place among the leading European nations.

Spain was unable to participate in the international power struggle that determined the European control of Near Eastern territories during the 19th century. Her political system was decadent and increasingly inefficient, her social, administrative and economic structures completely unprepared for modern times or society's new needs. Finally, the Disaster of 98 (the Spanish-American Civil War, Spain's enforced withdrawal from Cuba, and the destruction of the Spanish fleet in Manila Bay) produced a major shake-up in both culture and popular thought. All of these factors progressively weakened the country, as well as her status and position on the international scene.

Spain's attempts to provide an oriental (and particularly Egyptian) origin were motivated by the desire to emulate the French expeditions in the Mediterranean (Egypt, Morea and Algeria). The cultural and scientific context which made these expeditions possible arrived later in Spain, but both the official attitude towards new-found material, and the attempt to distort its own antiquity, betray an ambition to follow the French lead and to claim a place among the European powers.

CHAPTER 7

# 'TRANS-ATLANTIC PYRAMIDOLOGY', ORIENTALISM, AND EMPIRE: ANCIENT EGYPT AND THE 19th CENTURY ARCHAEOLOGICAL EXPERIENCE OF MESOAMERICA

*Isabel Medina-González*

## Introduction

> Looking around for a good man to accompany him in his expeditions, Stephens found in his friend Frederick Catherwood, a draftsman. Once again, we come across the same sort of fruitful partnership as that of Vivant Denon and the Egyptian Commission of the Napoleonic Wars ...

(Ceram 1951: 349)

In his classic book, Ceram (1951) makes a direct analogy between two legendary expeditions in the history of archaeology. He firstly alludes to the antiquarian investigations of Dominique Vivant Denon (1747–1825) – one of the French *savants* who joined the Commission of Science and Arts during Napoleon Bonaparte's invasion of Egypt (1798–1799) – and then to John Stephens' and Frederick Catherwood's 1840s explorations of the pre-Columbian ruins of south-east Mexico and Central America (Stephens 1841, 1843). Ceram provides no reason(s) to establish a link between these two expeditions separated considerably by time and space. In fact, however, their adventures do seem to share various common features. In the first place, some historical studies have recognized Denon's and Stephens' antiquarian campaigns as heralding the birth of modern Egyptology and Mesoamerican archaeology respectively (Curl 1994: 116; Daniel 1978: 271; Willey and Sabloff 1974: 57). A second similarity can be found in the political dimension of both enterprises. Many studies have discussed the links between the imperialist framework of Bonaparte's invasion of Egypt with the foundation and the works of the Commission (i.e. Said 1978: 80–87; Hassan Chapter 2, this volume). Equally, some scholars have argued that Stephens' and Catherwood's archaeological activities were influenced by the ideology of the Destiny Manifest and Monroe Doctrine (see Hagen 1950: 80–81; Hinsley 1993; Ortega y Medina 1962a, 1962b), and "enacted a complex of attitudes best described as 'imperial'" (Hinsley 1993: 110). Finally, it should be noted that the Napoleonic campaigns prompted an explosive interest in Ancient Egypt in early 19th century Europe that produced innovations in architecture, design, literature and art (Curl 1994: xiv; Grimal 1992: 8; Humbert and Price 2003). Stephens and Catherwood actively participated in this 'Egyptomania', exploiting its effects in archaeology.

Before their pre-Columbian expeditions, both had visited the ancient monuments of Egypt, producing accounts and illustrations. Stephens' (1837) were disseminated among the British and American public through travel-literature. Catherwood joined Robert Hay's 1834 Egyptian expedition, producing drawings that later served as the basis for the 'View of Thebes' displayed in Robert Burford's 'Panorama' in London's Leicester Square during 1835 and 1836 (Hyde 1988: 56; Paxton 1986: 11). From 1838 to 1842, this panorama was also exhibited in various cities in the USA (Bourbon 1999: 194; Oettermann 1997: 318).

This example is but one of the numerous 'connections' established between the study of Ancient Egypt and that of pre-Columbian cultures in the last 200 years. This chapter offers an analysis of this historical phenomenon. It examines the ways in which both Ancient Egypt and Egyptology served as a powerful reference/model for the investigation and interpretation of Mesoamerican prehispanic remains during the early 19th century. It also attempts to explain the rationale behind such incorporation of perceptions and experience, examining its associations with the intellectual development of archaeology.

## William Bullock's role in early 19th century interest in Ancient Egypt and Mexico

The interest in Egyptian and Mexican archaeology that arose in the early 19th century was intertwined with important local and global sociopolitical developments. After the Napoleonic invasion came to an end (1799), and especially during the government of Mohammed Ali and his successors, Egypt experienced a notable increase in European and American travellers who served as agents for business, diplomacy and politics (Brier 1992: 6; Grimal 1992: 9; Jeffreys Chapter 1 and Hassan Chapter 2, both this volume). A similar process took place in the aftermath of Mexico's independence from Spain in 1821 and the official opening of its borders (Estrada de Gerlero 1996: 185; Jiménez Cordinach 1996: 42–43; Ortega y Medina 1987: 3; Trigger 1989: 69). Linked with the rise of European economic and political expansionism, there was an explosion of European and American missions devoted to the study of geography, natural history and ethnology around the world, including in Mexico and Egypt (Pratt 1992: 5, 17–37). Pratt (1992: 4–5) has analyzed 18th and late 19th century western travel experiences associated with scientific enterprises, concluding that they evoked a eurocentric form of "planetary consciousness", which connected with practices and representations encoding and legitimizing the aspirations of economic expansion and empire. Surveying and collecting ancient Egyptian and Mexican antiquities was an intrinsic part of the latter enterprises (Braun 1993: 23; Reid 2002: 31–63).

The years 1809–1810 marked a turning point in the intellectual development of both Mexican and Egyptian archaeology, or, more precisely, of their revival among western audiences. This brief period saw the publication of the first volume of the Commission's *Description de l'Égypte* (1809–1829) and the work of Alexander Von Humboldt (1810). Offering a major re-evaluation of the history of ancient America, the latter raised European interest in pre-Columbiana to a "high scientific level" (Estrada de Gerlero 1996: 184; Keen 1971: 336; Ramírez 1982: 40). It also initiated a flux of European artists and writers who documented Mexican archaeology through the rest of the century (Ramírez 1982: 157–159). Although the idea of a glorified Mexican antiquity already "existed as a ideological construct" among the local intelligentsia, Humboldt was also a main transculturator of American antiquities for 19th century Mexican scholars (Pratt 1992: 134–135). During the 18th century, Creole intelligentsia formulated the idea of the Aztec world as an equivalent of 'Classical Antiquity' in Mexican history (Graham 1993: 53; Phelan 1960). During the 1820s, a nationalistic movement recalled the glory of the prehispanic world as a political and cultural unity, its usurpation by the Spanish conquest and its restoration by the Mexican Independence (Keen 1971: 319; Morales-Moreno 1994: 175).

An important figure in this early 19th century fascination for Egypt and Mexico was the British naturalist, traveller and showman William Bullock (ca. 1770–1849). In 1820, Bullock began promoting the Egyptian vogue that influenced the British learned and artistic circles at the time; for the construction of his 'London Museum' (at 12 Piccadilly Street), he selected an eclectic combination of 'Egyptianizing' architecture and decoration (Altick 1978: 236–237; Lancaster 1950: 94; Werner 2003: 83). Two colossal statues of Isis and Osiris, sphinxes, bulbous columns, prolific hieroglyphics and a huge cornice formed the imposing façade of this building that soon became known as the 'Egyptian Hall' (Figure 7:1; Werner 2003: Figure 5:3) (Bullock 1814; Curl 1994: 156–171; Honour 1954: 38; Mackenzie 1995: 78). According to its designer, Peter Frederick Robinson (1776–1858) – who was renowned as a 'connoisseur of styles'

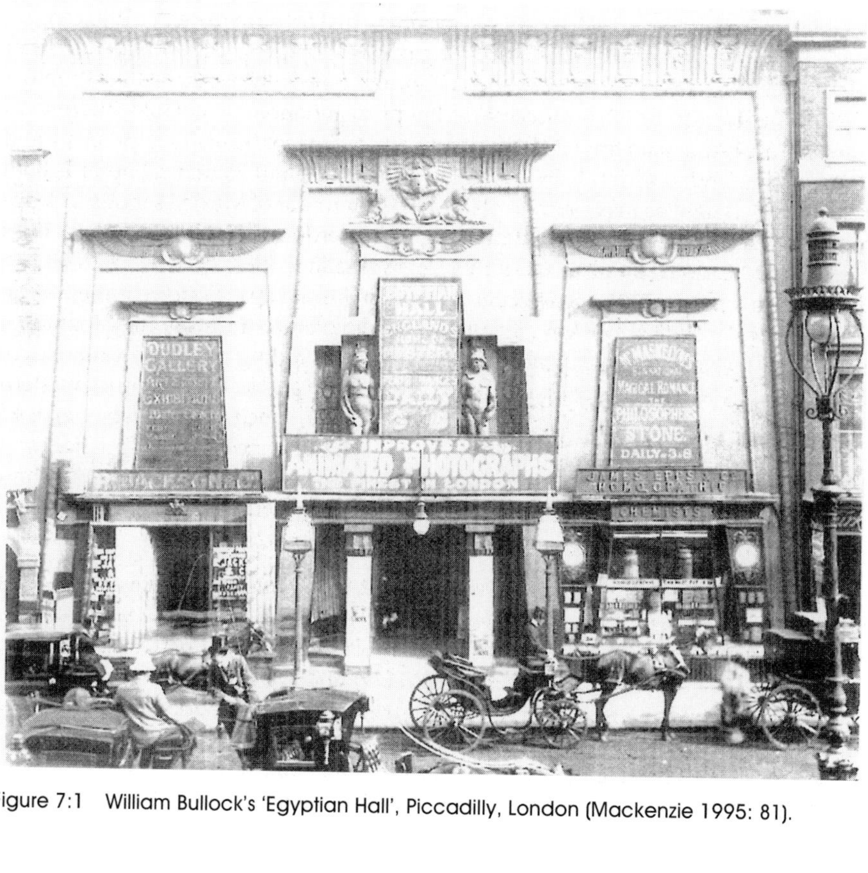
DUDLEY GALLERY
IMPROVED
ANIMATED PHOTOGRAPHS
STONE
DAILY 3.8
CHEMISTS

Figure 7:1 William Bullock's 'Egyptian Hall', Piccadilly, London (Mackenzie 1995: 81).

advising the Prince of Wales on the design of interiors in the Royal Pavilion at Brighton (Curl 1994: 156; Lancaster 1950: 94) – the composition had been "taken from Denon's celebrated work" (Denon 1802; Elmes 1827: 157). It was a free interpretation of the Temple of Hathor at Dendera, a "monument that epitomised the Egyptian architectural spirit as the Regency conceived it" (Altick 1978: 236–237).

In 1816, Bullock displayed Napoleon Bonaparte's military travelling carriage, which had been captured after the Battle of Waterloo; the Emperor's former coachman was employed as a guide (Bullock 1816a). This enterprise exploited the current fixation regarding Napoleon's defeat by British forces and, with the support of the press, it became one of the most popular and lucrative undertakings of Bullock's career, attracting 80,000 visitors (Altick 1978: 241). Amusing renditions of the show were depicted in the drawings of Thomas Rowlandson (Figure 7:2) and George Cruikshank. After taking the carriage on tour around England, Bullock set up a "Museum Napoleon" in the Egyptian Hall. These exhibitions formulated patriotic impulses, incorporating Bullock's expectations on the development of the British Empire, and featuring his personal ambitions as a collector. As the seventh edition of the *Companion to the London Museum* (Bullock 1816b: iv) stated:

> ... our unrivalled navy, and the extension of our colonies through the habitable world present such advantages to this Country ... that if the exertions [of the museum's proprietor] are seconded to the public ... he will very shortly be enabled to make a collection ... far surpassing anything of the kind [that exists] at the present ...

In 1819, the interiors of the Egyptian Hall were refurbished to form a series of galleries for exhibitions, auctions and events (King 1996: 117). John Papworth (1775–1847) then applied an 'Egyptian' décor (comprising paintings and Hathor-headed columns) to

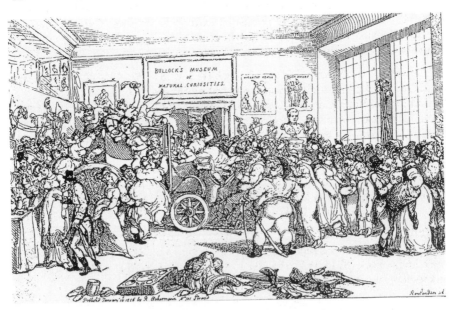

Figure 7:2 Drawing by Thomas Rowlandson of the Exhibition of Napoleon's carriage at the 'Egyptian Hall' (Altick 1978: 240).

the main gallery on the second floor, which was renamed the "Great Egyptian Room" (Werner 2003: Figure 5:4) (*Survey of London* XXIX: 266–270). Two years later, "a curious twist of fate determined that [this space] should house a magnificent exhibition of Egyptian artefacts brought to London by Giovanni Battista Belzoni" (1778–1823) (Curl 1994: 158). Several antiquities and models of pyramids were placed within a reproduction of the Theban Tomb of Seti I formed by casts, reproductions of murals and an original alabaster sarcophagus (Pearce 2000; Werner 2003: Figure 5:5). Belzoni's (1820) nationalistic appeal for British support to sponsor archaeological expeditions in Egypt served as a publicity stunt for the display. Although ancient Egyptian sculpture had been previously exhibited in country houses of the British aristocracy (Gilding 2001: 36), Belzoni's exhibit allowed large audiences to come into contact with Egyptian antiquities for the first time (Curl 1994: 159).

In 1823, Bullock embarked on a trip to Mexico. Its timing was more than opportune since in 1822 Spain had disowned the agreement of independence of Mexico, and the Mexican government had consequently turned to England, France and other western countries for recognition and support (Vázquez 1976: 3). Furthermore, Britain, like the rest of Europe, had followed the emancipation of Latin America with particular interest. This process implied reshaping the international balance of power, entailing a full-scale negotiation of political, economic and commercial relations between Spanish America and northern Europe in a new era of imperialistic expansion (Vázquez 1976). Humboldt (1811) – a work including statistical, political, economic and scientific information – provoked considerable interest among British speculators and entrepreneurs who were interested in Mexican commercial, industrial and mining opportunities (Ortega y Medina 1987: 7). The British press informed the public about Mexico's diplomatic and financial highlights, underlining Britain's role in them (Jiménez Cordinach 1996: 41; Medina-González 1998: 14). Periodicals frequently published extracts or reviews of voyages in Latin America: Mexico was the topic of hundreds of accounts by British authors in the course of the 19th century.

During his residence in Mexico, Bullock (1824a: 183–187, 328–342, 442) collected handicrafts, botanical, zoological and mineral specimens, as well as antiquities. With the support of the Mexican Minister of Domestic and Foreign Affairs, he (Bullock 1824a: 329) also borrowed a series of prehispanic codices (and copies) from the Mexican government that were claimed to have belonged to Lorenzo Boturini, who had visited New Spain between 1736 and 1742, collecting some 350 prehispanic manuscripts. Bullock's son produced sketches of attractive destinations, including a view of Teotihuacan (Figure 7:3). José Cayetana, an "Indian from Chytla near Texcoco" became Bullock's personal servant, agreeing to accompany him back to England (Bullock 1824a: 442–443).

Bullock's publication in 1824 was such that a second edition was printed within the year, and translations soon appeared in Dresden, Delft, Jena and Paris (Baquedano 1993: 259; Bullock 1824d, 1825a, b). His book also announced the public display of the articles that he had brought from Mexico.

Figure 7:3  Drawing by William Bullock Jr. of the pyramids of Teotihuacan (Bullock 1825a: between 410–411).

## 'Ancient Mexico': representing connections between Mesoamerica and Ancient Egypt

On 8 April 1824, Bullock opened the twin exhibitions 'Ancient Mexico' and 'Modern Mexico' in the Egyptian Hall (*The Times*, 8 April 1824: 2; *Literary Gazette*, 10 April 1824: 237). 'Ancient Mexico' was set up in the 'Great Egyptian Room', the most prominent exhibition space on the premises. According to the printed catalogue (Bullock 1824b) more than 60 objects were displayed, including casts of monumental Aztec sculpture, stone-sculptures, a series of ceramic and lithic artefacts, original and copies of prehispanic manuscripts, paintings, and a model of the pyramids of Teotihuacan. The gallery was refurbished in order to "convey some idea of the Temple of Mexico ... [displaying] whatever is related to the ancient religion" (Bullock 1825a: 9). The catalogue does not provide details about the physical organization of the collection; however, an engraved frontispiece by Agostino Aglio provides a panoramic view of it (Figure 7:4). The guide mentions that the Serpent's Head was located "at the west end" of the gallery, that the Teoyamique was placed "at the east end" of it and that the enlarged folios of the *Codice Boturini* encircled the room (see Bullock 1824b: 41–43). Aglio's engraving shows these monumental sculptures at opposite ends of the gallery. On the surface of the peristyle entablature that surrounded the gallery, images from the *Codice Boturini* appear. Such arrangements suggest that Aglio's panoramic view might have been an accurate depiction of the physical disposition and appearance of 'Ancient Mexico'.

'Ancient Mexico' formulated and disseminated a complex representation of the Aztecs through the display of an arranged collection and the exhibit's narrative (Medina-González 1998: 16–33; 2003). The presentation of a model of the Teotihuacan pyramids was of especial relevance for this exhibition. First, Bullock (1824b: 33)

Figure 7:4   Engraving by Agostino Aglio of the panoramic view of the 'Ancient Mexico' exhibition (Bullock 1824b: frontispiece).

explicitly prized the pyramids of Teotihuacan among the antiquities of Mexico. Second, the catalogue presents an extensive and detailed description of these monuments (Bullock 1824b). Finally, Bullock placed the model in a prominent position: it occupied the left-back corner of an enclosed composition of monumental casts that was followed by the rest of the collection (Figure 7:4).

The panoramic view of the exhibition shows that the model of the Teotihuacan pyramids reproduced all the formal characteristics of the original buildings except for size. It therefore derived from what Elsner (1994: 162) has termed the "microscopic method": a scaled-down representation standing for a real building. The use of a model as a technology of display was meaningful for three reasons. In the first place, models do not merely constitute a representational alternative for what cannot be reproduced in actual dimensions. Additionally, miniatures implicitly stand for objects of large size. This dialectic relationship between the idea of grandeur and models helped to formulate the notion of the monumentality of the Teotihuacan pyramids in Bullock's display.

Second, architectural models were highly praised by Bullock's contemporaries. At the beginning of the 19th century, the British architect John Sloane (1753–1837), who displayed models of Classical buildings in his private museum in London, clearly stated the powerful effect that models were thought to produce: "Large Models, faithful to the originals, not only in form and construction, but likewise to the various colours and materials would produce sensations and impressions of the highest kind, far beyond the powers of description and surpassed only by the contemplation of the buildings themselves. [Models were meant] to explain ... different modes of construction" (Sloane 1929: 191 in Elsner 1994: 164).

The guide to 'Ancient Mexico' did not provide details about the model itself, nor the aims of its display. Bullock was neither an architect nor an academic. However, since his exhibitions aimed to instruct as well as entertain (Bullock 1816a: 140), it can be speculated that by including details of the location, the arrangement and the construction of the Teotihuacan pyramids, Bullock might have tried to invite the visitor to reflect on the architectural techniques developed in prehispanic Mexico.

Third, as Elsner (1994: 171) has suggested, 'models memorialize famous monuments ... they freeze in material form in the here and now the desire for lost or distant grandeur'. This idea seemed to have been related to the presentation of the miniature of the pyramid of Teotihuacan in 'Ancient Mexico'. Bullock (1824b: 3) produced a replica of a structure that he considered to be the "most extraordinary of the antiquities that survived the conquest". The pyramids of the Sun and the Moon at Teotihuacan had become known to European scholars following publications by Humboldt (1810, 1811). In fact, Bullock quoted these works in the guidebook for 'Ancient Mexico'.

Brief details regarding the historiography of Humboldt's 1810 publication reveal that significant connections between the Mexican archaeological research on Mesoamerica and that of Ancient Egypt had been established long before the 19th century. Humboldt was a polymath whose scholarly pursuits benefited from travelling (Labastida 1999: 103). At the end of the 18th century, Humboldt's scientific interest markedly focused on Egypt: twice he attempted journeys up the Nile, joining both an English expedition and Napoleon's Commission (Pratt 1992: 116). After both enterprises failed to come to fruition (Pratt 1992), Spanish America became the alternative terrain for a five-year (1799–1804) scientific exploration (Labastida 1999: 368). In New Spain, the local intelligentsia collaborated in Humboldt's antiquarian investigations; for instance, Juan José de Oteyza (1777–1810) provided Humboldt with the results of his topographical survey of Teotihuacan (Gallegos 1997: 100 n. 27; Humboldt 1974: 42–58, 1984: 124–127). He may have known that Carlos de Siguenza y Góngora (1645–1700) had previously conducted research on prehispanic antiquities, concluding that Hebrews, Christians and Ancient Egyptians were the ancestors of Mesoamerican peoples (Keen 1973: 203). Siguenza had also postulated that prehispanic pyramids revealed evidence of an ancient Egyptian origin and had carried out antiquarian explorations in Teotihuacan. Humboldt reported on these explorations in the *Political Essay* (Bernal 1980: 50; Rojas Garciadueñas 1988: 49–50).

According to Keen (1973: 340), Humboldt's interpretation of prehispanic America reflected the belief in the psychic unity of humanity, and the principle of valuing each epoch and culture individually (thus rejecting comparisons that led to judgment). Using a comparative method, Humboldt aimed to establish the general outlines of cultural development through the ages, distinguishing local variation caused by environmental and historical factors (Florescano 1994: 85; Keen 1973: 341). A prime example of this approach was his analysis of the Teotihuacan pyramids. Although Humboldt never visited these monuments (Labastida 1999: 368), he acquired data from literature, reports and informants which he then compared to the characteristics of Egyptian pyramids, tracing analogies in building technique, the number of small pyramids that surrounded them and their arrangement in the urban layout (Humboldt 1974: 53). Observing that the monuments of Teotihuacan were aligned to the earth's meridians and parallels, Humboldt (1984: 126) reported that the British traveller Richard Pococke (1704–1765) had noted a similar alignment in the pyramids of Giza. Humboldt also addressed the analogies in the writing systems of both cultures, their similar chronological systems, and the resemblance between the headdress of Isis and that of an Aztec goddess (Keen 1971: 335). He (1974: 54) also noted the differences between Egyptian and Mexican pyramids, explaining that whereas the former had been employed as funerary structures, the latter had been used both as tombs and temples.

Scholars have debated whether Humboldt supported or opposed diffusionist theories (Keen 1973: 344). Ambivalence reigns over his analysis of the pyramids of Teotihuacan. On the one hand, he proposed that people at the dawn of civilization used actual mountains to erect their temples, shaping them into regular forms with stairs. He confirmed that this type of structure had been discovered all over the world. By using this argument and stressing the differences between Egyptian and Mexican pyramids, Humboldt appeared to suggest that the same architectural form could have developed independently in both the Old and the New continents. On the other hand, by questioning whether the builders of the pyramids of Teotihuacan had taken this type of construction from the Mongolian race, or from a common ancestor of the Chinese and Japanese, he appeared to support a diffusionist approach (Humboldt 1984: 126).

In 'Ancient Mexico', Bullock emulated Humboldt's approach by comparing the Aztecs and the cultures of the Old World, including Ancient Egypt. The model of the Teotihuacan pyramids proved to be a fruitful terrain for postulating links with the pyramids at Giza. The following range of strategies illustrates the ways in which language and modes of display were systematically manipulated in 'Ancient Mexico' in order to create connections and to justify them.

### Reference to size

As scaled-down representations, models require a reference to the dimensions that they are meant to represent. For models of buildings, the first point of reference is, of course, the human body (i.e. the observer). However, in order to indicate the actual size of Mexican pyramids, Bullock approached the unfamiliar through the familiar (Pagdem 1993: 21), proposing that these were "scarcely inferior to that of Cairo" (Bullock 1824b: 33). No exact dimensions were given. However, through the evocation of an already known prototype of grandeur, this model showed that prehispanic architecture was comparable to the monumental vestiges of another ancient culture.

### Reference to form

Bullock pointed out that the form of the Great Pyramid of Teotihuacan had a square shape as regular as that of the Great Egyptian pyramid (Bullock 1824b: 34). At the beginning of the 19th century, formal analysis in architecture (identification of similarity among types, forms and features) was employed to trace relationships between cultures, as well as to establish hypotheses regarding their development in history. For example, Maurice (1800 in Curl 1994: 94) argued that "India, with its zoomorphic deities, pyramid temples and decorative motifs had derived religion and architecture from Egypt".

### Reference to urban layout

Bullock (1824b: 34) noted the small structures that encircled the pyramids of Teotihuacan, pointing to their similarity to the structures that stood near the pyramids of Cheops and Mykerinos. Reviews published in the press not only supported this idea but elaborated upon it, proposing that the distribution of the Teotihuacan pyramids was just "in the manner of the structures of Giza" (London Magazine, May 1824: 522–523).

### Reference to historical events

The guidebook for 'Ancient Mexico' provided a romanticized account of the 16th century Spanish conquest of the Aztecs, including references to the defeat of the indigenous military forces in Otumba, a population near to Teotihuacan. None of the sources consulted by Bullock (writings of conquerors and historians such as Hernán Cortes (1777) and Bernal Díaz del Castillo (1800)) had reported that the Spanish troops had passed by the Teotihuacan pyramids. Nevertheless, the catalogue linked these monuments to the battle of Otumba (Bullock 1824b: 33). Bullock (1824a: 153) stated, "I believe that from the top of one of these [pyramids], Cortes noticed the arrival of the enemy's army". Although there is no direct evidence, it is possible that this claim was but an evocation of events recorded at the Battle of the Pyramids of Giza fought by Napoleon's army in July 1798.

'Ancient Mexico' also detailed other correspondences between Egyptian and Aztec cultural productions. Some assertions directly reproduced Humboldt's ideas; for example, Aztec and Egyptian hieroglyphic writing were described as "almost alike" (Bullock 1824b: 47). Other arguments elaborated analogies previously mentioned by Humboldt, but highlighting specific artefacts on display in order to develop both a sense of immediacy and an effect of scientific 'truth' by using 'material evidence'. For instance, the catalogue described the bust of a female as bearing "a strong resemblance to Isis"; another statue called the "Aztec Princess" gave "the appearance, at first sight, of the front of the Egyptian Sphinx, to which the resemblance of head-dress greatly contribute[d]" (Bullock 1824a: 38, 39). Other comparisons were Bullock's own innovations. For example, the guidebook linked the size of the "Great Kalendar" with that of the Zodiac of Dendera, an Egyptian monumental ceiling block (Bullock 1824b: 33, 1825c: 27). Significantly, the cast of the latter monument had been brought to London during the same year (*Gentleman's Magazine*, 1824, 94: 795). Finally, the recreation of a Mexican temple was superimposed on the original ornamentation of the 'Great Egyptian Room'. The blend of the two decorations not only evoked a prehispanic temple as a large solid structure with complex architectural elements (columns, decorations, etc.), but also contributed to the creation of a visual link between Aztec and Egyptian aesthetics. In the same year, Bullock (1824a: 394) claimed further relationships, stating that the religion, traditions and architecture of Texcoco resembled those of the "enlightened nation of Africa".

## The rationale of 'Ancient Mexico' and its socio-political agenda: diffusionism, Orientalism and the expectations of the British Empire

Bullock clearly departed from Humboldt's conclusions by proposing that Aztec and Egyptian cultures had a "kindred origin [that] can hardly be doubted" (Bullock 1824b: 47). Furthermore, he argued (1824b) that the cultural achievements of the former originated in the latter, assuming a theoretical position aligned with diffusionism. Judging from press reviews, it seems that 'Ancient Mexico' was quite effective in transmitting this message to the public. Reporters of the *New Monthly Magazine* (April 1824: 163–164) and the *London Magazine* (May 1824: 521–522) were convinced of the affinities and common origin of Aztecs and Egyptians: the latter even mentioned that in 'Ancient Mexico' "there was a Zodiac of Dendera [displayed] under the title of the Great Kalendar Stone". Addressing the similarities between Aztec and Egyptian cultural productions, the author of an article published in the *Classical Journal* (1824, 29: 189) speculated that Egyptians had colonized or conquered Mexico during prehispanic times.

Bullock's diffusionist approach embraced some principles of early 19th century British ethnology (embodied by the works of James Prichard) which, through comparisons, attempted to trace cultural derivation and origins (Stocking 1987: 51). 'Ancient Mexico' additionally followed a long-standing trend of European scholarship that, from the 16th century and throughout the 18th century, posed diffusionist hypotheses linking the development of Mesoamerica to the cultures of the Old World (e.g. Acosta 1590; Gemelli Carreri 1700; Clavijero 1807). Although such diffusionist interpretations varied considerably regarding the places/peoples of origin and routes of migration proposed, all echoed the long-accepted biblical view of history that was essentially monogenist and explained the spread of peoples (and their customs) through a series of dispersions (Trigger 1989: 33).

Newer currents in scientific thought also influenced the diffusionist interpretation formulated in 'Ancient Mexico'. From the late 18th century onwards, diffusion continued to play a major role in explaining cultural progress in history; emerging "general or scientific formulations of the idea of progress in civilization" stressed the importance of "the essentially diffusionary process of the intercommunication of ideas" (Stocking 1987: 16). In the exhibit, Bullock made no explicit attempt to demonstrate that the links between Ancient Egyptians and Ancient Mexicans had been the result of *migration*; rather, he pointed to similar cultural achievements, suggesting that these had been transmitted from Ancient Egypt to Mesoamerica. Such emphasis reflected the early 19th century broad sense of 'diffusion', which "implied both the migration of peoples *and the dissemination of ideas*" (Stocking 1987: 15, emphasis added).

Bullock's idea that Ancient Egypt could have been the source of Mesoamerican culture was also endorsed by the perceptions of historical development that dominated early 19th century thinking. Clavijero (1964: 49–51) calculated that 511 AD was the oldest date for Mexico; this marked the beginning of the migration of the Toltecs – held to be the builders of the pyramids of Teotihuacan – now dated 100–1 BC (Manzanilla 1995: 142–151). In 1822, Champollion's decipherment of Egyptian hieroglyphs demonstrated the *recent* origin of the Zodiac of Dendera, "thus putting an end to the disconcerting datings previously put forward" (15000–6000 BC) that contradicted chronologies based on the Bible and Classical texts (Donadoni *et al.* 1990: 135–138). The chronology (that "allowed 1663 years for pharaonic history before the Persian conquest" of 525 BC) suggested that the pyramids of Giza and Saqqarah (now dated 2700–2050 BC) had been constructed between 2000 and 500 BC (Anderson 1987: 8; Andreu 1997: 1). Considering these 'tight' interpretations of time in history, Bullock's and his contemporaries' belief that some sort of contact could have taken place between Ancient Egypt and Ancient Mexico is perfectly understandable.

The diffusionist approach of 'Ancient Mexico' underlined messages that were highly significant in the 19th century. Bullock recognized that Ancient Mexicans had possessed writing, calendar systems and monumental sculpture; however, he found it difficult to accept that indigenous peoples had developed such complex cultural achievements without external intervention. Similar stances have been detected in antiquarian research framed within colonialist paradigms (Trigger 1984, 1989: 104–147). Colonial North America saw the emergence of the myth of the Mound-builders: this proposed that an extinct race of inhabitants, unrelated to the native Americans, had erected the monumental constructions found in Ohio and the Mississippi valleys (Trigger 1985, 1989: 105; Willey and Sabloff 1974: 35). During the late 19th century, archaeologists proposed that Great Zimbabwe was the product of a foreign occupation (Galarke 1973: 15–16). What distinguishes Bullock's exhibition is that such argument, which denied the local capacity of cultural development and emphasized a static and hence 'uncivilized' nature of indigenous people, was developed to explain the past at a non-colonial stage.

Pointing to Ancient Egypt as the 'originators/creators' of cultural achievements and Ancient Mexico as the 'receiver', Bullock also placed these cultures along an axis of comparative categories: active/passive, superior/inferior. This idea was followed by an author in the *Classical Journal* (1824, 29: 189), who stated that the "Egyptians were a nation infinitely more enlightened than the Mexicans". Considering that 'Ancient Mexico' followed a Christian approach to history, it is not surprising that Aztec religion was held as being responsible for the 'cultural inferiority' of Ancient Mexicans. The catalogue stated clearly that "the worship of the Mexicans appeared to have been more monstrous and bloody than the Egyptians" (Bullock 1824b: 3). From analogies between buildings and representations of serpents in sculptures, Bullock (1824b: 3) proposed that the Aztec religion "resembled that of the Buddhist and Hindoo ... strengthen[ing] the hypothesis of a similar origin". These ideas underlined a set of distinctions and categorizations that were routinely used to promote the difference between the familiar (Europe, Western culture, 'us') and the strange (Orient, Eastern culture, 'them') (Said 1978: 43). By ascribing Aztec 'idolatry' to 'the Other' – non-Christian – reality, the Orient was held to be the source of 'barbaric' practices that had spread to the New World. By the same token, such explanation confirmed the supposed (moral) superiority of the west.

'Ancient Mexico' formulated various ideas that can be related to the network of practices and representations at the core of Orientalism. Said (1978) maintains that the Napoleonic Commission of Egypt constituted a benchmark in the development of western attitudes and perceptions that orientalized the Orient and that served as mechanisms of propaganda to justify its domination by the west. Apart from addressing the contributions of travel writing and exhibitions to the building of Orientalism discourse, Said (1978: 7, 99) draws attention to the considerable "support from the unearthing of dead Oriental civilizations". He also addresses the development of the idea of the "good Orient as an invariably classical period somewhat long-gone". Said (1978: 122–148) and Rashed (1980: 1–11) have also proposed that the following notions underlined the process of appropriation of ancient civilizations by 19th century western (Orientalist) scholarship. Modern inhabitants were described as either new interlopers themselves, or as the degenerate remnants of a lost 'high culture', and this belief was extended to argue that non-westerners (Orientals) were unfit to analyze their own culture. By contrast, Jean-François Champollion became a paradigmatic figure of "the (western) hero rescuing the Orient from obscurity, alienation and strangeness ... [whose] research reconstructed the Orient's lost languages, mores and even mentalities" (Said 1978: 121).

The narrative of 'Ancient Mexico' exhibited similar, although original, permutations of the ways through which the west formulated notions for the appropriation of ancient civilizations. Through the names of the exhibitions, Bullock shaped time into distinct periods: Mexican history was hence dissected into an ancient era and a modern era. The intermediate colonial period was not only practically excluded from representation in Bullock's displays, but the guidebook also pictured it as worthless, affirming that the Spanish rule had brought "Mexican History to ... utter doubt and darkness" (Bullock 1824c: 19–20). Such categorization could be associated with the conventional division of western history into three eras – Antiquity, Middle Ages, Modernity – and with the value judgments traditionally imposed on each period, expressed by the metaphors of light and darkness, day and night, wakeful and sleep (Calinescu 1987: 20). Hence prehispanic Mexico came to be perceived as a resplendent and distant world.

Bullock's interpretation of the effects of the Spanish invasion completed his conceptual image of Mexican antiquity. Apart from stating that the invaders had "annihilated the race of Moctezuma" (the Aztecs' emperor), several pages of the catalogue described the *conquistadores'* destruction of the splendid Aztec City and its extraordinary monuments (Bullock 1824b, c: 19–22). These ideas contributed to the representation of Ancient Mexico as a distant, vanished and once-magnificent world. According to Pratt (1992: 134–135), these perceptions resulted from the early 19th century process of "monumental reinvention" that took place simultaneously in Egypt and America:

> The European imagination produces archaeological topics by splitting contemporary non-European peoples off from their pre-colonial, and even their colonial, pasts. To revive indigenous peoples' history and culture as archaeology is to revive them as dead. The gesture simultaneously rescues them from European forgetfulness and reassigns them to a departed age.

To maximize the value of both his collection and the information presented in 'Ancient Mexico', Bullock (1824b: 2) explained that the "jealous policy of Old Spain had prevented Europe from acquiring correct information about Mexico, its condition and antiquities"; he "had rescue[d antiquities] from oblivion and safely transferred [them] to England". Bullock was transformed into a cultural hero. The *Classical Journal* (1824, 29: 186) stated that Bullock had "found [the antiquities] in the possession of the multitude, from whose destroying hands each work" had been obtained. This narrative thus attempted to vindicate the appropriation of the items under the guise of conservation obligations. As Coombes (1994: 121) has suggested, this rhetoric – based on the 'necessity of conservation and preservation' – was used to justify the development of ethnographic and archaeological collections as European imperialism peaked in the 19th century.

Greenhalgh (1988: 88) has demonstrated that "the obsession with authenticity of the object and the rationale of collection in science, not in plunder ... encourage[d] and justif[ied] the acquiring of objects from all over the world by the Western Museum". 'Constructing' the spectator as a serious observer and pointing to the scientific nature of his collection (Medina-González 1998: 20), Bullock ensured that education was seen as the central rationale for the exhibit's experience. As the catalogue stated, "The proprietor [has] tried to combine in the best manner ... all that he could gather to illustrate the ancient capital, its monuments, religion, inscriptions, feelings and customs ... promoting interest in science and learning" (Bullock 1824b: 5). This idea acquired an increasing importance during the Victorian period, culminating with the Educational Act of 1902: apart from museums, this rhetoric was also incorporated into other contemporary forms of 'instructional amusement', such as World Fairs and Panoramas (Coombes 1994; Greenhalgh 1988).

The account published in the *Classical Journal* facilitated the dissemination of Orientalist categorizations and imperialist expectations, merging such messages and complementing them to the contemporary rhetoric of science, collecting and the exhibition. Pointing to the general lack of knowledge about the Aztecs among the British public, the author commented upon the scant support given to antiquarian research in England, comparing it with the French system of patronage for antiquities' collecting and research that had led to the ground-breaking work of Jean-François Champollion (*Classical Journal* 1824, 24: 176; and see Bierbrier Chapter 3, this volume). The same reporter claimed that the value of overseas investigations lay in their potential utility for political and commercial enterprises, not only supporting the hypothesis that 19th century anthropology and its practitioners attempted to appear indispensable to imperialist pursuits, but that collecting met the interests of the state, the public and academia (Coombes 1994: 107). Furthermore, it demonstrated that such perspectives, representations and practices were also applied to non-colonial locales. The globalization of this phenomenon can be detected in the review of Bullock's exhibitions published by *The Times* (9 April 1824). Asking "Why is this collection so meagre? Why have we not a much greater assortment of objects to illustrate the civil and religious customs of these singular people?" the reporter suggested that "We might at least have had as much from Mexico as we have from Herculanaeum or Pompeii". Clearly, the press was also an outspoken supporter for the development of overseas archaeological collections during the 19th century.

The images and messages presented in 'Ancient Mexico' were complemented by the display 'Modern Mexico' (see Medina-González 1998: 33–36, 64–68). Bullock's interest in the future development of independent Mexico was represented as being intrinsically linked with the expansion of western enterprises, particularly the establishment of industries, arts and mining enterprises funded by British investment. As the catalogue stated:

> Mexico has thus become an object of Great European consideration; and to no country is it of such special import as to Britain. The enlightened policy of our Cabinet [has] virtually opened that incalculably extensive mart to the operations of our commerce, and even made the interior one vast field for the exercise of British capital, machinery, and industry. Already do we see mining and mercantile speculation largely at work; companies and individuals seek the scene; and in a very short period millions will be embarked in prosecuting those enterprises ...
>
> (Bullock 1824c: 4)

Bullock (1824c: 5) claimed that the Mexican exhibitions were created to address the lack of knowledge about Mexico and "to create an advantageous intercourse ... understanding of what Mexico wants from us, what she can return, where we can most effectively assist her, and how she can best repay our exertions". In this sense, 'Modern Mexico' was a predecessor of the late 19th century World Fairs that served to structure imperial rationale, transforming it into a product for public consumption and entertainment. The same can be said of the display of the Mexican Indian, José Cayetana, within Bullock's exhibits. For matching Britain's economic interest in Mexico, the catalogue represented the Indian as the archetype of the perfect potential worker, describing him as "docile and extremely intelligent, apt of learning whatever is proposed to him ... simple and content, his wants consequently few" (Bullock 1824b: 12).

'Modern Mexico' was also a "human show-case" that transformed a fellow being into material for examination (Greenhalgh 1988: 84). Whereas the catalogue referred to Cayetana as an "object to merit attention" (Bullock 1824b: 12), the reporter from the *London Magazine* (May 1824: 522) described him as "a living specimen ... the most interesting object in this collection of foreign curiosities". The 'objectification' of Cayetana might have been considered too obvious, and rather offensive, by those spectators still influenced by the principle of human unity derived from the philosophical stance of the 18th century Enlightenment (Trigger 1989: 57). This perspective was expressed by the reporter from *The Times* (9 April 1824: 5), who asked: "Is the Indian to be a fixture, like the stuffed birds and fishes [on display]?"

Cayetana's representation was the basis of many problematic, even conflicting, interpretations. Although the Indian was presented as part of 'Modern Mexico', advertisements (*Literary Gazette*, 2 April 1825: 22) created a connection to 'Ancient Mexico', describing him as "one of the only Mexican Indians who has visited Europe since the natives sent by Cortes to the King of Spain". By conveying a sense of continuity between prehispanic and modern Indians, without making any claims of degeneration for the latter, this representation differs from the conventional principles of Orientalism. Cayetana's role in the exhibits suggests another important difference between Bullock's display and the notions underlying the process of appropriating ancient civilizations proposed by Said and Rashed. As advertisements announced (*Literary Gazette*, 2 April 1825: 22) that Cayetana also performed as tour-guide of the display. Bullock (1825b: 12) stated that Cayetana was "well informed on the history and affairs of his country". Reporting that the Indian appeared "sensible and very communicative", the press appears to have been sympathetic towards Cayetana's image (*London Magazine* 1824: 522). The *New Monthly Magazine* (1825: 163) further reinforced the link of the Indian with his ancestors, by affirming that Cayetana could partially interpret prehispanic codices. All of these statements suggest that Bullock's exhibit was altogether exceptional. First, Cayetana occupied a relatively dignified position. Second, this living Indian was represented as capable of interpreting his own culture and antiquity to Europeans.

## Conclusions

In the contemporary climate of self-revision and criticism, partly inspired by post-processual approaches to archaeology, textual and visual interpretations of the 'past' have been brought into close scrutiny. Analysis has focused upon the styles and designs in which knowledge is produced, the political or ideological implications of the representations, and the role and the effects of their dissemination in society (e.g. Gathercole and Lowenthal 1990; Shanks and Tilley 1987). Initially centring on academic texts, research has recently expanded to include two- and three-dimensional representations, widely identified as 'popular', to form a new field of enquiry dubbed 'archaeological representation' (Moser 2001). This has slowly gained recognition in archaeology, including theoretical forum contributions (Hodder 2001). Critical analysis of the representations of the 'past' has achieved the following results. First, it has demonstrated that two- and three-dimensional representations (i.e. images, dioramas and displays) contribute to the research and interpretative process, having a dynamic role in the shaping of knowledge about the 'past' (e.g. Beard and Henderson 1999; Moser 1998, 2001). Second, it has proved that these are not only in close relationship with anthropological theory, but that they actually constitute theoretical arguments (Moser 1992, 2001) and reflect tensions between different models of understanding the past (Beard and Henderson 1999: 46). Researchers have also recently proposed that the study of representations of the past "cannot be divorced from a consideration of [both] the political and ideological context" of production/consumption and their role fulfilling contemporary interests (Champion 1997: 213–214; Shanks and Tilley 1987: 68–100). Similar conclusions have resulted from those few analyses focusing on representations of the past produced within historical displays (e.g. Medina-González 2003; Riegel 1996; Russell 1997; Stocking 1985). The latter works have increased awareness of the impact of exhibits in society by showing that their representations had a critical role in disseminating political messages (Russell 1997).

This chapter not only confirms these views, but it also demonstrates that the critical examination of historical displays constitutes a rich ground for understanding the 19th century development of regional archaeologies and their connections throughout the 19th century. By presenting the historiography of 'Ancient Mexico' and by analyzing its representations and its rationale, this chapter shows the ways in which Ancient Egypt and Egyptology served as powerful models for investigation and representation of Mesoamerica in the early 1800s.

Moser (2001: 266) considers that "we still need to know exactly how representations make their statements and create knowledge about the past". This chapter has approached this issue by examining the narratives and modes of display used in the case of 'Ancient Mexico' to propose a diffusionist interpretation that traced the origin of the cultural achievements of Mesoamerica to Ancient Egypt. This has revealed that Bullock employed specific exhibition techniques (such as models and recreation) and forms of narrative (references to form, urban layout, use, historical events, formal or functional similarities) for the formulation of notions (i.e. monumentality) and analogies that linked Ancient Egypt to 'Ancient Mexico'. It has also been demonstrated that as result of the systematic use of strategies, such interpretations appeared both feasible and justified. It is clear that Bullock followed a long-standing scholarly tradition proposing a common origin for both Egyptian and Mesoamerican cultures. However, using the comparative method to support a diffusionist interpretation, 'Ancient Mexico' incorporated new currents in scientific thought, making an important contribution to the 19th century intellectual study of Mesoamerica.

Through exploration of the political dimension of representations in 'Ancient Mexico', it is evident that connections with Orientalism and imperialist agendas were a common feature in the development of both Egyptian and Mesoamerican archaeology. Future research should attempt to elucidate whether this set of attitudes either spread from Egypt to Mexico, or developed simultaneously in these two parts of the world.

This chapter shows that the idea that the Napoleonic invasion of Egypt, the works of Denon's Commission and the development of Egyptology became powerful referents and sources of inspiration for imperialist expectations, projects and plans, notably for those involving antiquarian missions. Bernal (1980: 107) has already pointed out that the Commission Scientifique, founded on the occasion of the 1860s French intervention in Mexico (which included research on prehispanic cultures), was set up in imitation of Napoleon I's similar venture in Egypt. Furthermore, this chapter has demonstrated that the links between archaeological studies of Egypt and Mesoamerica can be traced back to early 19th century exhibitions and surveys. Johanssen (1985: 155) has argued that as American soldiers invaded Mexico in 1848 they sought for the ancient monuments and the location of Cortes' battles in order to satisfy their romantic fascination for antiquity and military history. It seems that Aztec ruins particularly touched these invaders who felt that "the army of Napoleon ... fighting in the shadows of Egypt's pyramids, could not have experienced more awe".

The proposed link between Mesoamerica and Egypt endured far beyond 'Ancient Mexico' and its "capacity to exert influence and to leave a legacy" (Champion 1997: 213). In 1828, the British Museum acquired Bullock's antiquities, which constituted the core of its Mexican collection that would grow erratically throughout the 19th century (Medina-González 1998: 68–73). By 1855, this institution "arranged [some Mexican figures] along the walls of the Egyptian room, where the student of ethnology could find the resemblance in posture and decoration" (Connolly 1855: 42). Two private exhibitions held in London during the same decade (Charles Young's display of Mexican Antiquities in Pall Mall and 'The Aztec Lilliputians Show') stressed links between the Aztecs and the Egyptians, presenting 'material evidence' and arguments reinforcing their connection (Altick 1978: 286; Medina-González 1998: 39–40). Diffusion-based hypotheses postulating a common cultural origin for Ancient Egyptians and Mexicans prevailed, especially during the mid-19th century. Evidence of their widespread acceptance can be inferred from the works of Stephens (1841) and Norman (1843), which contested studies linking prehispanic American and Egyptian material culture in order to propose an alternative hypothesis for an independent development of American aboriginal culture (Norman 1843: 287; Priest in Norman 1843: 282–287; Stephens 1969, 2: 442). At the turn of the 20th century, the British publication *The American Egypt* (1909) continued to deny any connection between Ancient Egypt and Mesoamerica, pointing to the differences of style, the difficulties of mapping a migration route and the lack of physical, mythological or philological analogies (Channing and Tabor 1909: 258). However, its authors did not abandon diffusionist theory, proposing that Central American peoples differed greatly from all other American Indians by their astonishing skill as architects and that their building capacities might have derived from outside sources (Channing and Tabor 1909: 242). *The American Egypt* additionally affirmed that the 'history of Yucatan is the History of Egypt' (Channing and Tabor 1909: 226). Equating the splendour of the Mayas with that of the Ancient Egyptians, these authors may well also have been aiming to elevate prehispanic culture to the level of ancient Egyptian civilization, this being prompted by eurocentric attitudes. A related attempt can be found in the work of Mexican geographer and writer García Cubas (1872) who published an exhaustive comparative analysis of the geographical, topographical and environmental locales of the sites of Teotihuacan and Giza. Tracing the similarities between the construction, urban arrangement and orientation of the pyramids, García Cubas concluded that those of Teotihuacan had been built either by descendants of the Ancient Egyptians, or by peoples who had acquired knowledge from them. By comparing Mexican and Egyptian pyramids, García Cubas was quite probably trying to boost national pride.

## Acknowledgments

I would like to thank Professor Peter Ucko for inducing me to write this chapter. Gratitude is also due to CONACYT and INAH Mexico, the generous sponsors of my doctoral research. This chapter benefited greatly from Xóchitl Medina's and Nick Merriman's knowledge and critical suggestions. Elizabeth Bloxam kindly answered my innumerable queries about Egyptology. I also thank Ariel Goldblatt for her support. I am particularly grateful to Lawrence Steward Owens for his invaluable editing and advice.

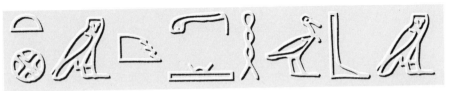

## CHAPTER 8

# EGYPT AND THE DIFFUSION OF CULTURE

*Timothy Champion*

For a brief period in the early 20th century Egypt played a central role in lively debates within prehistory and anthropology far outside the confines of the specialized discipline of Egyptology. From 1911 to the early 1930s the idea of Egypt as the unique origin of human civilization played a dominant, but hotly disputed, role in academic and more popular literature. At the time it was often referred to as the 'heliolithic' school of thought, a term coined to reflect the importance of sun-worship and megalithic architecture in its theories, and more recently it has been dubbed 'hyperdiffusionism' to convey the significance of Egypt as the point of origin and the extreme nature of these theories.

It was an episode that is now largely forgotten or dismissed as bordering on the lunatic fringe and an embarrassment to intellectual history (Daniel 1978). In that light it can be difficult now to understand the importance of this short-lived school of thought or to appreciate its attractions for the general public and the high esteem in which its proponents were held. For it was not just an academic conceit, but a vision of the past that caught the public imagination. It was very much a product of its time. It could only have happened at a particular juncture in the history of archaeology and anthropology, and the idea of human history that it projected had a particular appeal, especially in the decade after World War I. It was also very much an English phenomenon, and drew very little support from scholars in other countries.

It is an interesting reflection that none of the scholars involved in this movement was by professional specialism an Egyptologist. It drew heavily on the work of Egyptologists and indeed would have been impossible without the extensive and well documented archaeological record that had been assembled for Egypt by the beginning of the 20th century. The two main proponents were a pair of remarkable scholars, G. Elliot Smith and W. J. Perry.

## G. Elliot Smith

Grafton Elliot Smith (1871–1937) was born in Australia, the son of an English immigrant school-teacher (Dawson 1938; Elkin and Macintosh 1974). He showed an early interest in science, and studied medicine at the University of Sydney, where he began to establish a reputation as a neurologist. In 1896 he won a scholarship which took him to Cambridge. There he worked in the Department of Anatomy under

Professor Alexander Macalister, who had trained as a zoologist in Dublin and later moved to human anatomy. He also had an interest in Egyptology and biblical archaeology; he published several articles in these fields, and was the father of the archaeologist R. A. S. Macalister, who was already working in Palestine and in 1909 would become the first Professor of Archaeology at University College, Dublin. Cambridge at that time contained a group of scholars, some of whom had changed from one discipline to another mid-career and were leading the development of new fields of research. One such was A. C. Haddon, who in 1893 had switched from zoology to a junior post in physical anthropology, and played a major pioneering role in anthropology, eventually being appointed to a readership in ethnology. A major influence on Elliot Smith was W. H. R. Rivers, who had also come to Cambridge in 1893 to teach experimental psychology and had pioneered neurological and psychological approaches to sensory perception. In 1898 he took part in the landmark Cambridge Anthropological Expedition to the Torres Straits in order to study the islanders' psychology and physiology, in particular their sense of vision. He collected much oral evidence about genealogical relationships to compare with his physiological observations, and realized that this material contained important information about social questions as well. Thereafter he turned increasingly to social anthropology, producing important monographs on the Todas of India (1906) and on Melanesian society (1914). In 1911 he came out firmly in favour of diffusion over evolution and independent parallel development, laying the foundations for the short-lived domination of this theory in British social anthropology (Stocking 1996: 179–208).

Arriving in Cambridge in 1896, Elliot Smith thus found himself in an intellectual environment where anatomy and neurology were being studied in a context that also embraced physical and social anthropology and archaeology, and where there were good role models for enterprising scientists to cross the boundaries of the emerging disciplines. By 1900 he had further enhanced his reputation as a neurologist, becoming a world authority on the brain and on human evolution. That year was a turning point in his career. He was appointed to the first professorship of anatomy in the School of Medicine in Cairo. He returned to Britain as Professor of Anatomy at Manchester in 1909, and in 1919 moved to head the Department of Anatomy at University College London (UCL), where he remained until his retirement in 1936. Throughout this distinguished career he continued his work in human evolution, but he added to it an interest in Egyptian archaeology and the history of human social organization.

Elliot Smith's interest in Egyptology was aroused when his former Cambridge colleague, Rivers, visited Egypt to do research on the colour vision of the workmen engaged in an excavation being directed by David Randall MacIver and Anthony Wilkin, his former student who had also been a member of the Torres Straits expedition. Rivers encouraged Elliot Smith to extend his research, and pointed out the existence of preserved brain tissue in some of the mummies deriving from excavations. Elliot Smith originally turned his attention to the processes of mummification to pursue his neurological research, but he became progressively more involved in Egyptian archaeology. He contributed his expertise to the study of the many thousands of human remains being excavated, especially in the Aswan Dam project. He was fascinated by the processes of mummification and published a series of papers on them. He convinced himself that they were so complex that they could only have been invented once, and soon after his return to England he decided to take a further step into the world of anthropology.

The first substantial statement of his argument was made in his book, *The Ancient Egyptians and their Influence on the Civilization of Europe* (1911), later reissued as *The Ancient Egyptians and the Origins of Civilization* (1923). The 1911 publication presented the nucleus of his ideas of the unique invention of human culture and its diffusion from Egypt. It contained several elements that were to remain central to his ideas throughout his life. First, he put great weight on the complexity of the processes of mummification and the improbability that they could have been invented in more than one locality. Second, he saw a close relationship between mummification and the development of stone architecture for tombs. His argument was that the Egyptians conceived a desire to preserve their dead and saw how this was effected naturally in the dry environment of the desert sands. Seeking to enhance this natural process by constructing stone chambers to protect the dead, they were shocked to find that this had the opposite effect, since the dead were now removed from the environment that had preserved them. To compensate, they invented the processes of mummification. There was thus a close connection between the two technologies and the one could not have been invented without the other, or anywhere except in the Egyptian environment. Third, he believed that the stone architecture would have been impossible without the prior development of metalworking to provide the bronze tools necessary to work the stone. In the absence of much evidence for mummification elsewhere in Europe, Elliot Smith concentrated on megalithic architecture as the key indicator of the spread of culture from Egypt, but it was the close link to mummification that guaranteed the Egyptian origin of such structures. The mastaba tombs were regarded not only as the ancestors of the pyramids of Egypt, but also as the precursors of the stone-built dolmens and chambered tombs of western Europe.

Elliot Smith had also presented his results to the 1911 meeting of the British Association for the Advancement of Science and the annual gatherings of this organization were to become a battleground for the ideas of the diffusionists and their critics over the next few years. Elliot Smith developed his case in an annual series of papers, relying mostly on the evidence of megalithic architecture and dealing in detail with the Mediterranean region and western Europe. The discussion there and elsewhere was fierce and something of the tone of these debates can be gathered from the polemical way in which Elliot Smith (1915: 25) refers to the arguments of his critics as "casuistry not unworthy of a medieval theologian" or "incoherent recklessness", "dogmatic and often irrelevant assertions", and "a farrago of meaningless verbiage" (Elliot Smith 1915: 16). In 1914 the annual meeting was held in Melbourne, Australia, and he originally intended to give a paper extending the argument to a new geographical region, southern Asia and the Pacific, again using primarily megalithic monuments as the evidence. On his way to the meeting, however, he examined a mummy from the Torres Straits in the museum at the University of Sydney, and did further research on mummification techniques there. He became so convinced of the exact similarity of some of the specific techniques involved in the preparation of the body in the Torres Straits and in Egypt that not only was he confident of their uniquely Egyptian origin, but he was also able to suggest a date. He claimed that the precise techniques used were not known in Egypt until the twenty-first Dynasty and that the eastward spread of these ideas could therefore not have begun until after about 900 BC. In the light of this discovery, he abandoned his intended paper and spoke about the significance of mummification, provoking yet another confrontation with the evolutionists, led on this occasion by the Oxford archaeologist, J. L. Myres, and the Cambridge anthropologist, A. C. Haddon (Elliot Smith 1915: 25).

Elliot Smith's argument was now restated in another monograph (Elliot Smith 1915). The implications of his interpretation of the Torres Straits evidence had convinced him that there was a much greater chronological variation in the spread of culture outwards from the archaic civilization of Egypt. He had by then also begun his long-lasting academic collaboration with W. J. Perry, discussed in detail below, and Perry had sorted out the complexities of the south Asian evidence to his satisfaction and added a greater anthropological concern for a wider range of material culture and for questions of social organization. Elliot Smith's vision of the archaic culture package which was diffused around the world was now more complex. It included a vast range of cultural practices which he regarded as "remarkable", "exotic", "useless" or 'ludicrous', and therefore not likely to have been disseminated for rational or utilitarian reasons. These included, as well as mummification and megalithic architecture, the practices of sun and serpent worship, ear-piercing, circumcision, tattooing, couvade, massage, cranial deformation, the swastika symbol, creation myths, belief in a flood, the petrifaction of human beings, the divine origin of kings, and a chosen people sprung from an incestuous relationship (Elliot Smith 1915: 3). The bulk of this work, however, is concerned with the eastward migration of culture through Asia and across the Pacific to America, and it deals primarily with one cultural trait, mummification. It thus complements the earlier treatment focusing on the Mediterranean and Europe, though there the emphasis had been on megalithic architecture.

Elliot Smith's invocation of a much wider range of cultural practices as signs of diffusion was designed to impress by the sheer weight of evidence. He did not document these practices in detail, but presented distribution maps to show the alleged similarity of the occurrence of all the traits. The maps are drawn at a very small scale, and to modern eyes they seem rather crude in their use of symbols, but they represent some of the earliest examples of distribution maps in archaeology, and may well have been powerful evidence not only for the worldwide extent of these practices but also for the routes they were supposed to have followed. The use of so many different cultural elements also had its disadvantages, since Smith had to admit that some of them were not of Egyptian origin but had been adopted there and had become part of the package. In addition, not all of them were found everywhere together. He did not appear to regard these as significant problems that needed much discussion.

These publications of 1911 and 1915 were the foundation of Elliot Smith's case for the Egyptian origin of civilization, and the arguments he adduced there remained substantially the same throughout his work. He added one major element to the argument for Egypt, and that was agriculture. This had not been a part of his original case, though it featured much more prominently in Perry's research. By the early 1920s it had taken on a new importance due to the work of an Australian scientist, Thomas Cherry, of the School of Agriculture in the University of Melbourne. He had served with the Australian Medical Corps for five years in World War I, working in Palestine and Egypt (Elliot Smith 1930: 285). Cherry argued (1921a, b) that the natural cycle of flooding and climate in the Nile Valley suited the growth of cereals, especially barley and millet, and that these conditions existed nowhere else; these crops would have evolved in this environment before human interference. But "the most momentous event in human history probably began when Man first scooped shallow channels to enable the water to spread over a wider area" (Elliot Smith 1930: 291). For Elliot Smith, irrigation was inseparable from agricultural origins, and Egypt was the only place where these innovations could have occurred.

Elliot Smith paid comparatively little attention to the means by which these ideas and practices had been disseminated around the world. In 1911 he appealed to the idea of a Mediterranean race proposed by the anthropologist Sergi (1904) and to diffusion between the tribes of this race. He also envisaged diffusion of the knowledge of metalworking to other Near Eastern groups in contact with the Egyptians. A third mechanism was via migrant craftsmen who spread a megalithic culture throughout the Mediterranean and western European area, building megaliths as inferior copies of the Egyptian monuments. In 1915 he did not address the question of who had been the agents of diffusion. In later works he adopted more and more of the ideas of Perry discussed below.

One important addition to his ideas was first presented in another book, *The Evolution of the Dragon* (Elliot Smith 1919). Elliot Smith was searching for a psychological explanation for the diffusion of culture at the level of individual motivation. He appealed to the use of certain materials in magic rituals; whether as elixirs or as amulets, certain materials were vital for securing good luck in life and continued existence after death. He termed these items "Givers of Life" and regarded the search for them as a powerful stimulus to travel.

In his subsequent works Elliot Smith did little to develop his basic belief in Egyptian origins. His thesis was disputed by prehistorians and anthropologists, but largely ignored by Egyptologists, perhaps because it had very little to say about Egypt itself. He had already become involved in a bitter personal conflict with Flinders Petrie over the evidence for dismemberment and cannibalism, and although the two of them were colleagues in UCL for many years, they were scarcely on speaking terms (Drower 1995: 345–346; Murray 1963: 112–113). Manuscript comments in the margin of a copy of Elliot Smith (1923), now in the library of the Institute of Archaeology (UCL) and almost certainly in Petrie's handwriting (Daniel 1978: 417), include "the asserted facts are largely untrue and the vague statements unsupported". Elliot Smith maintained a familiarity with current work in Egypt and was in contact with Egyptologists, but was never again actively involved in primary research on Egyptian material. Nor was he particularly active in British or European prehistory: apart from a peripheral involvement in the Piltdown affair (Elliot Smith 1916; Woodward and Elliot Smith 1917), his contribution was limited to two other short papers on physical anthropology (Elliot Smith 1925, 1927).

Instead, he turned his attention more to arguing the general case for diffusion, especially across the Pacific to the Americas, in the face of constant opposition, particularly from American archaeologists and anthropologists. He also attempted to develop his vision of a holistic history of the human past, including both biological and social evolution. His work became less concerned with the detailed arguments for diffusion, and more focused on the bigger picture of human society and on the philosophical issues involved in the diffusionist debate.

## W. J. Perry

William James Perry (1888–1949) was born in England, also the son of a schoolmaster. He went to Cambridge in 1906 to study mathematics, but his major interests lay elsewhere and he attended lectures by Haddon and Rivers. He embarked on a career as a mathematics teacher after graduating, but had formed a close friendship with Rivers, who in 1913 encouraged him to begin anthropological research on Indonesia. Rivers himself was deeply engaged in his work on Melanesia and committed to a theory of the diffusion of some important cultural elements into Oceania from the west by migration. Any such movement would have had to pass through Indonesia, which thus became a critical testing ground for his theories. Perry's role was to provide such a test, and by 1914 he was beginning to publish on such topics as Indonesian megaliths and burial customs. The full account of his results (Perry 1918) showed the presence of megalithic architecture and the sun-cult in Indonesia, as required by Rivers' theories, but he attributed them in turn to migrants from yet further west, who had introduced them together with other cultural traits such as metal working, rice cultivation and irrigation agriculture. He also introduced an explanatory concept that was to prove very important in his later work: the migrants had come to Indonesia in search of gold and other forms of wealth.

Perry had by now come into Elliot Smith's circle, presumably through Rivers' connections, and they began a fruitful collaboration. Elliot Smith relied heavily on Perry's research to complete his study of the eastward spread of mummification. He not only facilitated the publication of Perry's book by Manchester University Press, but in 1919 he also secured him a post as Reader in Comparative Religion at Manchester University. When Elliot Smith moved to UCL in 1919, Perry followed him in 1923, taking up the post of Reader in Cultural Anthropology within the Department of Anatomy.

Thereafter, Elliot Smith and Perry worked closely together. They borrowed ideas and information from each other, though there were significant differences of interest. By the time of his next major work, *The Children of the Sun* (1923), Perry had adopted Elliot Smith's view of Egypt as the origin of these innovations. Working from the basis of his researches in Indonesia, he still concentrated on the diffusion of irrigation agriculture, metalworking and megalithic architecture, but these were now linked to a greater concern for patterns of social organization and for the agents of change. He documented in painstaking detail the cultural sequence in many different parts of the world, working mainly from evidence of traditional mythologies. On this basis he could claim that each region showed a similar sequence of development, and that this similarity was based on empirical evidence, not an assumed universal pattern of growth. Everywhere, the rise of civilization had been associated with food-producers practising irrigation agriculture, in contrast to the food-gathering 'primitive men' surrounding them. All of these regional expressions of civilization were derived from a common source, the 'archaic civilization' which he located in Egypt.

Following Elliot Smith's lead, he accepted the idea of "Givers of Life", and carefully documented the use of materials invested with magical properties throughout the world. Once again, he argued that all of these were derived from the set of materials in use in the archaic civilization, with no known material anywhere with a different cultural origin (Perry 1923: 383–405). Another important element of the theory was the recognition in many of the mythical traditions of the existence of "culture-heroes", who were responsible for bringing the various components of civilization to a particular region. These were "men who posed as incarnate gods" (Perry 1923: 145), and they, and the worship of the sun, played a key role in the diffusion of culture.

The archaic civilization, however, had within itself the seeds of its own decline: the rise of a warrior class, the growth of a class system, competitive rivalry among ruling groups. In his subsequent, and very popular, work, *The Growth of Civilization* (1924, 1926), Perry turned to more diachronic themes in the evolution of political institutions and the story of their decline. He was particularly concerned with the relationship between the societies of the archaic civilization and their neighbours, and with the decline of that civilization under the influence of more war-like groups. Egypt figured less prominently in this work, but it did provide one very good example of a civilized society threatened by war-like invaders. Though his theme was the understanding of the past, he had an obvious message for the present, and his book can be read as a lament for the state of decline in which 20th century Europe found itself.

## Egyptian origins

The names of Elliot Smith and Perry are regularly linked as the moving spirits of this school of thought. Though Perry is sometimes described as Elliot Smith's pupil, he never was, and indeed from their first contact was an active and equal collaborator, albeit somewhat younger. Their thinking developed over a period of about 20 years, and though their various works represent a recognizably distinct contribution to the study of the past, there were differences between them. Elliot Smith began with an interest in mummification inspired by his time in Egypt and his neurological expertise. This remained a constant theme, and it is scarcely surprising that he placed great emphasis on the role of Egypt as the location of innovation. He was less interested in exploring the mechanisms of diffusion, or identifying the particular agents involved. On this point he came to accept the ideas of Perry. Perry, on the other hand, had come into the project from an interest in diffusion in Indonesia, and the nature of the people and processes involved in the spread of culture was a key theme to his work. He also moved from a concern with the diffusion of cultural traits to a focus on the development of social organization, and a worldwide view of the interaction between societies with a more complex political organization and their neighbours.

Nevertheless, there are a number of key elements that became central to the thinking of the group as it developed. These include the ideas of Egypt as the point of cultural origin, of the search for the Givers of Life, and of the Children of the Sun.

Perry (1923: 428–466) followed Smith in citing the origin of culture in Egypt. For Smith it had been a matter of mummification, but Perry was interested in a wider range of cultural traits. One of the most important ideas for him was the essential connection of civilization and agriculture, and Cherry's arguments for agricultural origins in Egypt were fundamental to this acceptance. The archaeological evidence as it was then understood was not decisive, but it at least allowed this conclusion, and gave it an air of academic authority. Similarly, there was then no means of determining dates for prehistoric monuments in Europe or Asia independently of the traditional cross-dating methods, which all ultimately relied on the Egyptian evidence for an absolute chronology. There too, a derivation of all stone monuments from Egyptian prototypes was at least permissible.

The role of the Givers of Life was central to Perry's explanation of diffusion. Following Elliot Smith, he located the explanation for human exploration and expansion firmly in the field of individual human motivation and aspiration. He refused to see human populations in the grip of external determinants: "Man, from the earliest times of which there is knowledge, has lived near his supplies of raw materials, and has got his food locally. He has never, so far as can be told, occupied a new country because he was pressed for food. This supposition is baseless, and the sooner it is abandoned the better for science" (Perry 1923: 500). Though the nature of the raw materials being sought as Givers of Life was most often non-utilitarian in a modern sense, it occasionally seems as though the concept is being extended to include commodities such as metals, which may have other, non-magical uses. Nevertheless, the quest for sources of raw materials was seen as a spiritual enterprise, not a materialistic one.

Despite adopting them for the title of his book, Perry was somewhat vague about the nature of the Children of the Sun. They were clearly a social elite, who claimed descent from the sun god, culture heroes who were daring travellers and prospectors, but Perry clearly did not envisage them as some sort of super race, as some critics have supposed. But he did not explain in detail how this social group was reproduced. In some places he seems to suggest that at different times and places various known peoples acted as such culture heroes. He (Perry 1923: 501–502) cites the Phoenicians, for instance, as possible agents in this manner. In retrospect, the way in which the Children of the Sun and the Givers of Life were identified and named (and often, as here, given capital letters) may have added to the attractiveness of the hypothesis to those predisposed to accept it. To its critics at the time, and to later scholars, it has added to the fanciful and dated nature of the ideas.

## The Anatomy Circle at UCL

When Perry moved from Manchester to London in 1923, he took up a post as Reader in Cultural Anthropology within a Department of Anatomy. Such a juxtaposition of disciplines was at the heart of Elliot Smith's vision of an integrated study of the human past. That vision is perhaps best expressed in one of his later books, *Human History* (1930). In that work he tried to provide a seamless narrative of the human past, embracing the biological evolution of the species as well as the development of human society. He maintained that the proper study of mankind should have as its chief aim "the study of the actions of the whole organism, the behaviour of living men and women, in all its puzzling manifestations ... The thoughts and feelings that provide the motives for men's behaviour are the things that matter most". He also believed that "the structure of the human body only becomes intelligible when one investigates not merely the functional significance of the various structural arrangements, but also the history of the processes whereby they attained their present structure and proportions. The study of biology is in this sense essentially a discipline of history" (Elliot Smith 1930: 11).

In the inter-war years the Rockefeller Foundation was one of the major funding sources for anthropology and related disciplines (Kuklick 1991: 209–213). UCL was a major recipient of grants from the Foundation, and in particular its medical school, partly as a thank offering for the contribution of British medical science during World War I (Dart 1974b: 32): Elliot Smith and Rivers had both done important work with victims of shell-shock. A series of grants in the 1920s paid for a new building (Price and Humbert 2003: Figure 1:13) and for a very varied programme of research. Elliot Smith as Head of the Department of Anatomy was thus in a position to promote his own vision of research. In 1927, however, the Rockefeller Foundation decided to reallocate its funding towards a different strand of anthropological research, the fieldwork-based functionalism represented most prominently by Bronislaw Malinowski at the London School of Economics. Elliot Smith's funding dried up and his work was "torpedoed" (Kuklick 1991: 211).

Before that happened, however, Elliot Smith was able to gather together a circle of like-minded scholars to pursue his project. Perry was appointed in 1923, and the English writer, H. J. Massingham, whose work is discussed in more detail below, was a colleague from 1924 to 1927. Others, though not employed there, were drawn into the circle. These included the Australian-born archaeologist V. Gordon Childe (Trigger 1980), who from 1925 to 1927 was working in the library of the Royal Anthropological Institute in London before accepting the post of Abercromby Professor of Archaeology at Edinburgh. In 1925 he had published *The Dawn of European Civilization*, which was to remain in print through successive editions for 30 years, and adopted a diffusionist approach to the explanation of European prehistory. Another participant was the biblical scholar and historian of Near Eastern myth and religion, S. H. Hooke (Porter 1977). There was also a succession of postgraduate students studying for doctorates, several of whom went on to follow distinguished academic careers (Kuklick 1991: 55, 129). The Australian A. P. Elkin (1974) succeeded Radcliffe-Brown and Firth as Professor of Anthropology at Sydney. Raymond Dart, who was appointed to the University of Witwatersrand as Professor of Anatomy, became a leading figure in human evolution studies but also developed a diffusionist archaeology of Africa (Dart 1974a). The career of E. O. James culminated in the Chair of the History and Philosophy of Religion at UCL. Another who eventually returned to UCL was Daryll Forde, whose original specialism was prehistoric archaeology; he travelled with Gordon Childe through central and eastern Europe in 1926 (Trigger 1980: 57). He published a popular diffusionist work, *Ancient Mariners: the story of ships and sea routes* (1927), dealing with the role played by ships of Egyptian design in the diffusion of culture. Forde later went as a postdoctoral student to Berkeley in California to study social anthropology. He returned in 1930 first to the Gregynog Professorship in Geography and Anthropology at Aberystwyth and then after World

War II he was appointed to UCL as the first Professor of Anthropology when the teaching of the subject was reorganized. His later work, whether in prehistory or the anthropology of material culture, showed little sign of his earlier intellectual orientation towards Egypt.

The various members of this circle brought together a wide range of interests, knowledge and expertise, though it is interesting that none of them would be recognized as having a particular specialism in Egyptology; though Hooke and James had detailed knowledge of the religions of the Near East, and Childe of its archaeology, only Elliot Smith himself had first-hand experience or intimate acquaintance with the evidence from Egypt. That was derived from his brief stay in Cairo, and though he maintained contacts with Egyptologists, he himself would not have been able to claim specialist knowledge. Although there was an impressive array of intellectual talent assembled in the Department of Anatomy, there is nevertheless an inescapable impression that they were in some sense outsiders. They did not occupy leading roles in Egyptology, anthropology or archaeology.

There are two accounts of the atmosphere in the Department at the height of its activity in the mid-1920s. One is from Elkin (1974: 11), the other from Massingham (1942: 56). Both give a vivid picture of the social life of the Department, especially the daily gatherings for lunch in Perry's office. Massingham recalls "lunch in a large room filled with skulls, large-scale maps plotting out the routes of the ancient mariners and prospectors". On the wall was a drawing of the carved stone from Copan in Mexico, which Elliot Smith maintained was a representation of an elephant and therefore a key element in his derivation of American civilization from Old World origins. Elkin's memories include the gossip, mutual encouragement and informal instruction typical of a tight-knit academic community and emphasize the spirit of camaraderie that went with their sense of a mission to discover the truth of the human past. Elliot Smith had created a scholarly group which had a sense of purpose and worked well together, and whose members were able to learn from each other. He himself, known affectionately as the 'Old Man', was very much the synthesizer and theoretician, while Perry was seen as the gatherer of detailed factual information. Their collaboration is well evidenced by the dedications of two of their books: Perry dedicated *The Children of the Sun* to Elliot Smith "in memory of many happy hours", while Elliot Smith responded by dedicating *Human History* to Perry "as a tribute of admiration of his vision and courage".

The UCL circle was at its peak in the middle of the 1920s, but its decline was rapid. The cessation of the Rockefeller funding in 1927 was undoubtedly a major blow to Elliot Smith's ambition, but he was able to maintain his research in neurology. Massingham left, and Perry was increasingly the victim of ill health with the onset of Parkinson's disease. None of the postgraduate students succeeded directly to a post in anthropology or archaeology in Britain. Elkin returned to Australia and Dart went to South Africa, while Forde's eventual academic career in Britain was influenced more by his exposure to American anthropology in California than to the ideas of Elliot Smith. The intellectual legacy of the group was dissipated, and with the rise of a new wave of functionalist anthropologists in Britain it came to seem more and more old-fashioned.

## Egypt in Downland

The enthusiasm for the ideas of the hyperdiffusionists was limited almost entirely to England, and it was in the context of contemporary debate about the nature of England and Englishness that they found one of their most developed expressions, through the work of H. J. Massingham (1888–1952) (Matless 1998: 116–118; Moore-Colyer 2001). He later became a prolific writer of rather reactionary books on the English countryside, lamenting the decline of the countryside and of the nation. His themes included the ruin of the rural landscape through modern farming methods and suburban development, the breakdown of long-established patterns of rural life, the decline of ancient craft skills, and the loss of the traditional farming wisdom that had maintained both the landscape and the economy for so long. His target was the evils of his day, but these were contrasted with a lost paradise. When this idyllic past had existed was uncertain; many of his references seem to focus on a recent, but ill-defined, past, perhaps the idealized heyday of high Victorian farming before the economic slump at the end of the 19th century, but he also endowed the traditional knowledge of farmers with a more ancient and almost mystical value. As well as writing, Massingham was also involved more actively in campaigns to restore the countryside. Although he was passionately concerned for the fate of rural England, the landscape was also a metaphor for the soul of the nation. In the curious political world of England in the 1920s and 1930s, there was little space between the burgeoning environmental movement and more extreme attempts to restore the homeland.

For a short period in the 1920s Massingham (1942: 54–66) worked closely with Elliot Smith and Perry and became deeply interested in British prehistory. He was already deeply engrossed in environmental issues and the history of the English countryside when he began to appreciate the wealth of prehistoric earthworks and monuments surviving in the landscape. He began a correspondence with Perry, whom he presumably knew of through reading *The Children of the Sun*. He was eventually employed as part of the team in the Department of Anatomy at UCL, with "a roving commission to prospect the upland homes of prehistoric man in England" (Massingham 1942: 54). For a period of more than two years between 1924 and 1927 he played an active part in the project, including field survey of archaeological sites, until the funding from the Rockefeller grant ran out.

He describes his discovery of the idea of diffusion as though it were a religious revelation, asserting that "my association with Elliot Smith and Perry was the turning-point of my life" (Massingham 1942: 61). It provided him with a means of understanding the relationship of the past and the present and of explaining the evidence of the prehistoric occupation so visible in the English landscape. It offered him a vision of the past world and of the processes of social change: "when therefore I came into contact with the writings of Elliot Smith and Perry, it seemed to me that I had found the key to unlock the magic door into the past" (Massingham 1942: 55).

His ideas are briefly sketched in a popular pamphlet, *Pre-Roman Britain* (1927), and much more extensively in *Downland Man* (1926), one of the real oddities of British prehistoric literature. Massingham saw his task as documenting the story of England's idyllic past, its archaic civilization and subsequent corruption. He paints a picture of a neolithic paradise, with its capital at Avebury, where farming was intensively practised in a well-managed landscape, and people lived at peace with each other till warfare was rudely introduced by the barbarian Celts. Not only did these people live in harmony with each other and the landscape, they actually improved their environment, leaving "a mark upon nature more beautiful and yet stranger than she had been before" (Massingham 1942: 55). The origin of this utopian culture was of course Egypt, and one of his chapters in *Downland Man* is actually entitled "Egypt in Downland".

Massingham's debt to Elliot Smith and Perry, as well as to archaeologists such as Childe, is obvious and his writing then was very much a product of the time and of his collaboration with them. For him, there was a twofold value in their ideas: the theory of an archaic civilization gave him the proof of a lost English paradise and the concept of diffusion provided a mechanism for social change that avoided the perceived competitiveness and violence that had characterized the previous decades of European history. He was occasionally quite explicit about his anti-evolutionary purpose: his target is "the common interpretation of the Neo-Darwinian process as one of advances made through the media of accident and savagery", an idea which he wishes to see "go the way of the Ptolemaic system of astronomy" (1926: 15). Above all, he recognizes "the need to relate the story of megalithic England both to modern civilization and to human life, to look before and after, to show that this wonderful story, as it is by its own nature, has a definite meaning for us today" (Massingham 1926: 16). His argument, in short, was that "its (i.e. Avebury's) civilization was a cutting taken from the Egypto-Cretan stem before it had forfeited the primitive and natural peaceableness of the entire human race" (1926: 304), and that "the warlike temper was superimposed on, not planted in the soul of man. What a civilization, a miracle of beauty and freedom and joy might we not have achieved today but for the Fall of Lucifer!" (1926: 305).

Although Egypt was a central part of his thesis, Massingham displays little detailed knowledge of its history and archaeology. He was clearly well versed in European prehistory, but his Egyptian knowledge is at a much more general level. It was the idea of Egypt, of Egypt as the romanticized and idealized past, that appealed to him rather than the reality of Ancient Egypt. He also endowed the archaic civilization of prehistoric Britain, and by implication its Egyptian source, with surprisingly modern characteristics. It was a country with an efficient central government and an intensive but well-managed and environmentally friendly agricultural economy. Its capital, Avebury, was the counterpart of London as the centre of a developed transport system and the seat of government. The Egypt recreated in Downland was, in fact, not Egypt as known but England as wished for.

There is also a curious ambivalence in Massingham's attitude to archaeological evidence. Though he was dependent on the emerging discipline of archaeology for much of his evidence, and the references cited in his works show extensive familiarity with the work of a wide range of European scholars, he had no time for the increasingly technical discussions of the specialist literature. His was an alternative reading of the past, appealing to the insight of the ordinary readers who are encouraged to go out and see for themselves the truth as revealed in the English landscape. This anti-professional counter-culture would have struck a familiar note at the time. Some writers, including archaeologists, were encouraging people to go out and discover the past for themselves in the landscape (Matless 1998: 73–86) and themes of journeying through the countryside and exploring England were common in much English literature at the time, forming "internal voyages of national exploration" (Cunningham 1988: 225).

Massingham's interest and involvement in archaeology should certainly be seen as part of his wider long-term project of reflection on the declining state of the nation, but his focus on Egypt was a comparatively short-lived feature of his thinking in the mid-1920s. Though he continued to write for more than 20 years, Egypt never again played the same role. Though the evidence of the remote past in the English landscape was evoked in many of his later books, it was a less exotic, more indigenous past. Massingham's Egyptian phase reflected not just the episode of collaboration with the diffusionists, but a time in the 1920s in the aftermath of World War I, when he was absorbed in ideas of a peaceful society. As the 1930s rolled on, such ideas became less and less appropriate.

## Rise and fall of Egyptocentric diffusionism

Time has not been kind to the hyperdiffusionist theories of Perry and Elliot Smith (Daniel 1978). They are now largely ignored, or at best banished to a marginal place in the histories of archaeology and anthropology, so that it can be very difficult to see why they were so popular in their time, or why the scholars who espoused them were regarded as being at the leading edge of their disciplines. They are often regarded as indistinguishable from the lunatic fringe. Daniel and Renfrew (1988: 87), for instance, ask why people had tolerated "this academic rubbish", and suggest that it was only through a desire for a simple explanation; they then offer a devastating critique of Elliot Smith and Perry's 'unscientific' method. They were, however, highly regarded and very influential in their time (Morkot 2003: 156; Reid 2003: 70), and collaborated with other scholars who have not been similarly ridiculed. Elliot Smith was commissioned to write the article on anthropology for the 12th edition of the *Encyclopedia Britannica* in 1922, in succession to Tylor, and he also wrote non-specialist texts for such series as the *Thinker's Library*, popularizing his ideas in a way very similar to that of Gordon Childe a few decades later. When Perry's *The Growth of Civilization* went into a revised edition (1926), he gave credit to Gordon Childe for help in the revision, and this edition was again reprinted in very distinguished company in 1937 as one of the first blue-covered Pelican paperbacks. Stocking (1996: 208–220) provides a much more sympathetic attempt to place them in their contemporary anthropological context, but his primarily narrative and biographical approach does not deal extensively with the reasons for the power and popularity of their ideas.

The development of these ideas demonstrates something of the random chanciness of history. If Elliot Smith had not taken up his post in Cairo in 1900, it is doubtful whether he would ever have become so engrossed in mummification and the archaeology of Egypt or have turned from neurology to anthropology. If the Australian agricultural scientist Thomas Cherry had not served in the Middle East during World War I, he would probably never have turned his attention to the ecology of river valleys and the origins of irrigation, thus providing a key link in the argument. Other people might have done, however, and these events are both integral parts of the late imperial period in Britain, which also provided the context for the growth of archaeology and anthropology. The work of Elliot Smith and Perry should not be seen as something isolated from the mainstream of anthropological and archaeological thought, a perversion of the rational process. Instead, it was merely a fully and explicitly formulated expression of a more extreme version of ideas that were common at the time, derived from the academic traditions and disciplinary formations within which these scholars worked.

The decades at the end of the 19th and the beginning of the 20th centuries saw enormous changes in the way that the past was studied. New disciplines emerged, with their characteristic structures of journals, university posts and professional methodologies. By the end of the century specialist fields of archaeology, such as Classical Archaeology and Egyptology, were beginning to be well established with university posts and even rudimentary research funding bodies such as the Egypt Exploration Fund (Jeffreys Chapter 1, this volume). Prehistoric archaeology, however, lagged some way behind. For much of the 19th century a single discipline of ethnology had embraced the study of both the prehistoric past and the non-European societies of the present. By the 1920s, however, the picture was very different. A recognizably new form of anthropology was being practised, led by Malinowski at the London School of Economics (Kuklick 1991; Stocking 1996). In prehistoric archaeology, the refounding of the Disney Chair of Archaeology at Cambridge in 1926 (Clark 1989) and the establishment of the Abercromby Chair of Archaeology at Edinburgh in 1927 were symbolic expressions of the transformation of the discipline. Books published at this time, such as Burkitt's *Prehistory* (1921) or Childe's *The Dawn of European Civilization* (1925) and *The Danube in Prehistory* (1926) were simply of a different order from anything written previously; even some archaeologists found *The Dawn* too technical (Trigger 1980: 37–38). The disciplines also developed their standard research methods: in prehistory the role of excavation took on a new significance, while in anthropology fieldwork became the key element of professional practice. The Torres Straits expedition of 1898 had already shown the way to a new disciplinary methodology and by the end of the 1920s the old style of research, relying exclusively on published accounts, was completely out of fashion. Perry was perhaps the last exponent of a sort of anthropology that relied on available published sources rather than on primary observation in the field. He apparently only once undertook a period of fieldwork, among the Pondo of southern Africa, and that was cut short through ill health (Kuklick 1991: 211).

One consequence of these developments was the increasing separation of anthropology and prehistoric archaeology. Another was the progressive disappearance of topics related to anthropological and archaeological research from the mainstream of general public debate. As the methodologies and the jargon became more technical, and the size of the academic and professional communities engaged in the disciplines expanded, so the nature of their research became more specialized, more inward-looking and more exclusive. It is probably no coincidence that the work of the diffusionists, described by Kuklick (1991: 12) as "the last anthropological effort to integrate archaeological, physical and cultural research", was probably also one of the last projects to attract such popular interest among a non-specialist readership.

If Elliot Smith and Perry were some of the last representatives of a dying discipline, sidelined by the emergence of new and distinctive disciplinary formations, their ideas were nevertheless in tune with the prevailing ideology of the time, both in anthropology and in archaeology. As Stocking (1996: 179–232) has shown, their ideas were part of a wider, if short-lived, reaction in anthropology to the evolutionary philosophies that had dominated the previous 50 years. This was symbolized most dramatically by W. H. R. Rivers' adoption of diffusionism in 1911. Diffusionist explanations had in fact always been an essential part of anthropological thought, though largely submerged by the dominant evolutionism, which fitted the climate of rapid industrial progress and imperial expansion. Towards the end of the century, however, perhaps influenced by the increasing disenchantment with progress and empire, diffusionist ideas were accorded greater weight. The human capacity for creativity was questioned. The German geographer and ethnologist Friedrich Ratzel argued that invention and innovation were random rather than regular processes; his ideas were taken further by Fritz Graebner and Wilhelm Schmidt, who located all innovation in a single series of cultures in central Asia, whence they had spread throughout the world (Harris 1968: 382–392). Diffusionism prevailed, and although it was in turn rapidly overtaken by functionalist approaches, for two decades it held sway in British anthropology.

In European prehistory too, diffusionism played a dominant role (Trigger 1989: 150–155). For much of the 19th century most archaeologists had worked within an evolutionary approach. There was no appreciation of the chronological depth of the pre-Roman past, and prehistoric remains were generally attributed to an indigenous prehistoric population. Nevertheless, despite this prevailing orthodoxy within prehistoric archaeology, emphasizing parallel development, the question of Europe's indebtedness to the East never quite disappeared. The growth of historical linguistics and the recognition of the Indo-European family of languages put the problem in a new perspective: the languages had spread from a single source, and Indo-European speakers were not the original inhabitants. The work of the German ethnologists also had a major influence in archaeology, and by the beginning of the 20th century archaeologists were regularly seeking the explanation of change through an external origin, either by migration or by cultural diffusion, rather than an indigenous development.

The nature of the relationship of Europe to the Near East remained a major question. By the end of the 19th century a reasonably robust scheme of relative chronology was beginning to be worked out and the volume of material for the later prehistory of Europe had grown enormously, especially in the Mediterranean region. The work of Schliemann at Troy, Mycenae and elsewhere, and especially that of Evans at Knossos in Crete, had provided startling new evidence for the later periods of European prehistory, raising once again the question of cultural relations in the eastern Mediterranean region. There were various answers. At one extreme stood the Swedish scholar, Oscar Montelius, who argued (Montelius 1899) that Europe was heavily dependent on oriental precursors for its entire cultural development, while at the other was the Frenchman, Salomon Reinach, who regarded such external origins as a mirage and instead supported an essentially indigenous origin for European cultures in the Mediterranean and elsewhere (Reinach 1893). Others, such as Arthur

Evans and John Myres, took intermediate lines, neither totally diffusionist nor totally indigenist.

This blend of evolutionary and diffusionist archaeology characterizes the work of Myres, the ancient historian and anthropologist who was a major influence on the early work of Gordon Childe. For Myres, sedentism was the critical step that preceded agriculture and was a necessary precondition for its development. Thereafter, Myres (1911: 29–30) distinguished four phases in the growth of civilization:

> the first stage is one in which the centres of advancement are provided and defined, by great river valleys, with alluvial irrigable soil ... the common character of what historians group together as the Ancient East, is that of detached, riparian, essentially agricultural civilizations, in recurrent peril from the men of the grassland and the mountain, and only in intermittent touch with each other ... such, for our purpose, is the first stage of human history, the development, within the limits of alluvial river valleys, of self-centres and almost self-sufficient worlds, each with its own highly special type of civilization adapted to local conditions.

Although he may not have been the first to do so, Myres had recognized a connection between major river valleys and the emergence of civilization, and clearly believed in the multiple independent origins of such developments, which in turn became the centres of further diffusion. His treatment of Egypt re-emphasizes this connection: "Egypt is the gift of the Nile" (Myres 1911: 45). He has very little to say about the origins of agriculture, however, which did not play a major role in his vision of human development; he plays down the initial importance of irrigation, since he did not think that it was practicable before political unification (Myres 1911: 66). His emphasis is on technical and intellectual evolution: "with the art of pottery, however, Egypt, like many other countries, took the first great step towards civilization and history ... the only group of industries which can compare with potmaking in intellectual importance is that of the textile fabrics; basketry and weaving" (Myres 1911: 53–54). In these skills, however, Egypt was not the innovator: pottery was introduced from some other unknown region (Myres 1911: 55).

Myres' ideas thus combined a belief in evolution and parallel development with a recognition of the role played by diffusion. Egypt and Babylonia were two independent areas developing in ways that were generally similar though very different in detail. Together they formed a core area from which civilization was diffused to the west via Crete, Cyprus and Greece. Agriculture was not a central part of this debate, but that may have been because there was as yet little firm archaeological evidence for its origins. The archaeological record of Egypt was at that time much fuller and certainly better dated than that of Mesopotamia, and the current state of the archaeological knowledge of prehistoric Europe permitted or even encouraged the possibility of an Egyptian origin. The new focus in the 1920s on the importance of agriculture as a defining criterion of the Neolithic drew Egypt into the debate as a possible point of origin. The rival claims of Egypt and Mesopotamia continued to be debated, and the idea that the origins of agriculture lay in Egypt survived as at least a possibility. It remained so until after World War II, when the work of Braidwood at Jarmo in the years between 1948 and 1955 began to show definitively that developments had been earlier there, and most subsequent debate has revolved around the earlier case of Mesopotamia.

Agriculture had been a key part of Perry's early ideas about diffusion to south-eastern Asia, but was a late addition to Elliot Smith's theory of Egyptian origins. His emphasis had been on megalithic architecture as the trait that showed the diffusion of ideas from Egypt. Elliot Smith and Perry were by no means alone in regarding the worldwide tradition of megalithic architecture as a unitary phenomenon. These monuments are some of the most striking features of the archaeological record, and were an early focus of attention. The concept of 'megaliths' as a meaningful category has survived into the present (Joussaume 1987; Mohen 1989), even though the vast differences in age and function of the various monument types included in the term are now more clearly understood. The ready acceptance of this concept encouraged archaeologists to think in terms of a single point of origin for the phenomenon. The Scottish archaeologist James Fergusson (1872) looked on the megaliths as examples of a single architectural style and assigned them to the post-Roman period, but most other writers realized their prehistoric date. Baron de Bonstetten (1865) placed their origin in northern Europe, but others looked to the east. The Irish antiquary, W. G. Wood-Martin (1888: 9) wrote: "Inexorable modern research, patiently and by slow degrees making its way clear into the remoter past, traces an early and megalithic building race from the far East; this people were once spread over the greater part of Europe, Asia and the northern coast of Africa, and their usages had probably passed away before history began." Similarly in Portugal, the megaliths were regarded by some as the archaeological evidence for the Aryan migration from the east (Martins Sarmento 1933: 290–295, in an article first published in 1885). T. E. Peet (1912) also regarded the megaliths as the product of a single race or an immense series of migrations, though he could not decide whether their origin was to be located in northern Europe, Africa or the Near East. As late as 1963 Glyn Daniel was arguing for megaliths as a useful and unitary concept, and also saw their origin in the east Mediterranean, though not in Egypt: "the spark that set off the development of the collective-tomb architecture in western Europe ... was most probably the arrival of Minoans or Aegeans in the middle and west Mediterranean from the east" (Daniel 1963: 16–23, 134–135). It was only the advent of radiocarbon dating that finally separated the megaliths of western Europe from any eastern origin by showing that they were earlier than their alleged prototypes (Renfrew 1973).

Elliot Smith and Perry were therefore following a well established precedent in seeing the megaliths as a single phenomenon; though they were alone in locating their origin in Egypt, the idea of a single origin somewhere in the east was far from uncommon. Even those who criticized them did so on detail rather than from fundamental disagreement. Wheeler (1925: 68–104), for instance, writing about the megalithic tombs of Wales, accepted their concept of a single global tradition, but disputed the precise relationships between the different regional groups; he preferred to see a process of development, not simplification, and thought it more likely that the western dolmens were ancestral to the much more sophisticated monuments of Egypt. Gordon Childe in the early editions of *The Dawn of European Civilization* followed Elliot Smith and Perry much more closely. He accepted the east Mediterranean origin of the tradition, though not an Egyptian one.

Childe also accepted Perry's idea that the megaliths had been spread by prospectors. Although he never commented specifically on their ideas, and remained sceptical about Egyptian origins, he used the idea of prospectors more widely to explain the dissemination of architecture and metalworking throughout Europe and southern Russia. As Trigger (1980: 87–89) points out, Childe was never a supporter of Egyptocentric diffusionism, though his ideas did have something in common with those of Elliot Smith and Perry, and much of his work was a defence of a more moderate form of diffusionism. The Children of the Sun lingered on in his writing, especially in the context of the part played by prospectors for metal ores or magical substances in the spread of megalithic architecture, and were not finally expunged until the very last edition of *The Dawn of European Civilization* in 1956.

A further 70 years of research has not made the question of Europe's debt to the east an irrelevant or outdated one, but it has seriously redefined the question. Generic concepts such as civilization have given way to a more detailed consideration of particular cultural traits such as agriculture and metalworking. Since World War II radiocarbon dating has had an enormous and totally unpredictable impact on prehistoric archaeology. By the 1960s sufficient dates were available to show that European megalithic architecture could not have been adopted from the east, since its origins in the west were earlier than the prototypes from which it was supposed to have been derived. Similarly, an independent European origin for metalworking has been suggested. Much of the argument now focuses on the question of agriculture, and there the problem to be explained is Europe's relationship to the Near East, not to Egypt.

The ideas of Elliot Smith and Perry may have been more popular in the eyes of the general public than they were in academic circles (Schadla-Hall and Morris 2003). They must have struck a chord with the public, matching some strand in the intellectual spirit of the post-war years. Stocking (1996: 217) is surely right to situate diffusionism in the background of Britain's late imperial experience and to detect in its more extreme forms an air of pessimism associated with the trauma of World War I. Diffusionism provided a mythical charter and a validation for the project of empire, as the Children of the Sun became prototypes for Britain's imperialists. It also offered an account of social change that was more acceptable than that of evolutionism. Perry (1924: 3) wrote: "In its earliest stages human society was peaceful; warfare has developed as an accidental excrescence. Warfare has grown like a parasitic plant, until it now threatens to destroy the host on which it lives. If this book helps to turn men's minds seriously to the consideration of this topic I shall be well rewarded." The idea of the archaic civilization also offered an appropriate vision of the past for those such as Massingham who were lamenting the state of the present.

But, if the general nature of the diffusionist argument struck a chord with the general public of the post-war decades, the specific invocation of Egypt as the point of origin of the archaic civilization also had a powerful impact. Egyptian civilization, especially its iconic representation through the pyramids, was by then deeply ingrained in the popular memory, and Egypt undoubtedly stirred the imagination much more powerfully than any other area of the Near East. Despite a century of archaeological research in Mesopotamia, the sites and monuments of that area were far less well known than those of Egypt. It was perhaps not until the spectacular discoveries made by Woolley in the so-called royal cemetery at Ur in 1927–1928 that Mesopotamia began to occupy a more prominent place in public perception. Exploration in Egypt was also very much in the news in the early 1920s, and the discovery of the tomb of Tutankhamun in 1922 unleashed a wave of enthusiasm for all things Egyptian (Humbert and Price 2003; MacDonald and Rice 2003).

We can see, therefore, that the appeal of Egypt lay in its potential to offer an explanation for human development that rejected the perceived struggles and violence of social Darwinism. What was offered instead was an account of the past where human motivation was the prime mover, and where the motive for expansion was a primarily religious or spiritual quest rather than militaristic or economic self-aggrandizement; the bearers of the archaic civilization were more missionaries than conquerors. In this attempt to place human agency at the heart of archaeological explanation, though none of the authors would have recognized such terminology, their reaction to evolutionism seems very similar to some of the objections launched more recently to the functionalist and dehumanizing tone of the neo-evolutionary component of the New Archaeology of the 1960s and 1970s. Furthermore, by rejecting the generalizing theory of evolutionism, and substituting for it a single narrative account of the past, it was possible to argue that the course of human history could have been otherwise. Warfare was not inevitable, and thus there was hope that a future world could recreate the lost utopia of the past.

With the benefit of perfect hindsight we can see that Elliot Smith and Perry had the wrong answer. But they were at least trying to answer one of the big questions of European and world archaeology. They produced a grand narrative of human history. It was an ambitious project, and one that few archaeologists have subsequently dared to attempt.

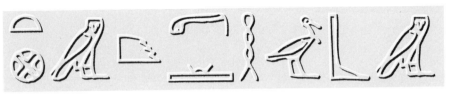

## CHAPTER 9

# APPROACHING THE PEASANTRY OF GRECO-ROMAN EGYPT: FROM ROSTOVTZEFF TO RHETORIC

*Jane Rowlandson*

The last decade or so has seen considerable academic interest in the intellectual background of Michael Rostovtzeff, one of the two greatest 20th century historians of the Greek and Roman worlds. This biographical interest was surprisingly slow to take off, given the obvious relevance of Rostovtzeff's experience, as a Russian intellectual who, already in middle age, left Russia in 1918 and after a brief stay in Britain settled in the United States, to the central themes of the two great multi-volume studies he produced there (Rostovtzeff 1926, 1941; see also Fikhman 1996; Marcone 1993; Rudich 2000). The most important earlier assessment of Rostovtzeff is that of Momigliano (1966), the only other 20th century ancient historian to rival him in scholarship and imagination. The intention here is not to add to detailed studies of Rostovtzeff's intellectual biography, but rather to offer some reflections on Rostovtzeff's impact on 20th century interpretations of the agrarian history of Greco-Roman Egypt, and the direction in which current interpretations are heading.

Shaw (1992), in his extended review of Wes's (1990) study of Rostovtzeff, has emphasized how the picture Rostovtzeff presents in both these major works (most unconvincingly in 1926, rather more subtly in 1941), of a circumscribed and beleaguered bourgeoisie attempting to preserve the benefits of Greco-Roman rationality and civilization from the mass of the uneducated and uncultured peasantry, precisely mirrors how the Russian intelligentsia of Rostovtzeff's generation saw their own position (Shaw 1992: 220). One could hardly, therefore, expect Rostovtzeff's approach to the Egyptian peasantry to show any degree of sympathy, let alone real empathy.

Nevertheless, Rostovtzeff (1910) is of critical importance in laying the foundation of interpretations of rural social relations in Ptolemaic and Roman Egypt. His deployment of the Greek papyrological evidence available at the time is comprehensive and authoritative, but he hardly draws on Egyptian texts at all; for even Rostovtzeff's formidably extensive range of historical skills did not extend to the Egyptian language, and the corpus of published demotic texts was still tiny (Depauw 1997: 49–50). He did briefly acknowledge that conditions in Ptolemaic Upper Egypt (as is evident even from Greek documents) seem at variance with his overall picture based on texts from further north (overwhelmingly from the Fayum) but was uncertain whether this was to be explained in terms of regional variation or chronological development (on Ptolemaic Upper Egypt, see Manning 1999, 2003). I have argued (Rowlandson 1996: chs. 2–3) for significant differences of detail even between the Arsinoite and Oxyrhynchite evidence. Thus Rostovtzeff's interpretation of Ptolemaic and Roman Egyptian land tenure which became the received view for over half a century is based on a range of documents which, though numerous, can hardly be considered representative. His project of tracing the origins of the Roman 'colonate' (after chapters on Ptolemaic and Roman Egypt, the book proceeds to studies of Sicily and Asia Minor, then Roman Africa) was concerned with finding evidence of 'unfreedom', and the oppression of the rural population in the interests of the state (Marcone 1993).

Until at least the 1960s, this picture of rural social relations remained canonical, with significant dissent only from A. C. Johnson. Both authors of monographs (such as Poethke 1969) and editors of texts continued to interpret the increasingly voluminous body of evidence within this model, even when this involved some 'shoe-horning'. For instance, the 'high land' (*ge epeiros* in Greek), attested predominantly though not exclusively in Upper Egypt, was interpreted as land requiring artificial irrigation, or '*sharaki* land' (borrowing a later Arabic term), since its tenure patently did not match the received picture of the tenure of the inundated *ge bebregmene*.

These basic assumptions persisted despite the progressive shift of focus, in the second half of the 20th century, away from a primarily legalistic approach, which looked to the formalities of land tenure as the key to the analysis of rural society. This development is paralleled in other historical fields, such as the declining influence in English medieval peasant studies of Rostovtzeff's compatriot Vinogradoff (Hilton 1975: 4), and the shift of focus in Roman political history from constitutional legalities to an emphasis on power relations and image projection. In all these cases the legal focus originated in 19th century German scholarship. Yet the study of Greco-Roman Egypt remained largely empirical in approach, and little affected by the burgeoning interest in comparative 'peasant studies' and attempts to construct theoretical models of the peasant economy (a notable exception is Banaji's 1997, 2002 work on late antique agrarian relations). The revision of Rostovtzeff's view instead started from detailed studies of textual evidence (in Greek): either by showing that newly published texts refuted his interpretation of a key institution (Vidal-Naquet 1967, on the so-called 'Crop Schedule', *diagraphe tou sporou*) or by radically revising the interpretation of existing texts (Bingen 1978). This work has, of course, assisted in the profound transformation in views of Ptolemaic Egypt as a whole (Marcone 1993: 185; Préaux 1939, 1978; Turner 1984), but its consequences specifically for the study of the rural poor, particularly of the Roman period, still do not seem to have been fully worked through. Studies by Rathbone of the Heroninus archive (1991), and by Kehoe of agricultural tenancy (1992), are both written primarily from the perspective of the landowner (although containing much invaluable discussion of the position of agricultural tenants and labourers), and are addressing the rather different agenda of 'economic rationalism'. Thus Rathbone, in particular, in his argument against Moses Finley's extreme Weberian position, returns to some common ground with Rostovtzeff, including an interest in the origins of the 'colonate' (Marcone 1993: 186).

The influence of Rostovtzeff in encouraging a negative view of the peasantry of Greco-Roman Egypt as irredeemably downtrodden is remarkably persistent, whether in the work of mainstream Greek or Roman historians (e.g. Cartledge 1997: 12), or in the interpretation of newly published texts.[1] Recently there has been a minor debate about whether Egyptian villages in late antiquity possessed any communal institutions or identity, revolving around the status of the village *koina* (councils) attested in various texts. Those who deny the existence of communal institutions argue that these *koina* are simply instruments of government imposed on the villages and made responsible (among other unenviable tasks) for administering the land imposed on the village for compulsory cultivation (Bagnall 1993: 137). The start of a lease by a *koinon* of an Oxyrhynchite village, recently published as *P. Oxy.* LXIII 4384, has been interpreted in this way, citing as a parallel a more complete early fourth century lease by a *koinon, P. Rain. Cent.* 82 (= *CPR* 1 41 re-edited), of land near the Herakleopolite village of Sobthis belonging to the village of Choinothmis '*logou epinemeseos*'. In late antique Egypt, *epinemesis* is customarily understood as land compulsorily assigned to villages, parallel to the earlier *epimerismos* and *epibole*, and there certainly are cases where an element of compulsion seems to be involved.

But this does not mean that in all instances it should be interpreted as 'compulsory assignment' rather than the more neutral 'assignment'. As is usual with *epimerismos*, the Herakleopolite *epinemesis* refers to land at one village being handled by a nearby village. Where land is not privately owned, and can thus be bought and sold, there needs to be an administrative mechanism for transferring responsibility for land if the population of one village falls while that of another increases. This may indeed involve compulsion if the population generally is falling, or the land is marginal, but does not necessarily do so; the receiving village may be glad to take on extra land. It is not the administrative mechanism as such, but the particular circumstances in which it is used, that would involve compulsion or oppression.

In *P. Rain. Cent.* 82, the level of rent and the fact that wheat was to be cultivated suggest that it was good quality land, which would yield a decent return; and moreover the rent level suggests that the *koinon* would be left with a net surplus once it had paid the government dues. There is nothing about this text, apart from the word *epinemeseos*, that carries any implication that the land was not commercially viable, and an asset rather than a burden on the village community. It also seems unwarranted to take the fragmentary Oxyrhynchite lease *P. Oxy.* LXIII 4384 as a case of compulsory imposition on the *koinon* in the absence of any reference to *epinemesis*. Scholars do still seem determined to take an exceptionally gloomy view of agrarian life in Greco-Roman Egypt.

Why is this? One problem is the strength of other influences, apart from Rostovtzeff's legacy, still pushing in the direction of viewing the rural population of the ancient world from the 'outside' or 'top down'. Scholars who approach Egypt from a training in Classics, and Greek or Roman history, understandably gravitate towards those aspects which Egypt shares with the wider Greek and Roman world, notably Hellenization and urbanization. From this perspective, as from Rostovtzeff's own, the countryside appears as the 'other', a potential hindrance to the glorious progress of Greek urban civilization. And Egyptologists, too, tend to focus attention on state organization, similarly devaluing by comparison the experience of the rural population (though there do seem to be some conspicuous exceptions to this; a few focus on rural themes in pharaonic Egypt – e.g. Eyre 1994, 1999; Katary 1989, 1999; Menu 1982).

In addition, a high proportion of the documentary evidence, particularly that in Greek, consists of administrative documents produced by, or at the demand of, government officials, and therefore inevitably produces an 'official', largely fiscal, perspective, in which the rural population exists to render its taxes unto Caesar (or Ptolemy), and should be coerced into doing so if necessary. For some parts of the period, and some areas, even the private texts are heavily slanted towards urban populations, and always there is a bias towards the relatively wealthy; the very poor would be illiterate in both languages, and could not afford to document their activities even if they wanted to (which perhaps they did; see below).

It is not easy to see how we can get to grips with a really 'empathetic' history of the peasantry of Greco-Roman Egypt – especially given the starting point of coming from the urban middle classes of northern Europe, and neither Egyptian nor peasant in origin. In an era of postcolonialism, it would surely be presumptuous to attempt such a project, appropriating other peoples' history as though we have a right to possess it. Mitchell (1990) has demonstrated how the distortion and ahistoricity of the image of the 'eternal peasantry' of Egypt is the construct of repeated and self-confirming application of 'orientalist' assumptions. But the modern world has equally taught us the danger of any country attempting to assert an exclusive prerogative over its own history. Herodotus and Polybius were already aware of the essential interconnectedness of the histories of different peoples and areas in their own day; how much more evident it is now, under the impact of globalization, that the ancient Mediterranean world, of which Egypt was part, is a shared cultural heritage.

If postcolonialism means that no one can now pretend to work on the history of Ancient Egypt in innocence of the fact that their underlying assumptions (however unconscious) and interpretations will carry implications for the present day, the sense of responsibility this engenders also encourages awareness of the potential for collaboration across the traditional disciplinary (and cultural and linguistic) boundaries. A seriously comparative approach to the agrarian history of Egypt through the entire period from the Old Kingdom to the 1992 tenancy law (Bowman and Rogan 1999) can show how to replace a mythologized 'eternal Egypt' with the critical exploration of how knowledge of one period may genuinely help to illuminate others, both by highlighting real continuities or parallels and by identifying what makes each period unique (Bagnall 2000; cf. also Scheidel 2001). The flourishing state of demotic studies, and increasing dialogue with Greek papyrology, not only banishes the one-sidedness of approach which characterized Rostovtzeff and his contemporaries, but also allows a much clearer appreciation of how the structures of the Greco-Roman period emerged from what preceded (Manning 2003; Thompson and Clarysse forthcoming).

The demographic and other basic structures of everyday life for the peasants of Greco-Roman Egypt are now on a firmer basis. However, rich though the papyrus documentation is, it almost never offers insight into villagers' perspectives of the kind that emerges from some notable studies in medieval and early modern European rural history. But the 'postmodern' fascination with the 'rhetoric' of texts, and emphasis on the indeterminacy and relativity of their meanings, encourages new perspectives on, and readings of, even the driest administrative document. Such an approach is hardly new; indeed, it is already evident in Crawford (1978), which explores the rhetoric of a Ptolemaic set of instructions to an official within the context of earlier Egyptian instruction literature (*P. Tebt.* III.1 703). While not wishing to deny that parts of the rural population often did in fact suffer oppression from tax collectors and other representatives of the state, and even from their close neighbours, it is also useful to look at the administrative texts as embodying a set of ideals of what ought to happen, as much shaped by the tradition of earlier literature, and by the need to respond to an immediately preceding text, as by the actuality of what was taking place in the fields. This is particularly true of Egypt, with its ancient scribal tradition, which the Ptolemaic and Roman governments were modifying rather than replacing.

How far the peasants themselves were prepared to accept the same set of assumptions about how rural society was, or should be, organized is an important question. The emphasis on meticulous record-keeping and bureaucracy revealed by the Greek papyri was hardly an alien phenomenon to the population of Egypt; given the demonstrable care taken by individual families to look after the legal documents related to their marriages and property dealings, the cultural importance of written texts seems to be common throughout the entire society. Thus a village woman and her son, presumably in pursuit of a dispute, thought it worthwhile to break into a neighbour's house and steal business documents relating to it (*P. Tebt.* I 52). On the other hand, there are a few texts that, particularly if read against the grain, do suggest that the bureaucratic perspective on landholding, with its elaborate categorization of land, and clearly defined rights, may coincide only partially with the way villagers themselves sometimes thought of their land. When they refer (admittedly in written petitions, or else we would not have the evidence) to the "ancestral rights" which a village held over some land or its water sources, and which were threatened by some big-wig coming in with a written lease for it, they may be referring to a system of customary rights underlying the clearly defined system of the legal and administrative documents (*P. Oxy.* XXIV 2410). Or, of course, they may be simply making a very weak case appear a bit stronger. Either way, it would be wrong to see such references to "ancestral rights" as necessarily reflecting real continuity from the pre-Ptolemaic period, subsisting beneath the system newly imposed by the foreign rulers. If there were 'popular' as opposed to 'official' traditions regarding rights to the land, the same disjunction is likely to have existed as long as there was a state to try to impose its own 'conceptual map' onto the Egyptian countryside.

To view bureaucratic or legal texts, not as straightforward reflections of an unproblematic social reality, but as constituting a self-referential and partial interpretative system which both interlocks and competes with innumerable other possible perspectives on human experience, encourages us to seek ways of exploring and overcoming their areas of reticence. The land leases, for instance, beyond their use in the economic discourse of rent levels, subsistence and profits, occasionally refer to gifts on occasion of the harvest or vintage, which can be set in the context of many other types of attestation of rural festivals (Perpillou-Thomas 1993). Or we can look to the corpus of magical papyri (normally studied separately from the 'documentary' texts), and to oracle questions, for elucidation of the plight of the partially-sighted Gemellus Horion, whose petition complained that neighbours had cast spells (apparently using a dead foetus) on both his tenant farmer and himself in their attempts to appropriate his crops (*P. Mich.* VI 423–424).

The material record from Egypt, both written and unwritten, is now so great that not even a historian of Rostovtzeff's stature could hope to command all of it. In any case, we now know better than to seek a definitive account of the peasantry of Greco-Roman Egypt (or any other topic), free of relativity of perspective and contingency of time. But the combination of specialist knowledge with interdisciplinary dialogue and awareness can provide an unprecedented opportunity for fruitful contributions to a better understanding.

## Note

1    Papyrus publications are abbreviated as in Oates *et al.* n.d.

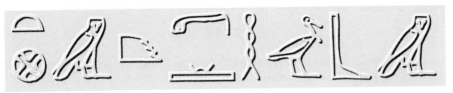

## CHAPTER 10

# THE BRITISH AND THE COPTS

*Mary Horbury*

## Introduction

Encounters with Egyptian Christians, the Copts, feature in a variety of sources accessible to the modern reader, from autobiographical accounts of colonial administrators and the jottings of tourists to the descriptions of scholars. Some of these sources from the 1820s to the 1920s are discussed below, and it is argued that the opinions expressed in such sources may have affected the discovery and interpretation of the Coptic material and textual past.

## *The setting*

Egypt was not exempt from Britain's imperial longings; it became an ideal setting in which to play out rivalries with France and, as the main gateway to India, was considered essential to the health of the rest of the British Empire. British interest in Egypt was finally formalized in 1882. This consisted of varying degrees of control, including martial law during World War I, until 1952 when the nationalist Free Officers overthrew the nominal Egyptian leader, King Farouk. The Suez crisis of 1956 illustrates how far Britain was prepared to go to maintain some kind of influence and control within Egypt (Jeffreys Chapter 1 and Hassan Chapter 2, this volume).

Britain's involvement with Egypt during the 19th and 20th centuries was not merely political. Cultural one-upmanship between the western powers of the day thrived, as Egypt's past was unravelled by western observers, and the subject of Egyptology was established. Competition for certain excavation sites was intense, as was the race to discover more and more about the splendours of Ancient Egypt. British tourists, officials, Egyptologists, missionaries and clergymen all played a role in revealing Egypt's past and present to western eyes. Arthur Weigall (1915: ix), whose academic work usually focused on ancient Egypt, wrote a history of modern Egypt because:

> Lord Cromer once remarked to me that no statesman can hope to understand the Egyptian Question unless he had made some study of ancient history; and with equal reason it may be said that no antiquarian can expect to interpret rightly the events of Egypt's mighty past unless he has been an interested spectator of Egyptian actions in modern times.

To those visiting Egypt, a variety of feelings were awakened on encountering the population. Egyptians were seen as in need of a civilizing influence, of education and improvement. Egyptian Muslims were viewed with the same ambiguity as Egyptian Christians: as both noble and degenerate. Links with the ancient Egyptian past were only made between the ancient and modern rural populations. The 'achievements' of the Ancient Egyptians, in particular the elite, were perceived as distant from the modern population. According to the nationalist Copt, Salama Musa, the history of Ancient Egypt was not studied by Egyptians because "the English had felt that it had better be left unstudied by the descendants of the Ancient Egyptians in the 20th century as it might incite in them an undue sense of pride and glory, and even foster the demand for independence" (Musa 1961: 50; and see El Daly 2003a: 143, 145, 149; Haikal 2003: 124–125; Hassan Chapter 2, this volume).

The majority of the Christians in Egypt are Copts, that is, those who follow the Monophysite doctrine that Christ's nature is indivisible. The proportion of those in Egypt thought to be Copts varies considerably according to the sources and is itself a political issue; in 1976 a nationwide census established that Copts formed 6 per cent of the whole population (Pennington 1982: 158).

## The Copts as sole heirs of pharaonic civilization and as sources for the study of Ancient Egypt

The alleged separateness of the Copts from the rest of the Egyptian people has been repeatedly emphasized – the key to this separateness being 'racial difference', religion and the Coptic language. With the decipherment of ancient Egyptian enabled by a knowledge of Coptic, British visitors to Egypt expected to find in the Copts unique descendants of the Ancient Egyptians, the language used in Coptic liturgies a living testimony to this 'fact'. Numerous accounts re-state this 'fact', from general histories and travel accounts of Egypt to leaflets promoting the case for the British government officially to recognize the Copts as a minority with rights.

A continual theme was that of the 'racial' link between the Copts and the Ancient Egyptians, in keeping with 19th and early 20th century preoccupations (Bayly 2002: 172–173). Copts encountered were stared at, their physical features noted and mentally compared to those of the Ancient Egyptians. Thus modern Copts were actively likened to mummified remains and stylized depictions of peoples who lived over 3,000 years previously, and with whom the only direct connection was that of physical landscape and location.

This is seen in two influential works. Edward Lane's *Manners and Customs of the Modern Egyptians*, written during 1833–1835, was eagerly read by British travellers to Egypt and ran into many editions. This work included a section, after the main text, on the Copts. Lane ([1836] 1842: 489) commenced this section by stating that "the fame of that great nation from which the Copts mainly derive their origin renders this people objects of much interest, especially to one who has examined the wonderful monuments of Ancient Egypt".

He then commented on how difficult it was for him to get to know the Copts due to the "aversion with which, like their illustrious ancestors, they regard all persons who are not of their own race", and went on to make clear that much intermarriage occurred in the early stages of Christianity in Egypt, de-romanticizing any notions of 'uniqueness'. While noting some physical similarities between the Copts and the Ancient Egyptians, he remained generally reserved on the point (Lane [1836] 1842: 489–491).

The first responses to encounters with Copts by British visitors seemed to consist of an almost instinctive comparison to the Ancient Egyptians, a comparison which the Copts themselves were aware of and doubtless played up to. This is demonstrated in Amelia Edwards' ([1877] 1993) seminal work *A Thousand Miles up the Nile*, which popularized travel to Egypt and stimulated interest in Ancient Egypt (Figure 10:1). While in Middle Egypt, close to Minya, Edwards' boat was hailed by monks from a monastery, who were renowned for approaching Nile tourist boats at this location. The monks swam towards the boat, proclaiming their Christian identity. One Copt was allowed into the boat, and Edwards gazed at him, mentally seeing a likeness between his appearance and those of the Ancient Egyptians in the tomb of Tiy: "and this is a Copt; a descendant of the true Egyptian stock; one of those whose remote ancestors exchanged the worship of the old gods for Christianity under the rule of Theodosius some fifteen hundred years ago, and whose blood is supposed to be purer of Mohammedan intermixture than any in Egypt" (Edwards [1877] 1993: 80).

Figure 10:1   A Coptic convent near Philae (Edwards 1877: 562).

Despite an awareness that the so-called 'racial link' between the Copts and the Ancient Egyptians was not simple or clear-cut, neither Lane nor Edwards were able to resist making physical comparisons between the two. This remained a continual theme in discussions about the Copts, and became part of the call for differential treatment under British rule.

Tourists to Egypt at the beginning of the 20th century avidly read Lane's and Edwards' works, and were also able to read a wide variety of more contemporary guidebooks. Authors of these guidebooks freely gave their opinions of the Egyptian people, and thus affected the responses of the tourists. In one such guidebook, readers were informed that the children in Old Cairo "are the true aboriginal Copts. Their features are wholly different to those of the Moslems who live outside this their narrow stronghold. Here and there you may even see a genuine Ancient Egyptian Pharaonic face, firm of line, hard and keen of eye" (Lamplough and Francis 1909: 64).

For British Christian visitors to Egypt, there could be a certain self-satisfaction gained from the belief that it was the Christians in Egypt, and not the Muslims, who were descended from the Ancient Egyptians. In the introduction to a widely read work about the history of Christianity in Egypt, its author, Edith Butcher (1879: vii), straightaway emphasized that "there are many now who have discovered that the true descendants of the ancient Egyptians are Christians, not Mohammedans". She was later among those who were to press for Coptic rights under British rule.

In a pamphlet issued by the Church Missionary Society, a Church of England organization, the Copts were described as "the true representatives of the Ancient Egyptian race" (CMS 1910: 7). This pamphlet was intended to provide information on Egypt and the Sudan, as well as to describe the work of the Anglican missionaries in these areas. It was written for consumption amongst Church of England congregations in Britain, and thus reinforced amongst those in Britain the idea that the Copts were 'racially' closer to the Ancient Egyptians than anyone else. In 1906, a book was produced by a member of the CMS mission in Egypt, full of photographs of the 'good works' being done in Egypt. This was intended to inspire donations from church-goers to the mission, and once more the point was emphatically made that "the Copts have a great racial interest also, as they are no doubt the purest descendants of the Ancient Egyptians. People long resident in Egypt can usually distinguish the Copts from the Moslems by their countenance, and some will even trace in their features the outlines long familiar in Egyptian monuments" (Gullock 1906: 34).

Such statements were not, however, without political overtones. These assertions of difference served to divide the population of Egypt in some British minds, and amongst some Egyptians as well. Thus there were those in Britain who actively supported the case for distinct Coptic representation (including electoral rights), made by prominent Copts. The *Church Times*, a Church of England newspaper, promoted the case for Coptic rights in Egypt, continually referring to the 'racial difference' of the Copts. For example, in an article from 1911, the writer stated that "the Copts represent the true native stock of the Egyptians. They trace their continuous descent to the time of the Pharaohs" (*Church Times*, 24 February 1911: 231). *The Times* also took a similar line, stating in an editorial, "The Copts represent the only

Egyptian stock which can trace its descent back to the times of the Pharaohs" (20 September 1910: 9).

Again and again this 'racial descent' seemed to be the key to the argument for Coptic status under the British. The Copts were not merely divided from other Egyptians by religion, but also by 'race'. This was repeated by Kyriakos Mikhail, a Copt who ceaselessly worked in London to promote the Coptic cause (see Bayly 2002). As part of his campaign, Mikhail (1911) edited a book about the 'Coptic Question', in which he enlisted the help of prominent individuals such as the clergyman and Near Eastern scholar, Archibald Sayce. In this book, Sayce (1911: viii) made clear that he thought the Copts were 'better' than all the other inhabitants of Egypt on account of their 'racial purity'.

The disputes engendered by these allegations of 'racial difference' were ongoing. At the same time as the above statements of difference, an English-language Egyptian newspaper argued that both the Copts and the Muslims "are of the same stock, indigenous to the soil, and have little if any blood relationship with the foreigners who have successively exercised power on the Nile" (*Egypt*, 11 April 1911: 11). So to deny one 'racial' argument, another was used.

The same argument had been used by Lord Cromer, Consul-General of Egypt between 1883 and 1907. In his book on modern Egypt, he minimized any 'racial difference' between the Copts and other Egyptians, saying that "the only difference between the Copt and the Moslem is that the former is an Egyptian who worships in a Christian church, whilst the latter is an Egyptian who worships in a Mohammedan mosque" (Cromer 1908: 206–207). This view was also asserted by Winifred Blackman, who lived in rural Upper Egypt for substantial parts of the year from the 1920s onwards: "the word 'Copt', it must be borne in mind, does not denote a racial, but rather a religious distinction" (Blackman [1927] 2000: 25). Instead, she compared the Upper Egyptians as a whole, whether Coptic or Muslim, with the Ancient Egyptians: "most of these still bear a striking facial resemblance to the ancient inhabitants of the land whom we see depicted on the walls of the temples and tomb-chapels and in the portrait-statues of the Old, Middle, and New Kingdoms" (Blackman [1927] 2000: 21–22).

The political motivation behind the alleged 'racial difference' of the Copts from the rest of the Egyptians was brought out by several commentators at the time. Such allegations of difference caused political divisions between Egyptians struggling for independence. The divisions within the Egyptian nationalist movement hampered its ability, hence helping to prolong the British occupation (Hassan Chapter 2, this volume). This was noted by Weigall (1915: 216), who, in his history of modern Egypt, stated that "these internal dissensions caused a set-back to Egyptian aspirations from which it will take many years to recover". Furthermore, it was pointed out at the time that, as the British occupation was beneficial to missionaries working in Egypt, it was in their interest as well to emphasize the differences between the Copts and Muslims (see *Egypt*, 11 April 1911: 11).

Set against the disputed background of how far the Copts were the unique descendants of the Ancient Egyptians, Egyptologists were frequently to draw on contemporary rural Egyptian life for parallels. The Copts featured in such parallels. In his memoirs, Flinders Petrie described an encounter with a Coptic landowner in 1894 while excavating in Upper Egypt. He compared the man's house with a Middle Kingdom home: "his house had all the business of the district going on in it, by his servants: the old scribe sat crooning over ancient airs as he cast up his accounts; it was the XIIth Dynasty still alive" (Petrie 1931: 151). Wallis Budge, the Egyptologist based at the British Museum during the late 19th and early 20th centuries, visited Egypt for the first time in 1886–1887. While there he stayed at a monastery near Port Said, and noted that "those who embalm the monks seem to be acquainted with a system of mummification uncommonly like that practiced by the Ancient Egyptians" (Budge 1920: 76). Such comparisons brought the subject alive for both the scholar and the reader: Ancient Egypt could be internalized, no longer distant in time, but as familiar as the cultures of ancient Greece and Rome, and easily accessible to the traveller to Egypt.

The Coptic language, with its roots in ancient Egyptian, served to heighten the perceived connection of the Copts with Ancient Egypt. This fascinated both scholars and travellers to Egypt. Amelia Edwards described an encounter between herself, her travelling companions, and a Coptic bishop in Luxor. A member of her group was keen to question the bishop about whether Coptic was ancient Egyptian or not. In response, the bishop confirmed that it was. Edwards ([1877] 1993: 463–465) went on to advise her readers to attend a Coptic service while in Egypt, as this provides a chance to "hear the last lingering echoes of that ancient speech read by the undoubted descendants of the Egyptian people". In 1907, when Storrs was working in Egypt, in the colonial administration, he went to a Coptic service in the church of Abu Sarga, Old Cairo. He was impressed by the service for the same reasons as Edwards, commenting that "there are not many rituals with an unbroken tradition of fifteen hundred years – that are chanted in Ancient Pharaonic, Greek and Arabic" (Storrs [1937] 1943: 53).

Thus, encounters with the Copts were seen by some as a way of discovering more about Ancient Egypt. Even more so than other Egyptians, the Copts were seen as a special link to a lost world which was slowly being reclaimed by scholar and traveller alike.

## The Copts as Christians

Under the British occupation and influence, the Copts were in the position of having a Christian power holding ultimate authority in Egypt for the first time since the Islamic Conquest. This placed both the rulers and the ruled in a complicated relationship, the Copts having been seen by Britain as both Christians from whom much about the early church could be learnt, and as Christians who were debasing Christianity with their degenerate ways. Likewise, the Copts took care not to appear to be collaborating with the occupying power, in case of endangering relations with their compatriots, but at the same time did take up governmental and administrative positions.

The fate of the first Coptic Prime Minister, Butros Ghali, was assassination by a Muslim in 1910 (Carter 1986: 12, 14). Storrs described the reactions of his Muslim friends to the appointment of Butros Ghali, and said that they were "as sick as the devil at the appointment of a Copt as Prime Minister", and he went on to note that Butros Ghali was "always subject to the taunt that he was the nominee of a Christian Occupation". After his assassination gangs of students sang songs in praise of Ghali's assassin, hailing him for having killed a 'Nazarene' (Storrs [1937] 1943: 71–73).

Outrage was also expressed in some quarters that the Copts did not receive special treatment under the British occupation. For example, Leeder (1918: 337–338), writing in 1913, forcefully questioned the policy of not allowing the Copts to have Sundays off work and school. This failure of the Copts to achieve recognition under the British occupation may, in part, be assigned to prejudice. Hence, the Copts were not officially recognised as a 'race' (Bayly 2002: 159), but were, nevertheless, depicted in unofficial governmental sources in the same negative light as Jews (Bayly 2002: 180). At the same time, an affinity between Jewish and Coptic religious practices had been explored in the works of the prominent British Jewish artist, Simeon Solomon. In 1865, he painted a picture of a Coptic baptismal procession (Figure 10:2) which was very closely related to that of an earlier work by him, the 'Procession with Scrolls of the Law', the rabbi replaced by Coptic priests (Weiner 2001: 18–19). Both paintings convey an impression of the age and solemnity of the rituals depicted in them.

The concern that the Copts were 'backward' or 'primitive' Christians was a constant theme in various sources, official and non-official, and was promoted in the widely-read descriptions of Egypt by colonial administrators (see Milner 1893: 398 ff). For example, Cromer (1908: 207) expressed the classic disappointment of a western Christian encountering an eastern Christian: "I fear it must be admitted that so far the Copt has stood before the world as a Christian who, by reason of adverse circumstances, has been unable to profit to any great extent by his Christianity." Not surprisingly, Cromer's views were condemned by anti-imperialists such as Wilfrid

Figure 10:2   Simeon Solomon's (1865) watercolour, 'Coptic Baptismal Procession' (Trustees of Cecil Higgins Art Gallery, Bedford).

Blunt (see Bayly 2002: 164). In a scathing review, reprinted by the English language Egyptian nationalist press, Blunt pointed out the agenda of Cromer's book: "it begins with an attack on the Mohammedan religion, which cannot but give the gravest offence, both in Egypt and India, and it goes on to deny all claim of intellectual or moral fitness for self-government, not only to the Mohammedans of Egypt, but to every section there of the native community, to Copts, Armenians and Syrians, all alike" (Blunt 1908: 84–85).

For those in the Church of England, the Copts presented a complex situation (Bayly 2002: 167–170). On the one hand, they were keen to instruct the Copts and improve their Christian knowledge, but at the same time shied away from direct proselytizing amongst a church which was far older than theirs. Furthermore, for some in the Church of England, the Copts were a welcome example of an ancient church independent of the Roman Catholic tradition.

In the early 19th century, there had been an attempt by the CMS to improve the Copts in Egypt. Once the Copts had been 'improved', it was hoped that they would then be able to influence the Muslims to convert to Christianity. In 1811, a letter was written by a Roman Catholic living in Malta to the CMS asking that they confirm the Christian faith "among the Ignorant members of the Oriental Churches" in the Levant (CMS 1910: 11).

In response to this letter, a mission was sent to the Mediterranean in 1815, and by 1825 several missionaries had started organized work in Cairo, although they found "the Copts generally indifferent to their message" (CMS 1910: 12). In contrast to this missionary work (later refuted by one of the CMS missionaries – see Campbell 1946: 206–207), another Church of England organisation, the Society for the Propagation of the Gospel, sought to carry out pastoral work. In 1819, on their behalf the Consul-General for Alexandria handed out Arabic bibles to the Coptic community (Pascoe 1901: 380*l*).

Florence Nightingale, visiting Egypt in 1849–1850, responded with the classic distaste of a devout member of the Church of England to the customs and behaviour of the Coptic population in Egypt. Her letters record her reactions to Egypt and its population; in all cases she was extremely scathing about the Copts. For example, her boat was accosted by monks at Minya, as described above with reference to Edwards. But Nightingale's reaction was far removed from that of Edwards:

> Alas! When I first saw the position of the convent, high on the cliffs of an impassable desert, and overlooking the valley of the dark and solemn Nile, it was such a situation for missionaries of the desert, ascetics of the Thebaid; and to see these wretched aquatic beggars, who I am sorry to say, bear a shocking character for robbing Dahabiehs, was such a fall. I was hardly ever so much disappointed or disgusted.

(Nightingale 1854: 50)

When writing from Qena, Nightingale (1854: 83) went so far as to claim that the Copts of Egypt could "hardly be considered as Christians", noting, "since we have been here, we have not been surprised at, but have heartily joined in, the Moslem contempt of Christians". Her letters, once published, reinforced the idea that something should be done about the parlous state of Christianity in Egypt.

By the mid-19th century in Britain, however, there was also a strong feeling that the Church of England should not proselytize amongst the Oriental churches; instead missionary work should be concentrated on Jews and Muslims. The CMS mission in Egypt had broken down, their only work in Egypt being financial support for a school to educate impoverished children (Whateley 1870). It was only with the assumption of formal British control of Egypt in 1882 that the stimulus came for the resumption of the CMS mission in Egypt.

In a pamphlet, a set of notes for instructing young people about Egypt put out by the CMS in 1909, the teacher was instructed to "stir the sympathy of the class for the much-tried Church of Egypt as it survives today" (Lunt 1909: 8). The pamphlet constantly reiterated the theme that the British occupation was of benefit to Christianity in Egypt, for example that the numbers of those in the Coptic church had increased and that measures in aid of religious toleration had been brought in. Such measures had, however, been initiated before the British occupation; in 1855 the *jizya* tax (a tax on non-Muslims) was lifted, and a Consultative Council was set up in 1866 (Carter 1986: 9). The presence of western missionaries in Egypt, despite the existence of a long established Christian church in Egypt, was justified by illustrating how the Copts needed help: the Coptic clergy were shown to be, in the majority of cases, ignorant (Lunt 1909: 9). In Gullock's (1906) book about the CMS mission in Egypt, the needs of the Coptic church and people were also emphasized: "through the centuries of oppression following on the Mohammedan invasion, the Copts, pitifully reduced in numbers, have yet preserved their integrity, and the handful of them that remains today in Egypt calls aloud for our sympathy" (Gullock 1906: 34).

The work of Church of England missionaries in Egypt was, however, focused on the Muslim population: British church-goers at this period appeared to have had no qualms about Muslims and Jews being converted to Christianity, but did claim to respect the rights of the Copts to follow their own religious beliefs. Their Christianity may have been far removed from that of the Church of England, but it was still Christianity. Thus the Society for the Propagation of the Gospel emphasized in its report from Egypt in 1888–1900 that "nothing will be done in the way of proselytism among the Copts, the friendly relations which exist between them and the English Church must tend to their benefit and enlightenment" (Pascoe 1901: 381).

Other missionary groups followed an overtly missionary stance towards the Copts. For example, the inter-denominational group, the Egypt General Mission, reported frequent disagreements with the local Coptic churches, while emphasizing the need for the Copts to learn more about Christianity. In Shebin el Kanater, the local Coptic church was opposed to the Egypt General Mission, the Coptic priest threatening to excommunicate those who went to the EGM bible class (Steel 1919: 58). An earlier report from Shebin el Kanater, from 1915, described a bible class for Coptic women, where the aim was improvement: "I am not sure that quite all who come understand their need of a change of heart, an idea which comes hardly to the Coptic mind" (Jameson 1915: 68). Nevertheless, despite worries over the religious health of the Copts, one missionary from the EGM was able to state, "It is so nice to have some 'Christians' to speak to, people who at least do believe the Bible to be the unadulterated Word of God, although their knowledge of the Book itself is next to nil" (Liblik 1919: 63–64).

This last sentiment seems to have been behind a lot of British ideas about the Copts. In articles supporting the right to Coptic status under the British, excuses were made for what was perceived as the sorry state of Coptic Christianity; nonetheless support for the Copts was urged (e.g. *Church Times*, 24 February 1911: 231). Coptic Christianity itself was rarely a source of direct spiritual inspiration to those from Britain; if services were attended, they were viewed more as a show, as a source of fascination (Storrs [1937] 1943: 53). This attitude was epitomized by Sladen (1908: 356) who described the Easter and Christmas processions of the Coptic church as "very oriental and picturesque".

Scholars of Ancient Egypt sometimes shared the feeling that the Copts were the civilized *Christian* element of Egyptian society, the least 'bad' element. According to Sayce (1911: x), "their morality and conception of the family is that of a Christian people, in other words, of Western European Civilization, and I see no reason why they should not take the same high place in the civilized world that was taken by their Pharaonic ancestors".

Petrie (1931: 208) shared similar views of the Copts as the least barbarous Egyptians, and blatantly asserted, "Egypt will never be a civilized land till it is ruled by the Copts – if ever". This comment was inspired by a visit to a Coptic village, where he had observed a Coptic service. He found the Copts far preferable to the Muslims, and his comments on Muslims were filled with orientalist stereotypes (Petrie 1931: 207–208).

Part of the acceptability of the Copts for such Near Eastern scholars was that they could be perceived as less foreign than other Egyptians (although the reverse was also true). When Copts converted to western Christianity, or became educated and westernized, then they could become even more acceptable. One of the most prominent Coptic families in Egypt, the Wissa family, having been converted by American Protestant missionaries in the 19th century, and having accumulated a great deal of wealth, integrated into the British way of life (Wissa 1994). Members of the family were educated abroad, at Oxford University and elsewhere (1994: 181). Esther Fahmy Wissa entertained British officials, and kept up a close correspondence with them, often protesting at political injustices carried out by the British (1994: 367–412). Superficially, at least, a situation had been reached whereby British administrators had entered into a friendship of sorts with a Coptic family. The case would doubtless have been very different had the Wissa family been rural dwellers such as those so despised by Nightingale.

## British responses to Coptic material and textual past

A kind of superiority infused all sorts of accounts describing encounters with the Copts; travellers were baffled by Coptic services, by the 'primitive' architecture and customs of fellow Christians, but at the same time were filled with awe at the great age of the Coptic church. This could be argued to have affected the ways in which the material and textual past of the Copts has been studied and treated.

An early record of the interest which could be stimulated by the Coptic Christian heritage in its own right is afforded by Curzon who travelled to Egypt in 1833, specifically to visit Christian sites and people as part of his travels in the whole of the Levant. Descriptions of his visit to the monasteries in Wadi Natrun convey great atmosphere, as well as details about the buildings and their inhabitants. The focus of his interest, however, was the textual heritage of the Copts; having managed to buy several Coptic manuscripts, including a copy of the gospels, from a monastery in Wadi Natrun (Souriani) he persisted in trying to see other manuscripts which the monks were initially not willing to let him see (Curzon [1849] 1955: 108–109). Here he made clear his aim in visiting the Coptic monasteries of Wadi Natrun: "I had been told by a French gentleman at Cairo that there were many ancient manuscripts in the monks' oil cellar; and it was in pursuit of these and the Coptic dictionary that I had undertaken the journey to the Natron Lakes" (Curzon [1849] 1955: 108).

Coptic monks and priests were well used to westerners visiting them in the hope of purchasing or otherwise acquiring manuscripts in Coptic, Greek or Syriac. By the time Curzon visited Egypt, he was following in a long tradition of scholarly travel. For one such traveller, purchasing Coptic manuscripts was a necessary aspect of his journeys (Clarke 1818: 272–273), although the greatest pleasure was derived from recording an inscription, thought to be in Arabic and Coptic, from behind the ear of the sphinx (Clarke 1818: 201–204).

What seemed to impress Curzon ([1849] 1955: 109) most about Coptic manuscripts was their great age. His accounts of finding and purchasing such manuscripts read like treasure hunts. In Thebes, for example, he was informed by a Copt about a library hidden in a ruined monastery. As a concession to Curzon's Christianity, and under an oath of total secrecy, the Copt agreed to take Curzon to the manuscripts (Curzon [1849] 1955: 129–130). In an ancient Egyptian tomb, the manuscripts were shown to him, but he was disappointed as they appeared to be 'merely' liturgical texts, and "not historical, nor of any particular interest, either from their age or subject" (Curzon [1849] 1955: 133).

The architectural heritage of the Copts was highlighted by Curzon when he visited the White Monastery, in Middle Egypt. This was where the 'father' of Coptic literature and monasticism, Apa Shenoute, had lived and worked in the fourth and fifth centuries AD. Curzon greatly admired the church in the White Monastery, and attributed its construction to the Empress Helena, placing the building firmly within the Greek Byzantine tradition: "the peculiarity of this monastery is, that the interior was once a magnificent basilica, while the exterior was built by the Empress Helena in the Ancient Egyptian style" (Curzon [1849] 1955: 137–140).

Apart from the sites of Old Cairo, Nightingale, visiting Egypt less than 20 years later than Curzon, was generally much less impressed. But she had a similar motivation to see as many biblical and early Christian sites as possible. Thus when in Memphis, she thought of Moses: "To-day I walked with Moses, under the palms" (Nightingale 1854: 259), and when near Qena, she thought of St Pachomius and wished that there was more evidence left of his monastic endeavours: "We passed the island of Tabenna, where once St Pachomius taught to pray twelve times a day, to labor; and to deny the body. Now no one prays, no one labors; and if they deny the body, it is because they have nothing to give it" (Nightingale 1854: 82). With the rest of her party, she also went to much trouble to see ancient monastic sites. For example, she tried to visit one of St Pachomius' monasteries on an island, but was disappointed with what she found:

> If the inhabitants were Copts, as most of the people are about there, they had not even a church – worse than the Mahometans. The crew carried Mr B. ashore on their backs, and us on their joined hands; we walked some distance, but could not even make the people understand that we wanted to see the ruins of a Deir (monastery). And yet here Christianity grew up ...
>
> (Nightingale 1854: 96)

It was Curzon's pioneering work which was to inspire later collectors and scholars to travel to Egypt in the hope of discovering more about the biblical past and the early church. Curzon's manuscripts were of central importance in the writing of a multi-volume work on the history of the eastern church (Neale 1850: xxv). Curzon's purchases thus resulted in knowledge about the Coptic church being disseminated. The stimulus for such research and manuscript hunts was the desire to find out about the Coptic church, its customs, history, and liturgies, with the other aspects of the Coptic past of little concern.

Curzon's work typifies later interest in the Copts: people were struck by their long textual heritage which had the potential for providing details and variant readings of early Christian texts, and by their ancient places of worship. Yet, like Nightingale, Curzon was also disparaging about contemporary Copts: they were a people incapable of looking after their own heritage 'properly', and who could be hoodwinked into selling their manuscripts if plied with enough alcohol.

Egypt remained a place for British people to visit and acquire antiquities, but the process became more complicated under the British occupation. When Budge visited Egypt for the first time on behalf of the British Museum (1886–1887) with the aim of supplying the museum with items for its Egyptian collections, he ran up against Cromer, and his successor, John Gorst (see Dixon Chapter 5, this volume). In his memoirs, Budge recounted their unease. For example, Cromer "thought that excavations made in Egypt by a British official were likely to 'complicate political relationships', and that the occupation of Egypt by the British ought not to be made an excuse for filching antiquities from the country, whether to England or to anywhere else" (Budge 1920: 81). Nonetheless, Budge was able, by various means, to acquire Egyptian antiquities, and described how he was assisted in this by certain Egyptians. For example, he related how the British Consul at Luxor, Mustafa Agha, helped him, saying that "he was devoted to the British, and wanted to make the British Museum 'the best in all the world'" (Budge 1920: 113).

Coptic antiquities and manuscripts were seen as worthy additions to museum collections, especially when they could be linked either with Ancient Egypt or early Christianity. A considerable part of Budge's time in Egypt was spent purchasing and excavating Coptic items on behalf of the British Museum. For example, he excavated the Monastery of St Simeon at Aswan. Here he uncovered many tombs, and was pleased to find in one what he identified as an episcopal staff. This crumbled into nothing as a rubbing of it was made, but Budge was excited by what he saw as "an attempt to unite the most sacred symbols of the Egyptian and Christian religions" in the design of the ornament (Budge 1920: 104–105). In an attempt to raise funds for the British School of Egyptian Archaeology, set up by Petrie, his wife Hilda wrote a book entitled *Six Notes on the Bible from Flinders Petrie's Discoveries*. One of the discoveries which she hoped would inspire people to donate money to the BSEA's excavations was that of a Coptic manuscript found in a late Roman pot at Qau el Kebir in Upper Egypt. The manuscript turned out to be a Coptic version of the gospel of St John (Petrie 1933: 36–41).

The Coptic non-textual past could also be a source of interest to the more casual observer, and tourist visits were made to sites under excavation. For example, the monastery of Apa Jeremias at Saqqarah was excavated by Quibell at the beginning of the 20th century, and the discoveries were admired by tourist and scholar alike. According to Quibell's wife, the church with its stone columns could be compared to Justinian's churches in Ravenna, and were "splendid examples of Coptic art" which must have been made "under Byzantine sculptors" (Quibell 1925: 58). A tourist to Egypt in 1909, Beatrice Gull, described a tea with Annie Quibell, at which she was shown some of the findings from Saqqarah: "we then called on the Quibells, he is an excavator and has found a very beautiful Coptic church and monastery about 500 AD. She showed us some of the capitals of the pillars etc. which were beautifully carved" (Gull 1909: x).

Coptic buildings which were still in use also formed part of the tourist trail, and were much admired. One of Storrs' roles as a colonial administrator was to escort notable British visitors round the sites of Cairo. Frequently the Coptic sites of Old Cairo were on the list of places visited (Storrs [1937] 1943: 19). Gullock, the CMS missionary, commented, "if you ask the average English tourist whether he has been to Old Cairo, he will reply, 'Oh, that is the place where all the Coptic Churches are, is it not?' And he certainly will have visited it" (Gullock 1906: 84; see also El Daly 2003a; Hassan 2003). Storrs argued for the preservation of Coptic churches on the grounds that: "here was a unique survival in design, in ornament and in liturgical language of Ancient Egypt" (Storrs [1937] 1943: 95). In a book addressing the political situation in Egypt as well as providing a guide to the sights, Sladen (1908: 325) wholeheartedly recommended a visit to Old Cairo as "the filthy Coptic town must be explored. Its fleas are numerous and welcome fresh pastures, but it is not a too high price to pay, for this Coptic city is unique".

The beauty of the churches and their great age were given by Sladen (1908: 325) as the main reasons for visiting Old Cairo. He described the screens within the churches as the "glory of Coptic art" and stated that the "sunken masonry, the brown wood, and fretted ivory bosses of the screens, the worn pavements convey the idea of an antiquity almost as old as Christianity" (Sladen 1908: 326). He singled out the Hanging Church as the most beautiful of the Coptic churches which "has only to fear comparison with the Cathedral of St Mark's at Venice and the Royal Chapel of Palermo. It's a gem of color and quaintness, harmony and proportion". His delight in Coptic monumental architecture and desire to recommend it to others is shown by his description of Islamic Cairo. In this he advised the reader to visit some Coptic churches on Sharia es Sureni, if the reader had not managed to see Coptic Cairo, as they are "of great importance and beauty, sufficient to give an idea of antique Coptic architecture and Coptic screens and painting to those who lack the time or the nerve to investigate the wonders of Old Cairo" (Sladen 1908: 348). Another bonus to be gained from visiting these churches as opposed to Old Cairo was that Sladen thought that the Coptic guides were more intelligent than those in Old Cairo.

Many tourists, including Edwards and Gull, chose to visit the rest of Egypt from a Cook's cruise of the Nile. On such cruises, British tourists could socialize with one another, eat British food, including bacon and eggs for breakfast, and view Egypt from a comfortable distance (see also El Daly 2003a). The Cook's tour decided what sites were visited, and made all the arrangements, so that the tourist could just sit back and wait to be taken to the site. The itinerary of a Cook's tour was thus central in forming a visitor's impression of Egypt, ancient and modern. Coptic sites could feature on such tours, although Sladen (1908: 426–427), with his interest in post-pharaonic sites, complained that the White and Red Monasteries (visited and admired by Curzon) did not form part of the itinerary.

That the Coptic material past was not a priority for the French-run Antiquities Service in Egypt is shown by the fact that Budge was allowed to remove Coptic antiquities from Egypt as "they would not be claimed by the Antiquities Service" (Budge 1920: 333). Indeed, the Antiquities Service had, at this period, been removing Coptic structures from sites with pharaonic remains. This was done in order to expose fully pharaonic structures which were given infinitely more importance than the Coptic past. Furthermore, the mudbrick structures of Coptic period sites were often removed by Egyptians for use as fertilizer in the fields. At Dendera this was undertaken with the permission of the authorities: Sladen described how the remaining section of the enclosure wall at Dendera was filled with Coptic buildings, but that it was "being quickly removed, since the farmers, who value it highly for manure, have been given permission to cart it away" (Sladen 1908: 435).

The combined effect of these actions often met with the approval of visitors to Egypt, who frequently complained of later additions to pharaonic temples, as well as Coptic graffiti on the walls of temples. Any destruction in temples was automatically assigned to the Copts. For example, Gull (1909) noted in her diary that the temple of Dendera "was dreadfully mutilated by the Coptic Christians", and found it a "wicked shame" that the Luxor temple had only been partially excavated. Even Annie Quibell, who praised the Coptic art in the monastery of Apa Jeremias at Saqqarah, saw fit to condemn the Coptic use of ancient Egyptian tombs at western Thebes: "too often do we see on the Sheikh Abdel Gurneh hill, a bit of beautiful XVIIIth Dynasty painting willfully defaced as heathenish and a cross splashed on above it in heavy red paint" (Quibell 1925: 57).

Visitors and scholars of Egypt made a distinction between the different elements of the Coptic material past, admiring the monumental and the artistic, but spurning that which might provide information on the social history of the Copts. Thus, visitors skirted round Coptic settlement sites with little or no interest, in order to reach pharaonic wonders (see e.g. Edwards [1877] 1993: 208–209). This of course reflected the focus of interest in the pharaonic era as well; Petrie was unusual with his rigorous recording of ancient Egyptian social history. But, in comparison to the treatment of pharaonic monumental structures, the monumental side of the Coptic past was removed without proper record by those keen to expose pharaonic remains, when at the same time Coptic monumental architecture was admired in Old Cairo. At Medinet Habu, the mortuary temple built by Ramesses III in western Thebes, a substantial church in the second court was totally destroyed by the Antiquities Service in 1859, and then between 1889 and 1899 the destruction of all Coptic structures within and immediately outside the temple was ordered by the Antiquities Service (Daressy 1897: vi). Naville undertook excavations at the site of Deir el-Bahri (Hatshepsut's mortuary temple) on behalf of the London-based Egypt Exploration Fund (Jeffreys Chapter 1 and Dixon Chapter 5, this volume). In the introduction to his preliminary report he condemned the Coptic monastery that had been built in Hatshepsut's temple, saying that "the destruction and the havoc wrought in this temple by the Copts is incalculable" (Naville 1894: 6). He ordered the Coptic remains to be knocked down, and by 1902 even the large Coptic monastic tower had been destroyed (Crum 1902: xiii), and Hatshepsut's temple was well on its way to being converted into one of the major tourist attractions on the west bank at Luxor.

Such destruction of Coptic monumental buildings was condemned at the time by some in the academic community. Somers Clarke, an architect turned full-time Egyptologist (see Reid 2002: 270–271), systematically recorded all the Christian antiquities in the Nile Valley. He openly criticised the ways in which the Coptic past had been destroyed, and stated, for example, that the loss of the Coptic church in the second court at Medinet Habu was due to the whim of the Antiquities Service: "this page of history did not please the gentleman who was director-general at that time so out the evidences must come. At no little trouble and cost the monoliths were dragged away and are to be seen lying outside the walls of the courtyard on its southern side. And not only so, but no plans, drawings or notes were published" (Clarke 1912: 189–190).

In 1884, Butler, an ardent supporter of the contemporary Copts, had urged that the scholarly world take an interest in the Coptic past. In his preface to his important work on the ancient Coptic churches of Egypt, he (Butler 1884a: vii–viii) cited the two familiar reasons as to why study of the subject was important: the links it provided to the ancient Egyptian past, and the information it could provide on the early church. Likewise he argued very strongly against the destruction of the Coptic past, and argued that it was as worthy of investigation as the pharaonic past, concluding his two volume work on ancient Coptic churches with very heartfelt words:

> ... remains so vast in extent, so venerable in years, so unique in character, so rich in known and unknown possibilities of interest, are surely as well worthy of research and exploration as the colossal monuments of pagan Egypt. Yet day by day they are perishing, unknown to western travellers, and little regarded by the Copts themselves, and nothing, absolutely nothing, has been done or is doing to rescue them from oblivion, or to save them from destruction.
>
> (Butler 1884b: 371)

Doubtless, Butler's zeal on behalf of the study of the Coptic past was influenced by his admiration for contemporary Copts and the ancient Christian rites preserved by the Coptic church. Butcher, also an outspoken supporter of the Copts, drew upon Butler's work for her history of the Coptic church. In this she reported that under Cromer, the ancient Coptic churches in Cairo were looked after by the Committee for the Preservation of Arab Monuments (1897: 400), and stated: "Lord Cromer said that the only serious danger to the antiquities of the Church of Egypt is the tourist" (1897: 401).

A real interest and desire to preserve some of the Coptic material and textual past was demonstrated by the founding of the Coptic Museum in Cairo in 1902. This was developed on the initiative of Morcos Simaika, the Vice-President of the Coptic Community Council, who catalogued and collected items that had been cleared out of the churches of Old Cairo (Reid 2002: 275–278). The museum was to include items witnessing to Coptic social, political and religious history. In his memoirs, Storrs ([1937] 1943: 95) noted how he helped out with the task of setting up the Coptic Museum in Old Cairo, and described how it was built in the form of a 16th century Coptic house, with the antiquities integrated into the very structure of the building. The project received support from the hierarchy of the Coptic church (Storrs [1937] 1943: 95–96).

Detailed recorded archaeological excavations of Coptic sites also began to gather pace. The majority of excavations, however, still tended to prioritize textual and 'artistic' finds which were seen as the most valuable and worthwhile, while other finds were consigned to spoil heaps (Crum 1902: ix). Petrie described an excavation he carried out in the Fayum in 1889 on behalf of some Coptic priests, in an area just outside his excavation permit. As soon as he began to find textual material the Coptic priests took over the site themselves, perhaps in order to profit from the sale of the papyri (Petrie 1931: 99).

Papyri such as those would then end up being bought by private individuals and those working on behalf of museums. For example, much of Budge's time in Egypt was spent purchasing manuscripts and these seemed to bring him the most pleasure, especially when the Coptic manuscripts involved were apocryphal texts or variant early readings of the Bible. He described the work of Upper Egyptian manuscript and antiquities dealers who carried out their own excavations (having received the permission of the Antiquities Service) in the hills near Edfu from 1907 onwards (Budge 1920: 371–372). In the course of these excavations apocryphal texts were found which Budge purchased for the British Museum. And texts found in this way did have a provenance of sorts, unlike the more unorthodox techniques also followed by Budge in the search for Coptic manuscripts. For example, on his first trip to Egypt in 1886 to 1887, he described a deal he made at Akhmim: "I found a very fine collection in the hands of a Frenchman who owned a flour-mill in Cairo, and he caused the police to be entertained at supper whilst he and I conducted our deal for Coptic manuscripts" (Budge 1920: 135).

The complicated pattern of networks enabling Egyptologists such as Budge to be so successful in the purchase of Coptic antiquities and manuscripts is revealed by the assistance he received from western clergymen. On one occasion, for example, he described how a clergyman, Chauncey Murch, took him to meet "some wealthy Copts" in Akhmim. The purpose of Murch's visit was to ordain a "native teacher". These "wealthy Copts" had a "good collection of Coptic manuscripts" (Budge 1920: 155). Contacts provided by the desire of the western churches to improve the Copts could thus facilitate the work of Egyptologists.

An unusual example of an excavation of a Coptic site which combined a desire to record textual and material finds is provided by the excavation of the Monastery of Epiphanius on the west bank at Luxor, carried out in the 1920s. Here Walter Crum worked in conjunction with Winlock and a team of archaeologists and epigraphists to excavate a group of monastic cells located in and around ancient Egyptian tombs. The wealth of discoveries, from ostraca to monastic baskets, were carefully documented, with the textual material treated alongside the non-textual, and a general study of other monastic sites in western Thebes was also made (Crum and White 1926; Winlock and Crum 1926).

Once discovered, Coptic texts were treated in various ways, some scholars delighting in the further information they provided on early Christianity, and others enjoying looking for similarities between ancient Egyptian and early Christian thought. For example, Petrie wrote a letter to Edwards, stating that he believed the Arian question stemmed from ancient Egyptian thought (Petrie 1931: 104–105). There were also those scholars who viewed Coptic writings from the context of what they perceived as the superior standpoint of the classical world. Bell saw the only interest of Coptic as showing how some early Christians had thought: "Coptic literature is dull enough in all conscience, and betrays an essential puerility in the Egyptian mind, but it is none the less of real importance as revealing the reaction of that mind to Christianity" (Bell 1922: 153). With the demise of the Byzantine influence on Egypt, and with the Islamic Conquest, Bell thought that Egypt had regressed, and clearly Coptic represented an aspect of such regression: "in this new world of dogmatism and religious bigotry, Christian or Mahommedan, there was no room left for the clear-eyed sanity of Hellas. Egypt had become once more a part of that Oriental world from which the fiery genius of Alexander had separated her for a thousand years" (Bell 1922: 154).

Even those who were utterly committed to the furtherance and development of Coptic studies felt that they had to 'excuse' certain aspects of the Coptic past and present. Thus, Butler (1884b: 247) agreed with the detractors of Coptic that there were no literary merits to Coptic, but argued that nevertheless the language should be studied due to its links with the ancient Egyptian and ancient Greek worlds. Butcher (1897: 425–426) agreed with the critics of the Copts that Coptic churches were not looked after, saying, "their churches are rarely cleaned, and their condition in the matter of order and cleanliness is generally disgraceful". She then went on to remind her readers that English churches used to be dirty as well.

Luckily not everyone took Bell's attitude towards the Coptic past, although such attitudes may have influenced those potentially interested in studying the subject. Certainly, it has remained very much a minority interest, either a sideline to Egyptological, theological or to Classical research, despite the best endeavours of early proponents of the subject such as Butler. In her memoirs, Murray (1963: 141) wrote that "the study of the Christian period of Egypt has been greatly neglected; the only interest shown is in the Coptic church and its liturgy, and in the language; the archaeology and art are hardly known".

## Conclusion

British encounters with the Copts and their past generated utterly opposed emotions, stretching from disgust and disinterest to admiration. A tourist could be uplifted by the churches in Old Cairo or by meeting a Coptic monk, but could also be exasperated by what was perceived as the 'uncivilized' behaviour of the Copts or the 'shapeless' ruins obscuring the greater glory of the pharaonic. Scholars, government officials and missionaries could also be affected by conflicting feelings. Coptic texts revealed little of what was thought to be 'literary' skill, but at the same time were thought to be linguistically fascinating. Early Coptic monumental art was admired, but was also thought to be 'primitive'. Coptic civil servants were not as 'useful' as the Levantine civil servants, but the British occupation could also sponsor a Coptic Prime Minister. Missionaries and clergymen could be appalled by the lack of biblical knowledge shown by the Copts, but could also feel respect for the antiquity of the Coptic church. Investigation and interpretation of the Coptic past was similarly approached with a variety of preconceptions and agendas, some of which were not far removed from political, ecclesiastical and touristic expediencies. In this, the pharaonic past of Egypt played a central role – either the Coptic past was seen as providing a vital link to Ancient Egypt, or it was seen as preventing the full wonders of the pharaonic past from being exposed. Today, Old Cairo is exposed for full exploitation by government and tourist, turned into a 'safe' enclave and guarded by an armed jeep. And so the recommended day trip in Cairo can still include a visit to the pyramids, to Islamic Cairo, and to the churches of Old Cairo, as it did at the turn of the last century. The ambiguity with which contemporary Copts and their past were approached lingers still, despite the changes in the political situation and in the priorities of academics.

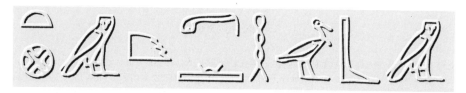

## CHAPTER 11

# ANCIENT EGYPT AND THE ARCHAEOLOGY
# OF THE DISENFRANCHISED

*Sandra A. Scham*

Egypt has become the cultural prize for two contending visions of the past – both of them facilitated by the current atmosphere of postmodern and postcolonial theorizing about history and archaeology (Scham 2001: 247). In a reaction against the western appropriation of their ancient past, Egyptians have begun to explore and value the glories of Ancient Egypt on their own terms (Kamil and Saad 2000; Spencer 1999). Meanwhile in Europe and America the rebirth of Ancient Egypt has taken a different form (see Hassan Chapter 2, this volume). The legacy of subjugation, which has heretofore created a rather truncated vision of the past for peoples of African descent, has been turned on its head by a new wave of appreciation, indeed adoption, on their part of the autocratic ancient Egyptian culture (Early 1998; Roth 1998). Egypt now represents for both of these groups the key connection between east and west as well as a reminder of the great civilizations that preceded those developed in Europe.

While the impetus behind these two perceptions of the ancient Egyptian past is similar, they differ in almost every other conceivable way. Modern Egyptians may identify with the global struggle against western domination, but they are eager for international funds to preserve sites and for international interest in those sites as tourist destinations. They also display a decidedly anti-global suspicion of any cultures or communities that come too close to similarly taking over their past – even if those communities are disenfranchized ones (Haikal 2003; Hana 1996; Hassan 1998).

In contrast, for peoples of African descent, there is no need to perform a balancing act between the local and the global – their focus is clearly universalist. Egypt belongs to all the people of Africa and African descent everywhere (Crawford 1994; James 1992). This astounding generalization may account for some postmodern scholars' frustrations with the 'Egypt in Africa' view of history and archaeology – when one would otherwise expect sympathy from them (for a review of some of this history and its implications, see O'Connor and Reid 2003a). In effect, the concept of Ancient Egypt 'for the ages' that informed Egyptology for so many years has been reborn in the 'Egypt in Africa' model.

## Egypt in Africa versus Egypt in Egypt

Modern Egyptian intellectuals never describe themselves as 'African', but self-identified people of African descent have for some time claimed to be, at least historically, Egyptian (Roth 1998). *Black Athena* (Bernal 1987, 2003) may have been a watershed in the formation of the 'Egypt in Africa' movement but this concept was explored well before Bernal's work – notably by Senegalese scholar Cheikh Anta Diop (1974) (MacDonald 2003). There are three well known accusations against the scholars of the past that are both explicit and implicit in Bernal's work. The first is that Classicists have undervalued the contribution of the Near Eastern cultures to western civilization. The second is that race, and racism, has played a part in the notions that led to an exaggerated emphasis on Classical Greek civilization as the progenitor of our own (North 2003). The third charge has only been inferred from Bernal's arguments – but it has become by far the most controversial of the three. Bernal suggests that the most important of our ancestor civilizations was Ancient Egypt and that Egyptologists have erroneously assumed (or intentionally implied) that Ancient Egyptians were white when, in fact, they were black – like other Africans (Bernal 1987, 2003). Diop's indictment of Egyptology is even more harsh than Bernal's. He claimed that white European scholars conspired to present an Egypt that was completely Caucasian in appearance and European in effect. The idea that Egypt was a part of Africa did not even enter into such traditional studies of the country's history (Diop 1974).

Egyptologists and Classicists have rushed to their own defence in countering these allegations (Lefkowitz 1996; Lefkowitz and Rogers 1996; North 2003). A less strident but nevertheless emphatic voice in this controversy has been that of native Egyptians (Hassan 1998) who have, thus far, avoided becoming too embroiled in the race debate. These mostly western-trained scholars want, as one put it, "the use of our own past" (Haikal 2003) not necessarily to the exclusion of other users but certainly to the extent of determining the presentation of this past to the rest of the world. Ostensibly, Egyptians do not really care if Akhenaten or Cleopatra were black – only that they are accepted as part of the Egyptians' history of continuous occupation of the land (Hana 1996). Nevertheless, some African American writers have suggested that, like other Caucasians, native Egyptians have attempted to eradicate any black African connections to ancient Egyptian civilization (James 1992).

Despite its prominence in current debate, the race question is not the most intriguing one that has been raised about what one scholar has called the "crucial links to contemporary concerns" (North 2003) being made about Ancient Egypt. Rather than discuss modern Egyptians' view of race, theirs or that of anyone else, a more significant question is whether average Egyptians, whose *per capita* income is among the lowest in the world, really identify with their 'pharaonic' past. Western scholars have long insisted that they do not, although there is at least some evidence to the contrary (Meskell 2000). Similarly, rather than discuss the issue (of rather dubious merit) as to what colour the Ancient Egyptians were, a more important concern is why Americans and Europeans of African descent, with a tragic history of slavery and class struggle, should wish to describe themselves as the heirs to this intensely hierarchical ancient society.

## Egypt in Europe

The Napoleonic Expedition to Egypt was a major contributor to European and western understanding of ancient Egyptian culture, however flawed that understanding might have been (Jeffreys Chapter 1, this volume). The *Description de l'Égypte* is a massive undertaking replete with detailed engravings of Egyptian pashas and peasants – all presented with loving attention to detail. The peasants do not receive the full 'orientalized' treatment that is reserved for the pashas, the latter shown reclining on pillows in their ornate houses. The other memorable images of the *Description* are those of hundreds of monuments – all of immense interest to the scholar of ancient Egyptian architecture. Gero and Root (1990) and Said (1993) speak of the unpopulated archaeological sites of colonialist antiquarians. The *Description* is undoubtedly the archetype for these. Many of the engravings show empty sites – or, more telling, sites populated by faceless 'natives' who are illustrated only in order to provide a scale. This forced separation of insignificant people from important places lives on in many discussions on the protection and preservation of archaeological sites today.

More important, the Napoleonic Expedition brought Egypt to Europe, which has controlled cultural production about it ever since. The great age of 19th century English explorers continued the tradition – by turning an avocation into a discipline – and, thus, Anglo-Saxon Egyptology was born. Contrary to Diop's charge that Egyptologists have consistently ignored the geography of Egypt, these English explorers knew precisely where it was located – in Great Britain! Even as recently as 1997, a reporter from *The Times* evoked this 'memory' of Egypt: "We know these places. The path to the Sphinx, the Corniche at Luxor, the drive to the Valley of the Kings are corners of a foreign field that have become forever England" (in Meskell forthcoming). It seems that little has changed since Balfour declaimed to the House of Commons on the necessity of Britain occupying Egypt: "We know the civilization of Egypt better than we know the civilization of any other country. We know it further back; we know it more intimately; we know more about it" (in Meskell 2000).

The images included in the published reports of the Napoleonic Expedition to Egypt were for many decades the only visions of Egypt known to the west. This French enterprise was simultaneously impressive and uninformed. In a sense, the same is true of the disciplines of archaeology and Egyptology. The 'patron saint' of Egyptologists, Sir Flinders Petrie, provides an example of both the brilliance and the naiveté (many would characterize it as more offensive than naive) of such scholarship. Petrie was the originator of pottery analysis and seriation in the Near East – a method that was to serve generations of future archaeologists – but, when writing about modern Egyptians, he expressed disbelief that the ancestors of this 'primitive' and poverty-stricken people could have been responsible for the splendour of Ancient Egypt (Montserrat 2000; and see Horbury Chapter 10, this volume). He was not alone in this; nor was Egyptology the only discipline whose practitioners held such racist views. These were the days when the sun never set on notions of British racial superiority. Indeed most archaeology of the past can be characterized as "the archaeology of the enfranchised" (Hamilakis 1999; Hodder 1999). In contrast, there is now the beginning of an archaeology of the disenfranchised, and this paradigm may fundamentally alter perceptions of Ancient Egypt.

## Locating Egypt on the postmodern map

The 'archaeology of the disenfranchised' (or archaeology of cultural identity) is a paradigm that countenances the assembled beliefs, associations, perceptions and theories about the past formed by minorities and formerly subjugated peoples (Scham 2001). Implicit is the assumption that the right of a people to define their own past should feature as part of those human rights that we so often defend, a right that often results in opposing western traditions. The dilemma occurs when there are conflicts between disenfranchised peoples who claim the same past. This was illustrated not so long ago by the clash between Greece and the newly emerging former Yugoslav Republic of Macedonia. Greeks who have only recently assumed ownership over their history (though not entirely, as the struggle for the Parthenon Marbles illustrates) were genuinely offended by the use of the name Macedonia as well as the famous 'Star of Vergina' on the Macedonian flag. They saw this, at the very least, as an attempt by the new country, composed mainly of Slavs and Albanians, to appropriate the great 'Greek' ruler Alexander the Great (Brown 1994, 1998; Kotsakis 1998).

By contrast, pharaonic Egypt appears to have a lower profile for modern Egyptians than ancient Greece for modern Greeks. For example, Sadat (1978), who had risen through the Egyptian political hierarchy from fairly humble village beginnings, mentions the Nile and Nile civilization in his book, but nowhere does he suggest that pharaonic Egypt was any part of the 'identity' for which he was in search. Nevertheless, Sadat's life and actions make it clear that he saw Egypt as distinct from the Islamic Arab world, the coalition of states that Nasser had envisioned (Hassan 1998). What appears to inform the average Egyptian notion of the difference between Egyptian society and that of other Arab states is that they have been fixtures in the same place for millennia and, despite much religious and cultural change, Egyptians cling to this historical 'certainty'.

More recently, Egyptian attitudes toward their past have begun to focus on a new concept of 'distinctness'. In the context of the Arab and Islamic Middle East, there is now a rather nebulous vision of Egyptian 'eternal uniformity'. A book review published by the Egyptian State Information Service proclaims that "The people of Egypt are only one people ... they formed from all of this mix [of cultures and peoples] a homogeneous human entity" (Hana 1996). Today's nationalism is, of course, a product of Egypt's distant past but at the same time it is also a product of its colonial past (Hassan Chapter 2, this volume).

Part of the colonialist enterprise all over the world has been the incorporation of many different indigenous cultures within one governmental structure and the creation of artificial borders that do not reflect traditional cultural divisions (Lowenthal 1989). The nationalism of formerly subjugated nations must thus both challenge colonial claims and, at the same time, accept some of their intellectual premises. Traditions within such nations are multi-cultural and multi-religious, but their envisioned pasts are mono-cultural.

Minorities within established nation-states are confronted by different problems. Their construction is no more the 'real' Ancient Egypt than are those of the nationalists. In the latter case, however, the objective is symbolically to opt to be within the majority culture (of power and influence) by creating a past that will fit the majority culture's perceptions of what is significant. The visions of the Frenchmen who painstakingly recorded the monuments and culture of the Egypt of the late 18th and early 19th centuries remain compelling for two reasons: first, because they formed the view of Egyptian culture for the succeeding centuries, and second, because they are the visions of conquerors.

Diop (1974) led the modern quest on the part of individuals of African descent to find an empowered past – a past that could counter the images of peoples of African descent as defeated, colonized and marginalized. Another motivation was to characterize generations of oppression as an elaborate conspiracy designed to deprive people of their dignity by depriving them of their history. However, attempts in such works as *Black Athena* (Bernal 1987, and see Bernal 2003) to correct such bias have been seriously critiqued. Thus Roth (1998: 220) believes that the main problem with such work is that, by viewing ancient Egyptian culture through an Afrocentric lens, they fail to examine the real nature of the society. Similarly, North (2003) suggests that Bernal's work is "deeply problematic" because of the connections that "Bernal makes (or allows to be inferred) to contemporary concerns ... first that the Egyptians were black; second that their blackness was connected with their being denied 'credit' in the evolution of culture; third, that the restoration of their 'credit' has relevance to relations between contemporary groups". He maintains, however, that "the problem for ancient historians is not just to say that this whole agenda is misconceived, but to define what would be a better one. Attributing colour to Egypt may be conceptually anachronistic; that does not destroy the power of the idea" (North 2003).

Most of the commentary on the 'Egypt in Africa' movement contend that race, *per se*, as well as our classifications and racial inferences, cannot be applied to Ancient Egyptians. When Egyptologists and Classicists utter such dire warnings they often do so when confronted with the assumption that Ancient Egyptians or famous Greeks were black. It is important to note, however, that there is a great deal more at stake than solely the misapplication of cultural categories. Thus, for example, Lefkowitz (1996: 125–126) fears that Afrocentrism "has a destructive side, which *cannot and should not* [emphasis added] be overlooked. First of all, it offers them a 'story' instead of history. It also suggests that African Americans need to learn only what they choose to believe about the past".

Race matters to individuals on *both* sides of this argument. Arguments such as Tritle's (1996: 1) dismissal of the notion that Herodotus was black, with the assertion that "surviving portraits of him reveal *without a doubt* [emphasis added] an individual of Indo-European, i.e. 'white' identity", are merely disingenuous. The appearance of individuals in ancient portraits is not persuasive evidence of cultural, racial or linguistic affiliation. Until very recently the United States Census Bureau labelled fair individuals with one-eighth African American ancestry as 'black'. To regard a seemingly 'Indo-European' person in ancient portraiture as 'black' makes no less (or more) sense than to label that person as 'white'.

## Napoleon and pharaoh

The differences between modern Egyptian views of the past and African American and European views of, ostensibly, the same past can be exposed in two anecdotes. The first is the reported statement by Anwar Sadat's assassin that "I have killed Pharaoh". This informs us of the problems inherent in extolling the pharaonic past in modern Egypt; not only is it a non-Islamic and non-Arab past – thus putting it out of touch with the modern population – but it is also a past that is actually denigrated by the newer traditions to which modern Egyptians adhere. In the Quran, 'Pharaoh' is a tyrant – not a cultural role model (Hassan 1998; but see El Daly 2003b).

The second anecdote holds that it was Napoleon's soldiers who were responsible for damaging the face of the Sphinx. Perhaps the soldiers were alarmed at the supposed African features of the statue. It suggests that it was a monumental depiction of Black Africa that was offensive to European eyes. The fact that most scholars believe that the Sphinx's destruction occurred in 1378 AD when a religious zealot found the depiction offensive to Muslim eyes (Roth 1998) is ignored by many African Americans and African Europeans who believe the story that the French were responsible for the damage.

Both instances reveal the re-telling of history. In the first case, it appears that Sadat's assassin was also attempting to kill Sadat's vision of modern Egyptian identity. If Sadat was a tyrant in the image of pharaoh (Champion and Ucko 2003: Figure 1:3) he was, by definition, a traitor to his religion and to the concept of Arab unity; in the second case, if it is inferred that Napoleon's army was shocked to find that Africans had been responsible for a great civilization. In this view the 'killing' of the history of Black African civilization is blamed on western imperialism. Both are synthetic folk etiologies that seem to explain and modify perceptions of the same time.

## Conclusion

Despite Bernal's (1987) claim that western civilization has never looked to Ancient Egypt for its roots, there is no doubt that the splendour of the ancient Egyptian civilization has been coveted by other cultures for generations. Subjected to military depredations and marauding 'scholars', Egypt has emerged in the 20th and 21st centuries as an economically struggling, often politically unstable but culturally distinct modern nation. Its history can be traced back thousands of years in the same place and, despite its chronicle of conquests and invasions, its current population clearly holds title to the magnificence of the ancient Egyptian civilization.

Nonetheless, Ancient Egypt belongs to Africa as well (see several chapters in O'Connor and Reid 2003a). Recently the Egyptian government has acknowledged its far-flung connections with neighbours to the south in the new (and somewhat controversial) Nubia Museum at Aswan (Meskell 2001). While it may not be historically accurate for peoples of West Africa to claim Egyptian roots (Folorunso 2003), the case of Ancient Egypt should be sufficient to counter any claim that Africa has not spawned any great civilizations. Ancient Egypt has become an icon of popular culture (MacDonald and Rice 2003), and all this has led to an over-emphasis on

Egyptian history in Afrocentrist perceptions, often leading to the ignoring of ancient African civilizations, such as Meroe, Axum and Great Zimbabwe (Reid 2003). As Davidson (2001) has recently pointed out, very little is known about the mechanism of influence and cross-influence between Egypt and the rest of Africa (see O'Connor and Reid 2003a). The narratives of many non-Egyptian African societies may well deserve 'credit' either for their contribution to Egyptian culture or for their contribution to western civilization.

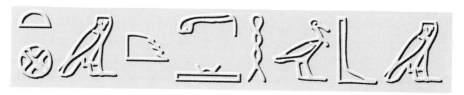

## CHAPTER 12

# FORGETTING THE *ANCIEN RÉGIME*: REPUBLICAN VALUES AND THE STUDY OF THE ANCIENT ORIENT

*David Wengrow*

The Musée Napoleon was born of three parents, republicanism, anti-clericalism and successful aggressive war.

... The Revolution had set up an idol which itself demanded the offerings that were made to it.

(Gould 1965: 13, 40)

That dead man is Old France, and that bier, the coffin of the Old Monarchy. Therein let us bury, and for ever, the dreams in which we once fondly trusted – paternal royalty, the government of grace, the clemency of the monarchy, and the charity of the priest; filial confidence, implicit belief in the gods here below.

(Michelet [1879–1880] 1967: 55)

## Introduction: the republican foundations of social thought in France

It is fascinating that Sigmund Freud, founder of modern psychoanalysis and author of *Civilization and its Discontents* (1930), chose largely Egyptian antiquities to line the shelves and cabinets of his office, which was also his consulting room (see Ucko 2001 for discussion and further references). By the early 20th century Ancient Egypt had come to symbolize many of the discontents and contradictions of Judeo-Christian, democratic, capitalist society. In this it was rivalled only by the 'primitives' of early ethnographic accounts who also fascinated Freud and, partly because of the evolutionary framework within which they were studied, feature heavily in his own theory of the development of the human psyche (e.g. Freud 1919).

Among these discontents are the repressed desire to abdicate responsibility for life to a higher authority, which satisfies both spiritual and physical needs; the desire for material rather than merely spiritual continuity after death; and the closely related desire to institute the social life of the living in some form of direct commerce with the dead (cf. Baudrillard 1993). Fustel de Coulanges (1864) speculated long ago as to how the repression of hereditary authority, and the cauterisation of its ancestral rites and institutions of dynastic rule, had provided the historical cornerstone of republican morality and rule of law. These institutions had made authority coterminous with particular forms of social relationship which through their restricted media and modes of transmission (the blood-line, the ancestral estate, etc.) were rendered the inalienable possession of a small elite. Their disappearance opened the floodgates which had stifled the flow of power between "ordinary people" and the political elite, and the Plebeians entered the 'Ancient City' of the Patricians.

Fustel de Coulanges was seeking to evoke the social conflicts at the heart of the ancient *poleis* of Greece and Rome, which his native France had sought to resolve in an entirely new way in 1789 through the violent destruction of the *Ancien Régime* to which he turned his scholarly attention in later life (Momigliano 1980: x–xi). The resemblance between that regime and the forms of government more recently described as 'archaic' or 'primitive' by anthropologists is traditionally underplayed in textbooks and popular dramatizations, but has been brought to light in studies such as Marc Bloch's (1924) *Les Rois Thaumaturges* and Ernst Kantorowicz's (1957) *The King's Two Bodies*. Anthropologist Sahlins (1985: 77) has similarly suggested that "the conception of divine kings we find in Hawaii or Fiji also happens to preside over the subterranean history of our own democracies".

The extent to which the memory of sacerdotal kingship has been eradicated from Europe's consciousness of its own social development, or replaced by a cosy nostalgia fostered through the pageant of modern monarchy, is apparent in the opening passage to Henri Frankfort's *Kingship and the Gods*: "The ancient Near East considered kingship the very basis of civilization. Only savages could live without a king. Security, peace, and justice could not prevail without a ruler to champion them ... But if we refer to kingship as a political institution, we assume a point of view which would have been incomprehensible to the ancients" (Frankfort 1948: 3). It was to the contemporary societies of Africa, rather than to Europe's own dynastic past, that Frankfort looked for guidance in understanding the functioning of ancient Egyptian and Mesopotamian forms of kingship. As Clastres (1987: 15, 205) reminds us, though, the earliest Europeans to reach Brazil considered the Tupinamba Indians savages precisely because they were "People without god, law, and king". When Frankfort (1948: x) asserted that "the achievements of the Greeks and the teachings of the Old and New Testaments" are the basis of modern Europe's alienation from the ancient Near East he was therefore presenting a partial view. As Dumont (1980) observed in his study of the Indian caste system, the Revolution had also played its part in making *Homo hierarchicus* incomprehensible to *Homo aequalis*.

The attitude of those early European explorers is now largely unrecognizable to us. The notion that genuine political participation begins where kingship and divinely sanctioned rule end has become a central feature of modern western thought, inscribed in the charters of its three great political revolutions: American, French and Russian. Despite their differences it is a common feature of these charters that any government worthy of the name must, as Giambattista Vico had already perceived, 'be conformable to the nature of the governed' rather than to that of the ruler, the cosmos, or the gods (cited in Wilson 1972: 11). The humanism of Vico's (1725) *Scienza*

*Nuova* differed profoundly from that of the 18th century Enlightenment in viewing the passage of social time as a cyclical process rather than a linear progression. The historical experience which, above all others, separated these two points of view – one essentially Medieval and the other Modern – was the French Revolution, and the rupture caused by this experience has been vividly evoked by Connerton (1989: 8–9; and see also Walzer 1974):

> The trial and execution of Louis XVI was not the murder of a ruler but the revocation of a ruling principle: the principle according to which the dynastic realm was the only imaginable political system. It had indeed been possible to envisage regicide within the terms of that system ... But whatever fate might befall individual kings, the principle of dynastic succession remained intact ... This form of regicide left the dynastic system unchallenged: the benchmarks of time were still the phases of dynastic rule. The death of the king registered a break in that public time: between one king and another time stood still.

And he goes on:

> The revolutionaries needed to find some ritual process through which the aura of inviolability surrounding kingship could be explicitly repudiated ... For thousands of years the kings of France had received at their coronation holy oil as well as the crown upon their heads, after the manner of the apostles' successors. The effect was to transform the enemies of royalty into apparently sacrilegious persons. This was the effect that the public regicide of Louis sought to undo ... The anointed head was decapitated and the rite of coronation ceremonially revoked. Not simply the natural body of the king but also and above all his political body was killed.

Revolutionary thought requires a sense of both the naturalness of its own aims, and the unnaturalness of what it seeks to overthrow. The experience of the French Revolution, and the chronic social instability and periodic relapses into old forms of authority which followed, raised urgent new questions (cf. Dumont 1980: 13–17; Giddens 1986: 11–24). How does a society function without rulers? What is the place and responsibility of the individual within the collective? Are forms of knowledge and organization based on secular principles adequate to replace the precepts of a hierocratic order? New ideas of social development were required to make the new vision of the present and future understandable as part of a natural evolution from the past.

A central theme of this chapter is that as a requirement of modernity the institution of kingship – especially in its sacerdotal forms – therefore had to be pushed to the margins of historical consciousness and rendered anomalous, exotic and moribund (cf. Ozouf 1988). This resulted, on the one hand, in the creation of a new European past rooted exclusively in an idealized image of classical antiquity, which encompassed both republican ideals and imperial ambitions (Bernal 1987; Hingley 2000). On the other it led to the construction of new and remote spaces of the imagination such as 'the Orient' (Said 1978) and 'primitive society' (Kuper 1988), incompatible with and subordinate to Europe's emerging self-image as a progressive society, onto which the collective memory of sacred kingship could be grafted. Said (1978: 42) has famously argued that "with Napoleon's occupation of Egypt processes were set in motion between East and West that still dominate our contemporary cultural and political perspectives". In discussing the themes outlined above I will attempt to situate these processes within a broader historical and cultural context, and to discuss their implications for the contemporary study of what was once habitually referred to as the ancient Orient.

## "Liberating" Egypt and exorcising the *Ancien Régime*

I have attempted to outline some of the social and ideological forces at play when Britain's growing hold on Mughal India and the eastern trade prompted Napoleon Bonaparte to invade Egypt in 1798. With the embers of the Revolution still smouldering, the chief servant of the Directory confronted the Ottoman Empire in the name of liberty and in the process encountered the ancient kings of the Nile Valley, a confrontation later visualized by artists such as Orange and Cogniet (Andreu *et al.* 1997: 19, fig. 4; Larsen 1994: 34, fig. 1). Faced with this spectacle, the general of the First Republic could not resist entombing himself briefly within the Great Pyramid. The irony was short-lived, however. It was not to a pharaonic legacy that Napoleon appealed in his victorious address to the people of Alexandria, but to an idealized Islamic past of flourishing cities and trade, free from the yoke of Mamluk tyranny. And it was with his domestic subjects, rather than the people of Egypt, in mind that Napoleon's *savants* were set to the task of documenting and appropriating the ancient monuments (Bret 1999).

The publication of the monumental *Description de l'Égypte* (1809–1828) was an event commemorated by the striking of a bronze medallion designed by J. J. Barre (Figure 12:1; Curl 1994: 132–133, fig. 81). It shows a masculine personification of Roman Gaul unveiling Ancient Egypt in the form of a suppliant woman. She holds a sistrum evoking the goddess Hathor (and hence female sexuality) whose temple at Dendera is faithfully depicted in the background, and fondles the muzzle of the crocodile upon which she reclines. While undoubtedly concerned at some level with discovery or appropriation (Larsen 1994: 36), the impression given by this allegorical

Figure 12:1   Bronze medallion commemorating the publication of *Description de l'Égypte*, 1826 (Curl 1994: 133, fig. 81).

image is also of the pacifying and feminizing of an alien power, metonymically represented by the pyramids which are visible behind the figure of Gaul.

The 'domestication' of Ancient Egypt also found expression in contemporary European fashions for interior design, instigated during the late 18th century by Giovanni Battista Piranesi's spectacular Egyptianizing fireplaces (Curl 1994: 87–97; Werner 2003). In France and Italy these fashions originated under the patronage of the *Ancien Régime* but were incorporated into bourgeois tastes during the early 19th century through the production of cabinets, clocks and more minor household articles such as teapots, which had been produced in Egyptianizing styles by Josiah Wedgwood for the mercantile middle classes of England as early as the 1770s (Curl 1994: 112–147; Humbert *et al.* 1994).

The democratizing of fine art and sculpture had commenced in France during the pre-Revolutionary period, when objects from the noble houses had first been placed on public display. In 1783 the Palais du Louvre, containing the royal collections, was opened as a public institution, the Museum Central des Arts. It subsequently became a venue for the display of an extraordinary quantity of art objects confiscated by Bonaparte's forces following their successful campaigns in Belgium (1794) and Italy (1796–1799) and was renamed the Musée Napoleon in 1803 (Gould 1965). In a letter to Bonaparte the Commissioner of Art, André Thouin, expressed his view that "the French spoliation of Italy was the reward of military virtue over decadence and that it was strictly comparable with what the Greeks are supposed to have done to the Egyptians and the Romans in their turn to the Greeks" (Gould 1965: 65).

Against this highly politicized background the display of Egyptian antiquities in the Musée Napoleon took on a particular social significance. A section of the museum devoted specifically to Ancient Egypt was first opened by Champollion in 1826 under the restored monarchy of Charles X, occupying the former chambers of the French queens (see Andreu *et al.* 1997; Humbert 1997). The extraordinary preservation of elite burials in the *salle funéraire* meant that any citizen could stand face-to-face with royalty and measure their own being against the exposed figure of a divine king, while at the same time measuring the human size of the latter against that of his boastful monuments. What was on display here was not merely the fantastic 'otherness' of Oriental civilization (cf. Mitchell 1991) but also the very embodiment of dynastic rule, displaced onto the inscrutable remains of an ancient culture and located safely behind the threshold of modernity. The guillotine had given way to the intrusive public gaze as a means of unveiling and laying to rest the ghost of monarchy (see, in this context, 19th century tableaux showing visitors to the Egyptian galleries; e.g. Andreu *et al.* 1997: 22–23, figs. 5–6). In this sense the museum anticipated in concrete form the grand themes of Michelet's (1879–1880) *Histoire de la Révolution Française*:

Another thing which this History will clearly establish and holds true in every connection, is that the people were usually more important than the leaders. The deeper I have excavated, the more surely I have satisfied myself that the best was underneath, in the obscure depths ... To find the people again and put it back in its proper role, I have been obliged to reduce to their proportions the ambitious marionettes whose strings it manipulated and in whom hitherto we have looked for and thought to see the secret play of history.

(Michelet in Wilson 1972: 24)

## The Renaissance background

Returning for a moment to the medallion commemorating the *Description* (Figure 12: 1) we also find an allusion to the image of the goddess Isis-Athena at Sais, described by Plutarch during the first century AD in his *De Iside et Osiride*. During the Renaissance, and on the basis of Plutarch's account, "the concept of the veiled figure of the goddess whom it is death to uncover became a frequent metaphor of revealed wisdom" (Whitehouse 1995: 20). At the heart of this Renaissance concept was a particular, pre-Revolutionary notion of the relationship between knowledge, art and power, in opposition to which the motif of 'unveiling Egypt' seems best understood. This earlier notion may be briefly explored by considering Gianlorenzo Bernini's 'Fountain of the Four Rivers', commissioned by Pope Innocent X as a foundation setting for the Egyptian obelisk he erected in the Piazza Navona in 1652, two years after its scheduled date of completion in the Holy Year 1650 (Curl 1994: 74; Hassan Chapter 2: Figure 2:25, this volume).

Schama (1995: 293) places Bernini's monument in its political context, noting that "in the age of sacred hydraulics, the way in which a papal dynasty effectively colonised a Roman piazza was by creating a new fountain". Innocent X had previously had the hieroglyphs on his obelisk studied by Athanasius Kircher, "an unreconstructed neo-Platonist obsessed with hieroglyphs as an allegorical and esoteric crypt" (Schama 1995: 300; cf. Curran 2003; Hassan Chapter 2, this volume; Iversen 1961: 89 ff). Bernini's sculpted setting for the obelisk expresses an appropriately holistic and mystical cosmology, framing it within four personified male figures of river-deities symbolising the Nile, Danube, Ganges, and Río de la Plata (Hassan Chapter 2, this volume: Figures 2:23, 2:25). The head of 'Nile' alone is shown veiled, suggesting its unknown source and reflecting the contemporary perception of Egypt as a locus of hidden knowledge. The top of the obelisk is crowned by a dove holding an olive branch and symbolizing both the Pamphili dynasty of Innocent X and the Holy Ghost (Schama 1995: 298).

Other dynasts, including Pope Alexander VI, claimed a more direct Egyptian ancestry by commissioning scholars to trace their family line back, via the Classical sources, to the mythical figure of Osiris (Iversen 1971: 183). This practice reached the western fringes of Renaissance culture where it was translated, none too subtly, into an early form of national agenda (Kendrick 1950: 65–72). Hector Boece's *Scotorum Historia*, published in 1527, revived a belief that his native Scotland has been named after Scota, daughter of the 'Pharaoh of the Oppression' and wife of a Greek prince. (He also claimed that King Arthur had died on the shores of the Humber, having promised Britain to the royal house of the Picts.) The English rebuttal came in the *Scriptorium Illustrium Majoris Britanniae* compiled by John Bale, Bishop of Ossory, and containing – in a second, expanded edition published in 1557 – a remarkable genealogy (Figure 12:2).

In his bold act of revelation, then, the figure of Gaul challenges not only the mystique of Egypt as a source of origin but also the very cultural basis of an old elite which, in republican eyes, had founded its authority upon an esoteric and unenlightened worldview. His gesture forms a symbolic counterpart to the physical transplantation of fine paintings and sculpture from the Italian heart of the Renaissance to the halls of the Musée Napoleon, shattering the 'art nexus' (Gell 1998)

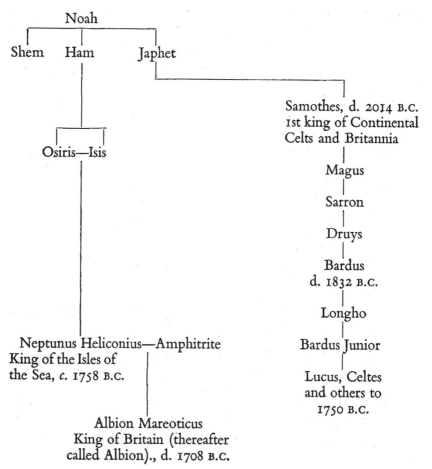

Figure 12:2   The origin of Britain according to John Bale, Bishop of Ossory (d. 1563) (after Kendrick 1950: 68).

which since the beginning of the Christian era had bound such objects and their associated meanings exclusively to the Church and the nobility (cf. Gould 1965: 13).

Another aspect of this transformation was the deconstruction of Egypt's special status as a source of high culture and wisdom (Ucko and Champion 2003), which had been cultivated by European elites since the 15th century, and its incorporation into what Whitehouse (1995: 16) has termed a "generalised oriental sphere" extending from China to the Mediterranean (cf. Said 1978: 42). The novelty of this view is highlighted by a consideration of the marked difference in Renaissance attitudes towards Egypt and the Near East. As Lundquist (1995: 67) points out, there had "never been a 'Babyloniamania' in western art, literature, architecture, or design to rival Egypt's hold on pre-modern Europe". This was due in large measure to the invisibility of Assyrian and Babylonian monuments prior to the beginning of large-scale tell excavations during the mid-19th century, as well as the local re-use of mud-brick over the centuries (Lundquist 1995: 67; and see Larsen 1996). It also reflected negative perceptions of the Near East conveyed to Renaissance scholars by their classical and biblical sources, the former crystallized in the Athenian response to the Great Persian War and the latter portraying Babylon as a site of urban corruption, idolatry and hubris (cf. McIntosh 1999). This biblical image was evoked in numerous depictions of Nimrod overseeing construction of the 'Tower of Babel', the most famous being the 1563 version by Pieter Brueghel the Elder (Klengel-Brandt 1982: 11, pl. ii).[1]

It is perhaps in this remote space of the Renaissance imagination that we find the germ of those attitudes characterized by Said as 'Orientalist', and only later extended to Egypt (cf. Lundquist 1995: 77). Such a view cannot be accepted uncritically, however. During the 16th century, negative images of the ancient Near East also resonated with contemporary rivalries between the ruling houses of Europe and the vast Ottoman Empire. The value attached to symbols of antiquity in this rivalry has been articulated through a study of the circulation of art objects between the Hapsburg and Ottoman elites (Jardine and Brotton 2000). The movement of artists, tapestries, medallions, horses, and other luxuries between courtly centres of Europe and the Orient reveals, not a distant perception of the exotic eastern 'Other', but a shared set of values within which dynastic rulers jostled for prestige: "East and West fixed each other with an equal, reciprocal gaze [which] was intensified and revised in the subsequent contests for power and legitimation that defined the escalation in inter-imperial confrontation in the course of the sixteenth century" (Jardine and Brotton 2000: 63). The common desire of Charles V and Süleyman the Magnificent to inhabit the image of Alexander the Great through the commissioning of art objects is particularly striking in highlighting the contests of power through which Europe took stock of its present cultural inventory (Figure 12:3).

In the ideological aftermath of the French Revolution the parameters within which material remains of earlier hierarchies, including those of the ancient East, were reconstituted and understood in Europe and America were profoundly altered (cf. Hughes 1995). No longer simply pawns in an ongoing game of dynastic one-upmanship, they now began to take up their new and often more paradoxical places in a self-consciously Occidental discourse of universal progress.[2] The transition is anticipated in a statement that concludes the entry for 'Egypt' in Diderot's *Dictionnaire Raisonné des Sciences, des Arts et des Métiers*, which appeared in 1751: "It was once a country to be admired; nowadays it is one to be studied" (cited in Gillispie 1987: 4; cf. Laurens 1999).

## *From Tribe to Empire*: reconciling the ancient orient with progress

When Georges Davy, a member of Emile Durkheim's inner intellectual circle, and the renowned Egyptologist Alexandre Moret decided to write a book together in the 1920s, they could have had little sense of its future impact – albeit largely indirect – on the development of archaeological thought. The result, which they called *From Tribe to Empire*, adding the subtitle 'social organization among Primitives and in the Ancient Near East' (Moret and Davy 1926), is an unintended monument to the conceptual gulf which, during the course of the 19th century, had come to separate the sociological study of human development from the older narrative history of kings, migrations and military clashes (Champion Chapter 8, this volume). It was not without diffidence

Figure 12:3   Detail from Pieter Coecke van Aelst's woodcut of 1533, 'Procession of Sultan Süleyman II through the Atmedan'. Note obelisk, top left (after Jardine and Brotton 2000: 151, fig. 62).

that the authors brought the monumental remains of ancient Egypt and Mesopotamia into a direct confrontation with the intellectual values of liberal, bourgeois republicanism:

> Why does this book, which is a history book and takes Egypt and the Ancient East for its subject, open with an introduction which is sociological and the scope of which extends far beyond Egypt and seems to embrace primitive institutions in general? ... Is it ... in the expectation of providing History with that absolute beginning which History

itself fails to offer us? ... however deep might be the interest of such an attempt, our contribution ... has more modest aims. It merely proposes to introduce the reader to an appreciation of the problems which the earliest history of Egypt and the Orient inevitably raises, being yet not committed to solve them.

(Moret and Davy 1926: 2)

What, then, were these profound evolutionary problems posed by the ancient East? They may be condensed into a single institution: kingship.

Based upon ethnographic accounts of native Australians, Africans and Americans, and heavily influenced by the work of Frazer, Maine, McLennan, Tylor, Morgan, Robertson Smith and Boas (see Kuper 1988), the scholars of the *Année Sociologique* had accepted a new point of origin for the development of human political institutions: the totemic clan. The clan was 'communistic' and 'democratic' but contained no true individuals. Its unity and egalitarianism derived rather from the common participation of all members in the religious essence of a unifying symbol, the totem. Consequently the early evolution of political institutions was merged with that of mythology and spiritual beliefs. The process by which hierarchy had emerged from undifferentiated unity had also involved issues of territorial rights, rules of property and inheritance, ritualized economic competition (the *potlach*) and gender ('the masculinization of kinship and authority'). At its core, however, was the theme of individualization, the absorption and embodiment of totemic force within a single person – the chief – whose power resided in his claim: "Le clan, c'est moi" (Moret and Davy 1926: 85).

It is not hard with hindsight to see from whence this scheme derived, and where it was leading. Individual authority, in its essential form, is nothing other than the transfigured spirit of the collective. Durkheim had been right: despotism, "at least when it is not a pathological or degeneration phenomenon, is nothing but a transformed communism" (Moret and Davy 1926: 111). It follows that in its pathological form despotism is tantamount to usurpation; a failure on the part of the ruler to perceive that his authority rests ultimately upon the will of his subjects. It will be clear by now that the primitive clan *was*, in fact, a charter of origin for republican society: the 'beginning' which conventional history had failed to offer. Behind the triumphal conclusion to Davy's contribution in *From Tribe to Empire*, we can still hear distant echoes of the Bastille falling:

This conclusion is just; for nothing comes out of nothing – Pharaoh's absolute kingship no more than any common-place natural product; and that is one of the first maxims we have laid down in these pages. Sovereignty has a "matter," and it cannot be created by a mere fiat of the sovereign's will. Such a will is, then, in this sense only a secondary cause. But history, *down to its latest self-revelation*, stands as a witness to warn us that a secondary cause is not necessarily an ineffectual cause, and that according as it assume this figure or that it can modify surprisingly the "form" of the "matter" in which it works.

(Moret and Davy 1926: 112, emphasis added)

The translator of *From Tribe to Empire*, and so of this oddly rendered passage, was V. Gordon Childe, and the rest as they say is 'what happened in history' (see Childe 1936; 1942; Champion Chapter 8, this volume; Rowlands 1994; Sherratt 1997: 64, "The writing of prehistory is still a dialogue with the ghost of Childe"). More deeply entrenched in Marx than his French contemporaries, Childe perceived technology rather than collective consciousness to be the 'matter' of which both despotic and free societies are made. But while technological capacity in itself is mere 'capital', so for Childe it was the "qualities of energy, independence, and inventiveness which distinguish the western world from Egypt, India or China" that transformed it into the instrument of liberty and progress (Childe 1925: xiii–xv).

## Contemporary archaeology and the idea of the Orient

As Trigger (1979) perceived, the problem of kingship remained a root cause of Egypt's isolation from the social sciences during the late 20th century (see also Lustig 1997). Once a cornerstone of social evolutionary thought, in the tradition set down by Frazer (1890) and Hocart (1927), kingship was marginalized from the neo-evolutionary theory of the 1960s–1980s which chose instead to ponder the transitions from 'tribe' to 'chiefdom' and from 'chiefdom' to 'archaic state'. Forms of status as diverse as 'warrior chief' and 'ritual leader' were subsumed within a single category, and a common criticism of the 'chiefdom' has since been that it spans too broad a range of social variation (e.g. Kristiansen 1998; Yoffee 1993).

At around the same time the anthropology of divine kingship took a semiological turn, inspired by Dumézil's analyses of Indo-European mythology and the structural anthropology of Lévi-Strauss (both grounded in comparative linguistics), and exemplified in de Heusch's (1972) study of Bantu myth and Sahlins's (1985) work on Oceania. There is no inherent reason why the study of Ancient Egypt or Mesopotamia should have been excluded from this theoretical enterprise, and many of its central concerns were anticipated in the work of Henri Frankfort (1948) which, as Trigger notes, attempted to discern the consistent patterns of mythical thought and symbolic practice underlying the different forms of kingship in these two regions (Trigger 1979: 32; cf. Wengrow 1999: 603 ff).

A notable attempt to break out of this self-imposed disciplinary isolation, which has already provoked ample secondary discussion (e.g. Rowlands 1989: 33–34; Larsen 1994: 29–33), is the debate involving K. C. Chang, G. Willey, K. Lamberg-Karlovsky and others published in the 1985 edition of *Symbols*, the journal of the Peabody Museum. These scholars broadly agreed that the Western attainment of technological progress, rational bureaucracy and secular political thought are rooted in the constitutional fabric of the ancient Mesopotamian city-state. They argued that its genesis during the fourth millennium BC represented a unique departure from a universal pattern of experience found in the other early civilizations of the Old and New Worlds, such as those of China, the Maya and Egypt. There political and economic life remained embedded within distinct cosmological systems that encouraged conformity to a pre-determined order encompassing both the human and non-human domains, and centred upon the mediation between kingship and divinity. By contrast, Mesopotamian civilization developed a cultural ethic based upon the conquering of nature by technological means, which was transmitted to modern Europe via ancient Greece and Rome, and upon which the values of individual freedom and rule of law are founded (Lamberg-Karlovsky 1985).

Quite apart from their obliteration of "Occidental despotism" from the historical record and their unusual interpretation of Mesopotamian kingship and cosmology, these accounts do not appear to consider whether concepts such as 'freedom' and 'progress' might themselves be "strategies of legitimation of a social order vis-à-vis the natural order" (Kus 1982: 53; cf. Pfaffenberger 1988). This was elegantly expressed in a Marxian vein by the anthropologist Franz Steiner in his 1944 essay, 'On the process of civilization':

> We have dropped the idea of measuring our powers with nature, as this is simply an allegory with the help of which predatory social elites transfigure the beliefs appropriate to their own technology. There is no such thing as the powers of nature on the one hand, those of 'the human being' on the other, an ensuing struggle, a growth of human powers, and finally a defeat of nature. That is simply the trite myth of capitalism.
>
> (Steiner, reproduced in Adler and Fardon 1999: 125)

The primary dissenter in the *Symbols* debate was a Professor of Latin who asserted that "the origin of the democratic concept of society did not reach Greece from contact with the Near East or Mesopotamia, where equity and justice were a gift of the ruler, not the right of the ruled, but stemmed from an Indo-European concept of social organization" (Hammond, cited in Larsen 1994: 33). The retention of this point of view among some classicists and ancient historians creates a problem for archaeologists seeking to respond constructively to Said's (1978) critique of 'Orientalism'. Such responses often take the form of a call for the deconstruction of historical narratives which value the study of the ancient East only in so far as it contributed to 'the rise of the West', a view symbolized on the relief which adorns the entrance to the Oriental Institute in Chicago (Larsen 1989, 1994; see also Bahrani 1998; Kohl 1989). Bahrani (1998: 163), for instance, regrets that "Countless texts from the Western historical tradition describe how civilisation was passed from the Near East through Greece and Rome to the modern West and this is hardly a point of contention any longer". But if so, then why has Bernal's (1987) *Black Athena*, a book which claims that Greco-Roman civilization had strong Near Eastern and Egyptian roots, generated such heated and lengthy controversy (e.g. Bernal 2001, 2003; Lefkowitz and Rogers 1996; North 2003)? There is an irony here. While archaeologists working in the core areas of "the Orient" are increasingly distancing themselves from eurocentric notions of progress in order to consider other pasts, many of those working in the Mediterranean region are still fighting a battle to prove how important oriental influences were in the formation of classical civilization. This latter enterprise has also taken a strange turn of late, which is worth exploring in the present context.

## Debating oriental influence in the ancient Mediterranean

The term 'orientalizing' has a confused history in the study of the ancient Mediterranean. It was introduced by art historians with reference to the appearance of objects, imagery, and techniques of Near Eastern or Egyptian derivation on the Greek mainland from the eighth to the sixth centuries BC, prior to the formation of classical culture (e.g. Poulsen 1912). These included figural images of real and fantastic animals, new skills in casting metal and clay figures, and unprecedented forms of monumental stone sculpture and architecture (Boardman 1964). In the 'pre-Said' era their impact upon Greek development was typically described in terms of a Hegelian opposition between the "spirits" of East and West, contrasting the active, self-conscious transformation of received knowledge by the Greeks with the 'banal', 'repetitive', 'stereotyped' products of the native Orient (e.g. Boardman 1973: 19–107, *passim*; and cf. Morris 1989: 41). In this sense the Orient has often served as the false conscience of global capital and 'coca-colonization', as well as of western political experience. It is particularly ironic that the desire of modern Greeks to 'occidentalize' through the consumption of mass-produced 'Americanalia' is perceived by Americans and northern Europeans as a betrayal of "traditional" Greek values (Herzfeld 1995).

More recently the concept of 'orientalizing' has been extended from the history of artefactual styles to a wider series of social and intellectual transformations in ancient Greece, including the inception of the aristocratic symposion, the introduction of the alphabet, and the encoding of a divine pantheon and body of myth (e.g. Burkert 1992; Murray [1978] 1993: 81–101). This coincided with the proposed restriction of orientalizing influences to a discrete chronological period (ca. 750–650 BC), a view which has since been subject to a sustained critique by Sarah Morris (1992). She marshals a wide range of evidence for oriental influences in the Aegean extending continuously from the late second millennium BC (Late Bronze Age) into the first millennium BC (Iron Age). To prehistorians who have traced the westward spread of Near Eastern innovations back into neolithic times this comes as no great surprise, but Morris' case is directed principally at scholars of classical antiquity.

The relationship between the concept of 'orientalization' and the discourse defined by Said as "orientalism" therefore seems best understood as one of opposition, the former referring to processes of concrete cultural interaction and the latter to the fashioning of a self-image predicated upon distance from an exotic 'Other'. What is less easily agreed upon is whether and (if so) how often there have been transitions from orientalization to orientalism (or vice versa) in Europe. To pose the question in this way might itself be viewed as an 'orientalist' conceit, introducing binary oppositions and false notions of cultural authenticity into what has always been a shifting constellation of identities spanning east and west (cf. Van Dommelen 1998). Orientalization and orientalism, today as in antiquity, may necessarily coexist (consider the highly successful use of traditional orientalist stereotypes in marketing Indian, Chinese and Middle Eastern food to western consumers). Nevertheless, the question has been posed and answered by a number of scholars. Said himself (1978: 55–73), in defining the scope of orientalism, cites Homer and Aeschylus as precursors to Flaubert and Nerval, implying a continuity of approach from Greco-Roman times to the present. More recently, Morris has argued explicitly that modern European attitudes to the Orient were prefigured in the Athenian response to the Persian Wars, which led Greeks to shun and stigmatize their own eastern heritage. This constitutes a significant revision of Martin Bernal's (1987) argument that the purging of oriental influence from Greek historiography is a consequence of modern European chauvinism: "Bernal's 'Aryan Model' began in the 5th century [BC], after the Persian Wars, and *not* in modern Europe, such that the object of study – classical culture – had already determined the mode of approach, long before the 18th century [AD]" (Morris 1992: xxii, cf. 1989: 40–41). Comparably, in the conclusion to his *Early Greece*, Oswyn Murray (1993: 301) writes, "The Persian Wars opened a new epoch. But they also closed an old one. Greek culture had been created from the fruitful interchange between east and west; that debt was now forgotten. An iron curtain had descended: east against west, despotism against liberty – the dichotomies created in the Persian Wars echo through world history ...".

Bernal and Morris also differ substantially in their reconstructions of the nature of oriental influence on Greece during the Bronze and Iron Ages. Little importance has been attached to these differences owing to the unsubstantiated character of many of Bernal's claims regarding ancient migrations into the Aegean and linguistic parallels between Egypt and Greece (see the commentaries in Lefkowitz and Rogers 1996). His strong emphasis upon Egypt as a source of Greek culture, which contrasts with Morris' focus on Levantine sources (for which he berates her; Bernal 2001: 300–305) is nevertheless of interest, because it stems from motives unrelated to his professional competence as a philologist or archaeologist. It is in fact intended to re-establish the validity of what he calls the "Ancient Model", the positive view which the ancient Greeks themselves held of their cultural debt to Egypt (Bernal 1987: 75–188).

The evidence for this view has recently been reconsidered by Bowman (forthcoming) who identifies five main strands to Greek perceptions of Egypt, all of which find parallels in modern western perceptions: Egypt as "the romanticised or idealised setting for ancient fiction", "the prime source of ancient wisdom and ritual", "a repository of ancient culture", a source of anthropological and ecological fascination, and a subject of historical study. As Momigliano (1975: 2–3) pointed out, it was natural, in the aftermath of the Persian Wars, that Greek attitudes towards Egypt should differ markedly from their perception of the Near East. Egypt was never treated by the Greeks as a political power, but rather as a repository of unusual knowledge. The Persian Empire was another story altogether: "it had ruled over Greeks".

We have therefore arrived at a paradox. In attempting to resurrect the "Ancient Model" Bernal has fallen prey to an ancient Greek prejudice, borne to us on Renaissance wings, which stigmatized the Near East but valourized many aspects of Egypt. Equally, in claiming an ancient precedent for Bernal's "Aryan Model" (and also for Said's "Orientalism"), Morris fails to problematize Europe's recent construction of its own special and exclusive relationship with classical civilization, which Bernal (1987) has documented as the "fabrication of ancient Greece, 1785–1985", and which she elsewhere concurs with (Morris 1989: 40–41). The final mystery is that Bernal (1989: 22, 2001: 296–298) appears to consider his lack of attention to the classical roots of modern European chauvinism a failure; as though the historical identification of modern Europe with ancient Greece was real rather than constructed. The recriminations of the Persian Wars may be "echoing down the corridors of time". But it is no longer clear who exactly is supposed to be listening.

## Conclusion

The contradictions and paradoxes implicit in the Napoleonic encounter with Ancient Egypt remain with us, in the uneasy coexistence of Egyptology with a strong public desire to retain a source of mystery, sensuous experience and self-knowledge (cf. MacDonald and Rice 2003; Roth 1998). They are also manifest in the ambiguous place which Egyptology itself continues to occupy between the humanities and the social sciences. The name given to the study of Egypt (like Assyri-*ology* and anthrop-*ology*) distinguishes it from that of Greco-Roman civilization (Bowman forthcoming) and incorporates it into a field of knowledge conceived as the scientific study of the 'other', but often practised as the humanistic search for 'self'.

In discussing the relationship between republican values and the study of the ancient orient I have also attempted to highlight the extent to which modern, western identity as a whole is anchored in the images and material remains of remote times and places. In Hollywood films, novels and fringe literature on the origins of extinct civilizations, western societies are still confronting fears about their own origins which manifest themselves as possessive demons, vampires, or other supernatural beings occupying the spaces between bourgeois consciousness and the ancient (and sometimes modern) East (MacDonald and Rice 2003). A common structural element within many of these narratives, from Bram Stoker's *Dracula* to William Blatty's *The Exorcist*, is the invasion of the western body by pathological forces from a hierocratic, dynastic past. Dumézil (at least in Sahlins's 1985: 73ff reading of him) might have argued for a deep Indo-European origin to the popularity of these stories, but undoubtedly they also express basic insecurities about the condition of modernity, and the integrity of 'the West'.

## Notes

1   The Renaissance portrayal of the building of the 'Tower of Babel', showing construction workers cowering before the magisterial figure of the king and pleading for respite, is a fascinating inversion of how ancient Mesopotamian rulers actually portrayed themselves (something unknown of course to Renaissance artists). In commemorative art and inscriptions the rulers of ancient Babylonia and Assyria are represented as the chief physical participants in the process of constructing monumental buildings, which constituted a basic act of royal mediation between humanity and divine will (e.g. Suter 2000). The gods are nowhere to be seen in the bright blue skies above Brueghel's tower.

2   Gillispie (1987: 4) suggests that the Marquis de Condorcet was "the first leader of opinion to use the term 'Occident', the West, in its modern sense, connoting the combination of cultural family with civilized norm".

## Acknowledgments

Parts of this chapter were presented at a symposium on 'Approaching orientalisation in antiquity' held at St John's College, Oxford in September 2002. I am grateful to Corinna Riva and Nick Vella for the invitation to participate. Much of the research was conducted during my time as Frankfort Fellow at the Warburg Institute, for which I thank its staff and members. Alan Bowman and Eleanor Robson also provided valuable references.

# References

Note: references to chapters and books in the *Encounters with Ancient Egypt* series are denoted in bold type.

Abbasi, A. B. el [1814] 1943, *Viajes por África y Asia*. Barcelona: Olimpo

Abd Alrazek, M., N. Abd Alsami'h and N. Sharobim 1984, Ramsses II Obelisk at Cairo Airport. *Alam Alathar* 5, 4–7

Acosta, J. de 1590, *Historia natural y moral de las Indias*. Seville: J. de Leon

Adalian, R. 1980, The Armenian Colony of Egypt During the Reign of Muhammad Ali (1805–1848). *The Armenian Review* 33, 115–144

Adams, W. Y. 1984, Science and Ethics in Rescue Archaeology, in R. Holthoer and T. Linders (eds), *Sundries in Honour of Torgny Säve-Söderbergh*, 9–15. Uppsala: Uppsala Universiteit

Adler, J. and R. Fardon 1999, *Orientpolitik, Value, and Civilization. Franz Baermann Steiner, Selected Writings,Vol. 2*, New York and Oxford: Berghahn

Altick, R. 1978, *The Shows of London*. Cambridge, Mass: Harvard UP

Amador de los Ríos, J. 1862, Algunas Consideraciones sobre la Estatuaria durante la Monarquía Visigoda. *El Arte en España* I, Madrid

Anderson, R. 1987, Introduction, in R. Anderson and I. Fawzy, *Egypt in 1800, Scenes of Napoleon's Description of Egypt*, 7–8. London: Barry and Jenkins

Anderson, R. and I. Fawzi 1987, *Egypt in 1800: Scenes from Napoleon's Description de l'Égypte*. Cairo: American University in Cairo

Andrés Espala, G. 1870, *Del Manzanares al Nilo y el Jordán*. Madrid: Diego Valero

Andreu, E., M-H. Rutschowscaya and C. Ziegler 1997, *L'Égypte ancienne au Louvre*. Paris: Hachette

Andreu, G. 1997, *Egypt in the Age of the Pyramids*. London: Murray

Arthur, G. 1932, *General Sir John Maxwell*. London: John Murray

Asprey, R. B. 2000, *The Rise and Fall of Napoleon Bonaparte. I: The Rise*. London: Little, Brown

Bagnall, R. S. 1993, *Egypt in Late Antiquity*. Princeton: Princeton UP

Bagnall, R. S. 2000, Egyptian Agriculture in Historical Perspective. *Journal of Roman Archaeology* 13, 707–711

Bahrani, Z. 1998, *Conjuring Mesopotamia: Imaginative Geography and a World Past*, in L. Meskell (ed.), *Archaeology Under Fire: Nationalism, Politics and Heritage in the Eastern Mediterranean and the Middle East*, 159–174. London: Routledge

Baines, J. and N. Yoffee 1998, Order, Legitimacy and Wealth in Ancient Egypt and Mesopotamia, in G. M. Feinman and J. Marcus (eds), *Archaic States: A Comparative Perspective*, 199–260. Santa Fè, New Mexico: School of American Research

**Bakos, M. M. 2003, Egyptianizing Motifs in Architecture and Art in Brazil, in J-M. Humbert and C. Price (eds), *Imhotep Today: Egyptianizing architecture*, 231–246. London: UCL Press**

Baldasano y Topete, A. 1870, *De la puerta del sol a las pirámides: viaje al istmo con escala en Jerusalén*. Madrid: T. Fortanet

Ball, J. 1932, The 'Description de l'Égypte' and the Course of the Nile between Isna and Girga. *Bulletin de l'Institut d'Égypte* 14, 127–139

Banaji, J. 1997, Modernizing the Historiography of Rural Labour: An Unwritten Agenda, in M. Bentley (ed.), *Companion to Historiography*, 88–102. London: Routledge

Banaji, J. 2002, *Agrarian Change in Late Antiquity*. Oxford: OUP

Baquedano, E. 1993, William Bullock viajero, coleccionista y museografo del siglo XIX, in A. Garritz (ed.), *Un hombre entre Europa y América. Homenaje a Juan Antonio Ortega y Medina*, 353–360. Mexico: UNAM

Baudrillard, J. 1993, *Symbolic Exchange and Death*. London: Sage

Bauval, R. and A. Gilbert 1994, *The Orion Mystery: Unlocking the Secrets of the Pyramids*. London: Heinemann

Bayly, C. A. 2002, Representing Copts and Muhammedans: Empire, Nation and Community in Egypt and India, 1880–1914, in L. T. Fawaz and C. A. Bayly (eds), *Modernity and Culture: From the Mediterranean to the Indian Ocean*, 158–203. New York: Columbia UP

Beard, M. and J. Henderson 1999, Rule(d) Britannia: Displaying Roman Britain in the Museum, in N. Merriman (ed.), *Making Early Histories in Museums*, 44–72. Leicester: Leicester UP

Bell, I. 1922, Hellenistic Culture in Egypt. *Journal of Egyptian Archaeology* 8, 139–155

Belzoni, G. B. 1821, *Voyages en Egypte et en Nubie*. Paris: Atlas, Libraire Française et Étrangère

Belzoni, S. 1821, *Fruit of Enterprise Exhibited in the Travels of Belzoni in Egypt and Nubia: Interspersed with the Observations of a Mother to her Children*. London: Harris and Son

Bernal, I. 1980, *History of Mexican Archaeology*. New York: Thames and Hudson

Bernal, M. 1987, *Black Athena: The Afroasiatic Roots of Classical Civilization. Vol. 1, The Fabrication of Ancient Greece, 1785–1985*. London: Free Association Press

Bernal, M. 1991, *Black Athena: The Afroasiatic Roots of Classical Civilization. Vol. 2, The Archaeological and Documentary Evidence*. London: Free Assocation Press

Bernal, M. 1994, The Image of Ancient Greece as a Tool for Colonialism and European Hegemony, in G. C. Bond and A. Gilliam (eds), *The Social Construction of the Past: Representations as Power*, 119–128. London: Routledge

Bernal, M. 2001, *Black Athena Writes Back: Martin Bernal Responds to his Critics*. Durham, NC: Duke UP

**Bernal, M. 2003, Afrocentrism and Historical Models for the Foundation of Ancient Greece, in D. O'Connor and A. Reid (eds), *Ancient Egypt in Africa*, 23–30. London: UCL Press**

Bierbrier, M. L. 1983, The Salt Watercolours. *Göttinger Miszellen* 61, 9–12

Bierbrier, M. L. 1999, The Acquisition by the British Museum of Antiquities Discovered during the French Invasion of Egypt, in W. V. Davies (ed.), *Studies in Egyptian Antiquities. A Tribute to T. G. H. James*, 111–113, Occasional Paper 123. London: British Museum Press

Bietak, M. 1979a, Urban Archaeology and the 'Town Problem', in K. Weeks (ed.), *Egyptology and the Social Sciences*, 97–144. Cairo: American University in Cairo

Bietak, M. 1979b, The Present State of Egyptian Archaeology. *Journal of Egyptian Archaeology* 65, 156–160

Bingen, J. 1978, *Le Papyrus revenue-laws. Tradition Grecque et adaptation hellénistique*. Opladen: Westdeutscher

Blackman, W. S. 1927, *The Fellahin of Upper Egypt*. London: Harrap

Blackman, W. S. [1927] 2000, *The Fellahin of Upper Egypt. With a new foreword by Salima Ikram*. Cairo: American University in Cairo

Bloch, M. 1924, *Les Rois Thaumaturges: étude sur le caractère surnaturel attribué à la puissance royale particulièrement en France et en Angleterre*. Oxford: OUP

Bloch, M. 1987, The Ritual of the Royal Bath in Madagascar: the Dissolution of Death, Birth and Fertility into Authority, in D. Cannadine and S. Price (eds), *Rituals of Royalty: Power and Ceremonial in Traditional Societies*, 271–297. Cambridge: CUP

Blunt, W. 1908, Review of Lord Cromer's Modern Egypt. *The Egyptian Standard*, 14 March, 84–85 (reprinted from the *London Evening News*)

Boardman, J. 1964, *The Greeks Overseas*. Harmondsworth: Penguin

Boardman, J. 1973, *Greek Art*. London: Thames and Hudson

Bosworth, C. E. 1974, Henry Salt, Consul in Egypt 1816–1827 and Pioneer Egyptologist. *Bulletin of the John Rylands University Library of Manchester* 57, 69–91

Bourbon, F. 1996, *Egypt Yesterday and Today. Lithographs by David Roberts.* New York: Stewart, Tabori & Chang

Bourbon, F. 1999, *The Lost Cities of The Maya. The Life, Art and Discoveries of Frederick Catherwood.* London: Swanhill

Bowman, A. forthcoming, Recolonising Egypt, in T. P. Wiseman (ed.), *Classics in Progress.* London: British Academy

Bowman, A. K. and E. Rogan (eds) 1999, *Agriculture in Egypt: from Pharaonic to Modern Times.* Oxford: OUP

Brasseur-Capart, A-M. and A. Brasseur-Capart 1974, *Jean Capart, ou le rêve comblé de l'Egyptologie.* Brussels: Editions Arts et Voyages

Braun, B. 1993, *Pre-Columbian Art and Post-Columbian World. Ancient American Sources of Modern Art.* New York: Harry Abrams

Bret, P. 1999, *L'éxpedition d'Égypte: une entreprise des lumières, 1798–1801.* Paris: Technique et Documentation

Brewster, P. G. 1960, The Egyptian Game Khazza Lawizza and its Burmese Counterparts. *Zeitschrift fur Ethnologie* 85, 211–213

Brier, B. 1992, *Egyptomania.* New York: Hillword Art Museum

Brown, K. 1994, Seeing Stars: Character and Identity in the Landscapes of Modern Macedonia. *Antiquity* 68, 784–796

Brown, K.1998, Contests of Heritage and the Politics of Preservation in the Former Yugoslav Republic of Macedonia, in L. Meskell (ed.), *Archaeology Under Fire: Nationalism, Politics and Heritage in the Eastern Mediterranean and Middle East,* 1–12. London: Routledge

Bruce, J. 1813, *Travels to Discover the Source of the Nile.* Edinburgh: Blackwood

Budge, E. A. W. 1920, *By Nile and Tigris. A Narrative of Journeys in Egypt and Mesopotamia on Behalf of the British Museum between the Years 1886 and 1913.* London: John Murray

Bullock, W. 1814, *A Descriptive Catalogue of the Different Subjects Represented in the Large Water Colour Drawings, by Chevalier de Barde, now Exhibiting at Mr Bullock's Museum, The Egyptian Hall, Piccadilly. London.* London: James Bullock

Bullock, W. 1816a, *Narrative of Jean Horne, Military Coachman to Napoleon Bonaparte.* London: London Museum

Bullock, W. 1816b, *A Companion to Mr Bullock's London Museum and Pantherion, Containing a Brief Description of Upwards of Fifteenth Thousand Natural and Foreign Antiquities and Productions of Fine Arts, now Open for Public Inspection in the Egyptian Temple Piccadilly. London.* London: James Bullock

Bullock, W. 1824a, *Six Months' Residence and Travels in Mexico.* London: James Bullock

Bullock, W. 1824b, *A Description of the Unique Exhibition, Called Ancient Mexico.* London: James Bullock

Bullock, W. 1824c, *Catalogue of the Exhibition called Modern Mexico, containing a Panoramic View of the City with Specimens of the Natural History of New Spain and Models of the Vegetable Produce, Costume andc., andc., Now Open for Public Inspection in the Egyptian Hall, Piccadilly.* London: James Bullock

Bullock, W. 1824d, *Atlas historique pour servir au Mexique en 1823,* Paris: Emery

Bullock, W. 1825a, *Six Months' Residence and Travels in Mexico.* 2nd edition, London: J. Murray

Bullock, W. 1825b, *Sechs Monate in Mexiko oder Bemmer Jungen über den Gegemärtingen.* Dresden: Hillchefchen Büchandung

Bullock, W. 1825c, *A Descriptive Catalogue of the Exhibition, Entitled Ancient and Modern Mexico. Containing a Panoramic View of the Present City, Specimens of the Natural History of New Spain. Models of Vegetable, Habitations, Costume andc., andc.* London: James Bullock

Bunsen, B. von 1844–1857, *Egypt's Place in Universal History.* London: Longman, Green and Co

Burkert, W. 1992, *The Orientalizing Revolution: Near Eastern Influence on Greek Culture in the Early Archaic Age* (trans. M. E. Pinder and W. Burkert). Cambridge, Mass: Harvard UP

Burkitt, M. C. 1921, *Prehistory: A Study of the Early Cultures in Europe and the Mediterranean Basin.* Cambridge: CUP

Bury, C. 1908, *The Diary of a Lady-in-Waiting.* London: John Lane

Butcher, E. L. 1897, *The Story of the Church of Egypt being an Outline of the History of the Egyptians under their Successive Masters from the Roman Conquest until now.* London: Smith, Elder and Co

Butcher, E. L. 1911, In the House of Bondage: A Short Sketch of Coptic History, in K. Mikhail, *Copts and Moslems under British Control (Egypt). A Collection of Facts and a Resumé of Authoritative Opinions on the Coptic Question*, 1–13. London: Smith, Elder and Co

Butler, A. J. 1884a, *The Ancient Coptic Churches of Egypt Volume 1.* Oxford: Clarendon

Butler, A. J. 1884b, *The Ancient Coptic Churches of Egypt Volume 2.* Oxford: Clarendon

Butler, W. 1911, *An Autobiography.* London: Constable and Co


Caballero y Morgay, F. 1828, *La Turquía, teatro de la guerra presente.* Madrid

Calinescu, M. 1987, *Five Faces of Modernity: Modernism, Avant-Garde, Decadence, Kitsh, Postmodernism.* Durham, NC: Duke UP

Cameron, A. and A. Kuhrt 1983, *Images of Women in Antiquity.* London: Croom Helm

Campbell, J. M. 1946, *Christian History in the Making.* London: Press and Publications Board of the Church Assembly

Cannadine, D. and S. Price (eds) 1987, *Rituals of Royalty: Power and Ceremonial in Traditional Societies.* Cambridge: CUP

Capart, J. 1935, Le Cercueil et la momie de Boutehamon. *Bulletin des Musées Royaux d'Art et d'Histoire* 3ème série, t. VII, 111–113

Capart, J. 1936a, *Le Temple des Muses.* Bruxelles: Musées Royaux d'Art et d'Histoire

Capart, J. 1936b, *Travels in Egypt, December 1880 to May 1891, The Letters of Charles Edwin Wilbour.* Brooklyn: Brooklyn Museum

Cartailhac, E. 1886, *Les Ages préhistoriques de l'Espagne et du Portugal.* Paris: C. Reinwald

Carter, B. 1986, *The Copts in Egyptian Politics.* London: Croom Helm

Carter, H. 1998, *Tutankhamun: The Politics of Discovery.* London: Libri

Cartledge, P. 1997, Introduction, in P. Cartledge, P. Garnsey and E. S. Greun, *Hellenistic Constructs: Essays in Culture, History and Historiography*, 1–22. Berkeley: University of California Press

Ceram, C. 1951, *Gods, Graves and Scholars.* New York: Knopf

Champion, T. C. 1997, The Power of the Picture: the Image of the Ancient Gaul, in B. Molyneaux (ed.), *The Cultural Life of Images. Visual Representation in Archaeology*, 13–29. London: Routledge

Chancellor, J. 1982, *The Flowers and Fruits of the Bible.* Exeter: Webb Bowen

Channing A. and F. Tabor 1909, *The American Egypt. A Record of Travel in Yucatan.* London: Hutchinson

Cherry, T. 1921a, The Discovery of Agriculture. *Journal of the Department of Agriculture of Victoria*

Cherry, T. 1921b, The Discovery of Agriculture. *Report of the Australian Association for the Advancement of Science*

Childe, V. G. 1925, *The Dawn of European Civilization.* London: Kegan Paul

Childe, V. G. 1926, *The Danube in Prehistory.* Oxford: OUP

Childe, V. G. 1936, *Man Makes Himself.* London: Watts and Co

Childe, V. G. 1942, *What Happened in History.* Harmondsworth: Penguin

Church Missionary Society 1910, *The Egypt and Sudan Missions*. London: Church Missionary Society

Clark, J. G. D. 1989, *Prehistory at Cambridge and Beyond*. Cambridge: CUP

Clarke, E. D. 1818, *Travels in Various Countries of Europe, Asia and Africa. Part the Second Greece, Egypt and the Holy Land Section the Third, Volume the Seventh*. London: Cadell and Davies

Clarke, S. 1912, *Christian Antiquities in the Nile Valley: A Contribution Towards the Study of Ancient Churches*. Oxford: Clarendon

Clastres, P. 1987, *Society Against the State: Essays in Political Anthropology*. New York: Zone

Clavijero, F. [1807] 1964, *Historia antigua de México*. México: Porrúa

Clay, E. 1976, *Sir William Gell in Italy: Letters to the Society of Dilettanti 1831–1835*. London: Hamish Hamilton

Clay, E. 1979, *Lady Blessington at Naples*. London: Hamish Hamilton

Cohen, A. 1981, *The Politics of Elite Culture. Explorations in the Dramaturgy of Power in a Modern African Society*. Berkeley: University of California Press

Commission des Sciences et Arts d'Égypt 1810–1829, *Description de L'Égypte, ou, Recueil des observations et des recherches qui ont été faites en Égypte pendant l'expedition de l'Armée française, publié par les ordres de Sa Majesté l'Empereur Napoléon le Grand*. Paris: Imprimerie Imperiale

Conner, P. 1983, *The Inspiration of Egypt. Its Influence on British Artists, Travellers and Designers, 1700–1900*. Brighton: Brighton Borough Council

Connerton, P. 1989, *How Societies Remember*. Cambridge: CUP

Connolly, J. 1855, *The Ethnographical Exhibitions in London*. London: John Churchill

Coombes, A. 1994, *Reinventing Africa. Museums, Material Culture and Popular Imagination*. Yale: Yale UP

Cortes, H. 1777, *Letters of the History of the Conquest of Mexico*. London: Dilworth

Crawford, C. 1994, *Recasting Ancient Egypt in the African Context: Toward a Model Curriculum Using Art and Language*, Trenton: African World Press

Crawford, D. 1978, The Good Official of Ptolemaic Egypt, in H. Maehler and V. M. Strocka (eds), *Das Ptolemäische Ägypten Akten des Internationalen Symposions 27–29 Sept 1976 in Berlin*, 195–202. Mainz: Philipp von Zabern

Cromer, Lord 1908, *Modern Egypt*. London: Macmillan

Crown, C. 1982, The Memphis State University Egyptian Collection. *Interpretations* 13/2, 1–25

Crum, W. 1902, *Coptic Ostraca from the Collections of the Egypt Exploration Fund, the Cairo Museum and others*. London: Egypt Exploration Fund

Crum, W. and E. White 1926, *The Monastery of Epiphanius at Thebes, Part II*. New York: Metropolitan Museum of Art

Cunningham, V. 1988, *British Writers of the Thirties*. Oxford: OUP

Curl, J. S. 1994, *Egyptomania: The Egyptian Revival*. Manchester: Manchester UP

**Curran, B. 2003, The Renaissance Afterlife of Ancient Egypt (1400–1650), in P. J. Ucko and T. C. Champion (eds), *The Wisdom of Egypt: changing visions through the ages*, 101–132. London: UCL Press**

Curzon, R. [1849] 1955, *Visits to Monasteries in the Levant*. London: Arthur Baker

D'Alton, M. 1993, *The New York Obelisk, or How Cleopatra's Needle came to New York and What Happened When It Got There*. New York: Metropolitan Museum of Art

Dain, B. 1993, Haiti and Egypt in Early Black Racial Discourse in the US. *Slavery and Abolition* 14, 139–161

Dalfes, H. N., G. Kukla and H. Weiss 1997, *Third Millennium BC Climate Change and Old World Collapse*. London: Springer

Daniel, G. 1978, *A Hundred and Fifty Years of Archaeology.* London: Duckworth

Daniel, G. and C. Renfrew 1988, *The Idea of Prehistory.* 2nd edition, Edinburgh: Edinburgh UP

Daniel, G. E. 1963, *The Megalith Builders of Western Europe.* 2nd edition, Harmondsworth: Penguin

Daressy, G. 1897, *Notice Explicative des Ruines de Medinet Habu.* Cairo: Imprimerie Nationale

Dart, R. A. 1974a, Cultural Diffusion from, in and to Africa, in A. P. Elkin and N. W. G. MacIntosh (eds), *Grafton Elliot Smith: the Man and his Work,* 160–174. Sydney: Sydney UP

Dart, R. A. 1974b, Sir Grafton Elliot Smith and the Evolution of Man, in A. P. Elkin and N. W. G. MacIntosh (eds), *Grafton Elliot Smith: the Man and his Work,* 25–38. Sydney: Sydney UP

Davidson, B. 2001, *African Civilization Revisited.* Lawrenceville, NJ: Africa World Press

Dawson, W. R. 1938, *Sir Grafton Elliot Smith: a Biographical Record by his Colleagues.* London: Cape

Dawson, W. R. and E. H. Uphill 1972, *Who Was Who in Egyptology. A Biographical Index of Egyptologists.* London: Egypt Exploration Society

Dawson, W. R. and E. H. Uphill. 1995, *Who Was Who in Egyptology.* 3rd edition, revised M.L. Bierbrier, London: Egypt Exploration Society

de Bonstetten, A. 1865, *Essai sur les Dolmens.* Geneva: Fick

de Heusch, L. 1972, *The Drunken King or the Origins of the State.* London: Routledge

**Delamaire, M-S. 2003, Searching for Egypt: Egypt in 19th Century American World Exhibitions, in J-M. Humbert and C. Price (eds), *Imhotep Today: Egyptianizing architecture,* 123–134. London: UCL Press**

Denon, V. [1802] 1990, *Voyage dans la Basse et la Haute Égypte: Pendant les Campagnes du Général Bonaparte.* Cairo: Institut Français d'Archéologie Orientale

Depauw, M. 1997, *A Companion to Demotic Studies.* Papyrologica Bruxellensia 28, Brussels: Fondation Égyptologique Reine Élisabeth

Description 1809–1828, *Description de l'Égypte, ou Recueil des observations et des recherches qui ont été faites en Égypte pendant l'expedition de l'Armée française.* Paris: Imprimerie Impériale

Díaz del Castillo, B. 1800, *True History of the Conquest of Mexico.* London: Wright

Diaz-Andreu, M. and T. C. Champion 1996, *Nationalism and Archaeology in Europe.* London: UCL Press

Diop, Cheikh A. 1974, *The African Origins of Civilization: Myth or Reality* (trans. M. Cook). Chicago: Lawrence Hill

Diop, Cheikh A. 1997, *The Peopling of Ancient Egypt and the Deciphering of the Meroitic Scripts: Proceedings of the Symposium held in Cairo from 28 January to 3 February 1974.* Cairo: Karnak House

Donadoni, S., S. Curto and A. M. Donadoni Roveri 1990, *Egypt from Myth to Egyptology.* Milan: Fabri

Drower, M. S. 1985, *Flinders Petrie: a Life in Archaeology.* London: Gollancz

Drower, M. S. 1995, *Flinders Petrie: a Life in Archaeology.* 2nd edition, Madison: University of Wisconsin Press

Dumézil, G. 1968–1973, *Mythe et Épopée.* Paris: Gallimard

Dumont, L. 1980, *Homo Hierarchicus: the Caste System and its Implications.* Chicago: University of Chicago Press

Dunham, D. 1935, Four New Kingdom Monuments in the Museum of Fine Arts, Boston. *Journal of Egyptian Archaeology* 21, 147–151

Durrell, L. 1971, *Spirit of Place: Letters and Essays on Travel.* London: Faber

Dykstra, D. I. 1979, *Egypt in the Nineteenth Century: the Impact of Europe upon a Non-Western Society.* Ann Arbor: University of Michigan Press

Dykstra, D. I. 1998, The French Occupation of Egypt, 1798–1801, in M. W. Daly (ed.), *Cambridge History of Egypt. Volume 2: Modern Egypt from 1517 to the End of the Twentieth Century*, 113–138. Cambridge: CUP

Early, G. 1998, Adventures in the Colored Museum: Afrocentrism, Memory, and the Construction of Race. *American Anthropologist* 100, 703–711

Edwards, A. B. [1877] 1993, *A Thousand Miles up the Nile*. London: Darf

**El Daly, O. 2003, What do Tourists Learn of Egypt?, in S. MacDonald and M. Rice (eds), *Consuming Ancient Egypt*, 139–150. London: UCL Press**

Elgood, P. G. [1877] 1924, *Egypt and the Army*. Oxford: OUP

Elkin, A. P. 1974, Sir Grafton Elliot Smith: the Man and his Work: a Personal Testimony, in A. P. Elkin and N. W. G. MacIntosh (eds), *Grafton Elliot Smith: the Man and his Work*, 8–15. Sydney: Sydney UP

Elkin, A. P. and N. W. G. MacIntosh (eds) 1974, *Grafton Elliot Smith: the Man and his Work*. Sydney: Sydney UP

Elmes, J. 1827, *Metropolitan Improvements, or London in the Nineteenth Century*. London: Jones

Elsner, J. 1994, A Collector's Model of Desire: the House Museum of Sir John Sloane, in J. Elsner and R. Cardinal, *The Cultures of Collecting*, 155–176. London: Reaktion

Empéreur, J. Y. 1998, *Alexandria Rediscovered*. London: British Museum Press

Engel, A. 1892, Rapport sur une mission archéologique en Espagne (1891). *Nouvelles Archives des missions scientifiques et litteraires* III, 204

Estrada de Gerlero, I. 1996, El tema anticuario en los pintores viajeros, in *Viajeros Europeos del siglo XIX en México*, 183–201. Mexico: Fomento Cultural Banamex

Eyre, C. 1994, Feudal Tenure and Absentee Landlords, in S. Allam (ed.), *Grund und Boden in Altägypten*. Akten des internationalen Symposions Tübingen 18–20 Juni 1990, 107–133, Tübingen

Eyre, C. 1999, The Village Economy in Pharaonic Egypt, in Bowman and Rogan (eds), *Agriculture in Egypt: from Pharaonic to Modern Times*. Proceedings of the British Academy 96, 33–60, Oxford: OUP

Fahmy, K. 1998, The era of Muhammad 'Ali Pasha, 1805–1848, in M. W. Daly (ed.) *Cambridge History of Egypt. Volume 2: Modern Egypt from 1517 to the End of the Twentieth Century*, 139–179. Cambridge: CUP

Fannon, F. 1968, *The Wretched of the Earth*. New York: Grove

**Fazzini, R. and M. E. McKercher, 'Egyptomania' and American Architecture, in J-M. Humbert and C. Price (eds), *Imhotep Today: Egyptianizing architecture*, 135–160. London: UCL Press**

Fergusson, J. 1872, *Rude Stone Monuments in all Countries: their Age and Uses*. London: Murray

Fernández de Avilés, A. 1949, Las Primeras investigaciones en el Cerro de los Santos, *Boletín de la Sociedad Española de Arqueología y Antropología*. Madrid

Fikhman, I. F. 1996, Retour à Rostovzeff. *Chronique d'Égypte* 71, 169–175

Florescano, E. 1994, The Creation of the Museo Nacional de Antropología of Mexico and its Scientific, Educational and Political Purposes, in E. Boone, *Collecting the Pre-Columbian Past*, 49–80. Washington, DC: Dumbarton Oaks

**Folorunso, C. A. 2003, Views of Ancient Egypt from a West African Perspective, in D. O'Connor and A. Reid (eds), *Ancient Egypt in Africa*, 77–92. London: UCL Press**

Forde, C. D. 1927, *Ancient Mariners: the Story of Ships and Sea Routes*. London: G. Howe

France, P. 1991, *The Rape of Egypt: How the Europeans Stripped Egypt of its Heritage*. London: Barrie and Jenkins

Frankfort, H. 1948, *Kingship and the Gods: a Study of Ancient Near Eastern Religion as the Integration of Society and Nature.* Chicago: University of Chicago Press

Frankfort, H. 1951, *The Birth of Civilization in the Near East.* Bloomington: Indiana UP

Frazer, J. G. [1890] 1911, *The Golden Bough: a Study in Magic and Religion.* London: Macmillan

Freud, S. 1919, *Totem and Taboo: Resemblances between the Psychic Lives of Savages and Neurotics.* London: Routledge

Freud, S. 1930, *Civilization and its Discontents.* London: Hogarth

Fustel de Coulanges, N. D. [1864] 1980, *The Ancient City: a Study on the Religion, Laws and Institutions of Greece and Rome.* Baltimore: Johns Hopkins UP


Galarke, P. 1973, *Great Zimbabwe.* London: Thames and Hudson

Gallegos, R. 1997, *Antología de documentos para la historía de la arqueología de Teotihuacan.* Mexico: Instituto Nacional de Antropología e Historía

Garcia Cubas, A. 1872, Ensayo de un estudio comparativo entre las pirámides Egipcias y Mexicanas, que dedica al Señor Licenciado don Ignacio Ramírez en testimonio a su gratitude. *Anales de la Sociedad Humboldt* 1, 49–98

García-Romeral Pérez, C. 1995, *Bio-Bibliografía de viajeros Españoles (siglo XIX).* Madrid: Ollero y Ramos

Gathercole, P. and D. Lowenthal 1990, *The Politics of the Past.* London: Unwin Hyman

Gell, A. 1998, *Art and Agency: an Anthropological Theory.* Oxford: Clarendon

Gell, W. 1804, *The Topography of Troy and its Vicinity.* London: Longman and Rees

Gell, W. 1807, *The Geography and Antiquities of Ithaca.* London: Longman, Hurst, Rees and Orme

Gell, W. 1810, *The Itinerary of Greece.* London: T. Payne

Gell, W. 1817–1819, *Pompeiana: the Topography, Edifices, and Ornaments of Pompeii.* London: Rodwell and Martin

Gell, W. 1834, *The Topography of Rome and its Vicinity with Map.* London: Saunders and Otley

Gell, W. and A. Nibby 1820, *Le Mura di Roma Disegnate da Sir William Gell.* Rome: Presso Vencenzo Poggioli Stampatore Camerale

Gemelli Carreri, F. 1700, *Giro del Mondo.* Naples

Gero, J. and D. Root 1990, Public Presentations and Private Concerns: Archaeology in the Pages of *National Geographic,* in P. Gathercole and D. Lowenthal (eds), *The Politics of the Past,* 302–314. London: Unwin Hyman

Ghali, I. 1986, *Vivant Denon.* Cairo: Institut Français d'Archéologie Orientale

Giddens, A. 1986, *Durkheim on Politics and the State.* Cambridge: Polity

Gilding, R. 2001, *Marblemania. Sculpture Galleries in England.* London: Sir John Soane Museum

Gillispie, C. C. 1987, Historical Introduction, in C. C. Gillispie and M. Dewachter (eds), *Monuments of Egypt. The Napoleonic Expedition: The Complete Archaeological Plates from La Description de l'Égypte,* 1–29. Princeton: Princeton Architectural Press

Gillispie, C. C. and M. Dewachter (eds) 1987, *Monuments of Egypt. The Napoleonic Expedition. The Complete Archaeological Plates from La Description de l'Égypte.* Princeton: Princeton Architectural Press

Godlewska, A. 1995, Map, Text and Image. The Mentality of Enlightened Conquerors: a New Look at the *Description de l'Égypte. Transactions of the Institute of British Geographers* 20, 5–28

Goedicke, H. 1971, *Re-Used Blocks from the Pyramid of Amenemhet I at Lisht.* New York: Metropolitan Museum of Art

Gould, C. 1965, *Trophy of Conquest: the Musée Napoléon and the Creation of the Louvre.* London: Faber and Faber

Grafton, A. 1993, *Rome Reborn: the Vatican Library and Renaissance Culture*. Yale: Library of Congress

Graham, I. 1993, Three Early Collectors in Mesoamerica, in E. Boone (ed.), *Collecting the Pre-Columbian Past. Symposium at Dumbarton Oaks, 6 and 7 October 1990*, 49–80. Washington, DC: Dumbarton Oaks

Greaves, J. 1646, *Pyramidographia, or a Description of the Pyramids in Egypt*. London: G. Badger

Greenhalgh, P. 1988, *Ephemeral Vistas. The Expositions Universelles, Great Exhibitions and World's Fairs*. Manchester: Manchester UP

Grenfell, F. n. d. [1925], *Memoirs of Field Marshall Lord Grenfell*. London: Hodder and Stoughton

Grimal, N. 1992, *A History of Ancient Egypt*. London: Blackwell

Gull, B. 1909, A Visit to Egypt, 1909, January 27th to April 2nd 1909, unpublished journal, copy presented to the Egypt Exploration Society by her nephew, D. C. Knollys, October 1979

Gullock, M. C. 1906, *River, Sand and Sun, Being Sketches of the C. M. S. Egypt Mission*. London: Church Missionary Society

Haarmann, U. 1980, Regional Sentiment in Medieval Islamic Egypt. *Bulletin of the School of Oriental and African Studies* 43, 55–66

Haarmann, U. 1996, Medieval Muslim Perceptions of Pharaonic Egypt, in A. Loprieno (ed.), *Ancient Egyptian Literature: History and Forms*, 605–627. Leiden: Brill

Habachi, L. 1984, *The Obelisks of Egypt: Skyscrapers of the Past*. Cairo: American University in Cairo

Hagen, V. W. von 1950, *Frederick Catherwood, Architect*. New York: OUP

**Haikal, F. 2003, Egypt's Past Regenerated by its Own People, in S. MacDonald and M. Rice (eds), *Consuming Ancient Egypt*, 123–138. London: UCL Press**

Hall, H. R. H. 1915a, Letters of Champollion le Jeune and of Seyffarth to Sir William Gell. *Journal of Egyptian Archaeology* 2, 78–79

Hall, H. R. H. 1915b, Letters to Sir William Gell from Henry Salt, (Sir) J. G. Wilkinson, and Baron von Bunsen. *Journal of Egyptian Archaeology* 2, 133–167

Halls, J. J. 1834, *The Life and Correspondence of Henry Salt*. London: Richard Bentley

Hamilakis, Y. 1999, La Trahison Archéologues? Archaeological Practice as Intellectual Activity in Postmodernity. *Journal of Mediterranean Archaeology* 12, 60–79

**Hamill, J. and P. Mollier 2003, Rebuilding the Sanctuaries of Memphis: Egypt in Masonic Iconography and Architecture, in J-M. Humbert and C. Price (eds), *Imhotep Today: Egyptianizing architecture*, 207–220. London: UCL Press**

Hana, M. 1996, Character – Exclusive to Egypt. *Egypt Magazine*, summer

Harfield, A. (ed.) 1986, *The Life and Times of a Victorian Officer, Being the Journals and Letters of Colonel Benjamin Donisthorpe Alsop Donne CB*. Wincanton: Wincanton Press

Harris, M. 1968, *The Rise of Anthropological Theory*. New York: Crowell

Hartleben, H. 1906, *Champollion: sein Leben und sein Werk*. Berlin: Weidmannsche Buchhandlung

Hartleben, H. 1909, *Lettres de Champollion le Jeune*. Paris: Ernest Leroux

Hassan, F. A. 1998, Memorabilia: Archaeological Materiality and National Identity in Egypt, in L. Meskell (ed.), *Archaeology Under Fire: Nationalism, Politics and Heritage in the Eastern Mediterranean and the Middle East*, 200–216. London: Routledge

**Hassan, F. A. 2003, Selling Egypt: Encounters at Khan el-Khalili, in S. MacDonald and M. Rice (eds), *Consuming Ancient Egypt*, 111–122. London: UCL Press**

**Haycock, D. B. 2003, Ancient Egypt in 17th and 18th Century England, in P. J. Ucko and T. C. Champion (eds), *The Wisdom of Ancient Egypt: changing visions through the ages*, 133–160. London: UCL Press**

Hekekyan, J. 1863, *A Treatise on the Siriadic Monuments*. London: Hekekyan

Herold, J. C. 1963, *Bonaparte in Egypt*. London: Hamish Hamilton

Herzfeld, M. 1995, Hellenism and Occidentalism: the Permutations of Performance in Greek Bourgeois Identity, in J. G. Carrier (ed.), *Occidentalism: Images of the West*, 218–233. Oxford: Clarendon

Heuzey, L. 1890, Statues Espagnoles de style Gréco-Phénicien. Question d'authenticité. *Revue d'Assyriologie Orientale* III, 94–114

Heyworth-Dunne, J. 1939, *An Introduction to the History of Education in Modern Egypt*. London: Frank Cass

Hilton, R. 1975, *The English Peasantry in the Later Middle Ages*. Oxford: Clarendon

Hingley, R. 2000, *Roman Officers and English Gentlemen: the Imperial Origins of Roman Archaeology*. London: Routledge

Hinsley, C. 1993, In Search of the New World Classical, in E. Boone (ed.), *Collecting the Pre-Columbian Past. Symposium at Dumbarton Oaks, 6 and 7 October 1990*, 105–122. Washington, DC: Dumbarton Oaks

Hocart, A. 1927, *Kingship*. Oxford: OUP

Hodder, I. 1999, *The Archaeological Process: An Introduction*. Oxford: Blackwell

Hodder, I. 2001, *Archaeological Theory Today*. Cambridge: Polity

Hoffman, M. 1984, *Egypt After the Pharaohs*. London: Ark

Hoffman, M., H. Hamroush and R. O. Allen 1986, A Model of Urban Development for the Hierakonpolis Region from Predynastic Through Old Kingdom Times. *Journal of the American Research Center in Egypt* 23, 175–187

Hogg, E. 1835, *Visit to Alexandria, Damascus and Jerusalem*. London: Saunders and Otley

Honour, H. 1954, Curiosities in the Egyptian Hall. *Country Life* 115, 38–39

Hornung, E. 2001, *The Secret Lore of Egypt: its Impact on the West*. Ithaca: Cornell UP

Howe, S. 1998, *Afrocentrism: Mythical Pasts and Imagined Homes*. London, New York: Verso

Huebner, E. 1876, Notes on the Discurso of Rada. *Jenaer Literaturzeitung* 185

Huebner, E. 1888, *La Arqueología en España*. Barcelona

Hughes, P. 1995, Ruins of Time: Estranging History and Ethnology in the Elightenment and After, in D. O. Hughes and T. R. Trautman (eds), *Time: Histories and Ethnologies*, 269–290. Michigan: University of Michigan Press

Humbert, J-M. 1998, *L'Égypte à Paris*. Paris: Action Artistique de la Ville de Paris

**Humbert, J-M. 2003, The Egyptianizing Pyramid from the 18th to the 20th Centuries, in J-M. Humbert and C. Price (eds), *Imhotep Today: Egyptianizing architecture*, 25–40. London: UCL Press**

Humbert, J-M., M. Pantazzi and C. Ziegler 1994, *Eyptomania. L'Égypte dans l'art occidental 1730–1930*. Catalogue d'exposition Paris 20 janvier–18 avril 1994, Paris: Réunion des Musées Nationaux

Humboldt, A. von 1810, *Vues des cordillères et monuments des peuples indigènes de l'Amérique*. Paris: Librerie Grecque-Latine

Humboldt, A. von 1811, *Essai Politique sur la royaume de la Nouvelle-Espagne*. Paris: F Schoell

Humboldt, A. von 1974, *Vistas de las cordilleras y monumentos de los pueblos indígenas de América*. Mexico: Secretaría de Hacienda y Crédito Público

Humboldt, A. von 1984, *Ensayo Político sobre el reino de Nueva España*. Mexico: Secretaría de Hacienda y Crédito Público

Hunter, F. R. 1998, Egypt under the Successors of Muhammad Ali, in M. W. Daly (ed.), *Cambridge History of Egypt. Volume 2: Modern Egypt from 1517 to the End of the Twentieth Century*, 180–197. Cambridge: CUP

Hyde, R. 1988, *Panoramania! The Art and Entertainment of 'All-Embracing View'*. London: Trefoil and Barbican Centre

Hymans, H. 1913, Schayes (Antoine-Guillaume-Bernard). *Biographie Nationale*, 21, col. 619, Brussels

Ibrahim, H. A. 1998, The Egyptian Empire, 1805–1885, in M. W. Daly (ed.), *Cambridge History of Egypt. Volume 2: Modern Egypt from 1517 to the End of the Twentieth Century*, 198–216. Cambridge: CUP

Iversen, E. 1961, *The Myth of Egypt and its Hieroglyphs in European Tradition*. Copenhagen: Gad

Iversen, E. 1968, *Obelisks in Exile, 1, The Obelisks of Rome*. Copenhagen: Gad

Iversen, E. 1971, The Hieroglyphic Tradition, in J. R. Harris (ed.), *The Legacy of Egypt*, 170–196. Oxford: Clarendon

Iversen, E. 1972, *Obelisks in Exile, 2, The Obelisks of Istanbul and Britain*. Copenhagen: Gad

Iversen, E. 1993, *The Myth of Egypt and its Hieroglyphs in European Tradition*. Princeton: Princeton UP

James, G. 1992, *Stolen Legacy: Greek Philosophy is Stolen Egyptian Philosophy*. Lawrenceville, NJ: Africa World Press

James, T. G. H 1982, *Excavating in Egypt: the Egypt Exploration Society 1882–1982*. London: British Museum Publications

James, T. G. H. 1992, *Howard Carter: The Path to Tutankhamun*. London: Kegan Paul

Jameson, J. S. 1915, Shebin-el-Kanater. *E. G. M. News, the Official Paper of the Egypt General Mission* 15, 68–70

Jardine, L. and J. Brotton 2000, *Global Interests: Renaissance Art Between East and West*. London: Reaktion

Jeffreys, D. G. forthcoming, *Survey of Memphis. Vol 6: The Hekekyan Papers, and Other Written and Graphic Sources for the Survey*. London: Egypt Exploration Society

Jiménez Cordinach, G. 1996, La Europa aventurera, in *Viajeros Europeos del siglo XIX en México*, 39–50. México: Fomento Cultural Banamex

Johanssen, R. W. 1985, *To the Halls of the Montezumas. The Mexican War in the American Imagination*. Oxford: OUP

Joussaume, R. 1987, *Dolmens for the Dead: Megalith-Building throughout the World*. London: Batsford

Kamil, J. and R. Saad 2000, Egyptology: Weighing the Issues. *Al-Ahram Weekly Online* 476

Kantorowicz, E. H. 1957, *The King's Two Bodies: a Study in Mediaeval Political Theology*. Princeton: Princeton UP

Katary, S. 1989, *Land Tenure in the Ramesside Period*. London: Kegan Paul

Katary, S. 1999, Land-tenure in the New Kingdom, in Bowman and Rogan (eds), *Agriculture in Egypt: from Pharaonic to Modern Times*. Proceedings of the British Academy 96, 61–82, Oxford: OUP

Keen, B. 1971, *The Aztec Image in Western Thought*. New Brunswick: Rutgers UP

Keen, B. 1973, *La Imagen Azteca en el Pensamiento Occidental*. México: Fondo de Cultura Económica

Kehoe, D. 1992, *Management and Investment on Estates in Roman Egypt During the Early Empire*. Bonn: Habelt

Kemp, B. J. 1984, In the Shadow of Texts: Archaeology in Egypt. *Archaeological Review from Cambridge* 3, 19–28

Kendrick, T. D. 1950, *British Antiquity*. London: Methuen

King, J. 1996, William Bullock, Showman, in E. Trabulse (ed.), *European Traveler-Artists in the Nineteenth Century in Mexico*. Mexico: Fondo Cultural Banamex

Kircher, A. 1650, *Obeliscus Pamphilias*. Rome: Grigorius

Kircher, A. 1652–1654, *Oedipus Aegypticus*. Rome: Vitalis Mascardi

Kircher, A. 1666, *Oedipus Aegypticus*, Volume 3. Rome: Vitalis Mascardi

Kitchen, K. A. 1973, *The Third Intermediate Period in Egypt (1100–650 BC)*. Warminster: Aris and Phillips

Klengel-Brandt, E. 1982, *Der Turm von Babylon: Legende und Geschichte eines Bauwerkes*. Berlin: Koehler and Amelang

Kohl, P. 1989, The Material Culture of the Modern Era in the Ancient Orient: Suggestions for Future Work, in D. Miller, M. J. Rowlands and C. Y. Tilley (eds), *Domination and Resistance*, 240–245. London: Unwin Hyman

Kohl, P. L. and C. Fawcett (eds) 1995, *Nationalism, Politics, and the Practice of Archaeology*. Cambridge: CUP

Kotsakis, K. 1998, The Past is Ours: Images of Greek Macedonia, in L. Meskell (ed.), *Archaeology Under Fire: Nationalism, Politics and Heritage in the Eastern Mediterranean and Middle East*, 44–67. London and New York: Routledge

Kristiansen, K. 1998, Chiefdoms, States and Systems of Social Evolution, in K. Kristiansen and M. Rowlands (eds), *Social Transformations in Archaeology: Global and Local Perspectives*, 243–267. London and New York: Routledge

Kristiansen, K. and M. Rowlands (eds), 1998, *Social Transformations in Archaeology: Global and Local Perspectives*. London and New York: Routledge

Kuklick, H. 1991, *The Savage Within: the Social History of British Anthropology, 1885–1945*. Cambridge: CUP

Kuper, A. 1988, *The Invention of Primitive Society: Transformations of an Illusion*. London: Routledge

Kus, S. 1982, Matters Material and Ideal, in I. Hodder (ed.), *Symbolic and Structural Archaeology*, 47–62. Cambridge: CUP


Labastida, J. 1999, *Humboldt. Ciudadano universal*. Mexico: Siglo XXI

Lacouture, J. 1988, *Champollion: une vie de lumières*. Paris: Bernard Grasset

Lamberg-Karlovsky, C. C. 1985, The Near Eastern 'Breakout' and the Mesopotamian Social Contract. *Symbols*, spring, Cambridge, Mass: Peabody Museum

Lamberg-Karlovsky, C. C. 1997, Colonialism, Nationalism, Ethnicity and Archaeology: Part I. *Review of Archaeology* 18, 1–14

Lamberg-Karlovsky, C. C. 1998, Colonialism, Nationalism, Ethnicity and Archaeology: Part II. *Review of Archaeology* 19, 1–11

Lamplough, A. O. and R. Francis 1909, *Cairo and its Environs*. London: Sir Joseph Causton and Sons

Lancaster, C. 1950, The Egyptian Hall and Mrs Trollope's Bazaar. *Magazine of Art* 43, 94–96,112

Lane, E. [1836] 1842, *An Account of the Manners and Customs of the Modern Egyptians*. London: Charles Knight and Co

Lane-Poole, S. 1919, *Watson Pasha*. London: John Murray

Larsen, M. T. 1989, Orientalism and Near Eastern Archaeology, in D. Miller, M. Rowlands and C. Y. Tilley (eds), *Domination and Resistance*, 229–239. London: Unwin Hyman

Larsen, M. T. 1994, The Appropriation of the Near Eastern Past: Contrasts and Contradictions. *The East and the Meaning of History: International Conference (23–27 November 1992)*, 29–51, Università degli studi di Roma "La Sapienza"

Larsen, M. T. 1996, *The Conquest of Assyria: Excavations in an Antique Land, 1840–1860*. London: Routledge

Lasalde, C. 1871, Los Primeros Pobladores de España, *La Ilustración de Madrid,* year II, 29,67–69 and 30,91–94

Lasalde, C., T. Sáenz and M. Gòmez 1871, *Memoria sobre las notables excavaciones Hechas en el Cerro de los Santos.* Yecla: P. P. Escolapios

Laurens, H. 1999, Les Lumières et l'Égypte, in P. Bret (ed.), *L'éxpedition d'Égypte: une entreprise des lumières, 1798–1801.* Paris: Technique et Documentation

Leeder, S. 1918, *Modern Sons of the Pharaohs: a Study of the Manners and Customs of the Copts of Egypt.* London: Hodder and Stoughton

Lefkowitz, M. R. 1996, *Not Out of Africa: How Afrocentrism Became an Excuse to Teach Myth as History.* New York: Basic Books

Lefkowitz, M. R. and G. M. Rogers 1996, *Black Athena Revisited.* Chapel Hill: University of North Carolina Press

Leitch, J. 1855, *Miscellaneous Works of the Late Thomas Young.* London: John Murray

Liblik, A. 1919, Women's Work. *E. G. M. News, the Official Paper of the Egypt General Mission* 19, 63–64

López, F. 1993a, *Yecla y el padre Lasalde.* Murcia.

López, F. 1993b, El padre Lasalde y los descubrimientos del Cerro de los Santos. *Boletín de la Asociación Española de Amigos de la Arqueología* 33

Lowenthal, D. 1989, Conclusions, in P. Gathercole and D. Lowenthal (eds), *The Politics of the Past,* 302–314. London: Unwin Hyman

Lundquist, J. M. 1995, Babylon in European Thought, in J. M. Sasson (ed.), *Civilizations of the Ancient Near East, Vol. 1,* 67–80. New York: Charles Scribner's Sons

Lunt, T. R. W. 1909, *Talks on Egypt: An Outline of Six Missionary Instructions, with Illustrations and Recitations, for Young People.* London: Church Missionary Society

Lustig, J. 1997, *Anthropology and Egyptology: a Developing Dialogue.* Sheffield: Sheffield Academic Press

**MacDonald, S. 2003, Lost in Time and Space: Ancient Egypt in Museums, in S. MacDonald and M. Rice (eds), *Consuming Ancient Egypt,* 87–100. London: UCL Press**

**MacDonald, S. and M. Rice (eds) 2003, *Consuming Ancient Egypt.* London: UCL Press**

Mackenzie, J. 1995, *Orientalism. History, Theory and the Arts.* Manchester: Manchester UP

Madden, R. R. 1829, *Travels in Turkey, Egypt, Nubia and Palestine, in 1824, 1825, 1826 and 1827.* London: H. Colburn

Madden, R. R. 1855, *The Literary Life of the Countess of Blessington.* New York: Harper

Magnus, P. 1958, *Kitchener: Portrait of an Imperialist.* London: John Murray

Malek, J. and M. Smith 1983, Henry Salt's Egyptian Copies and Drawings. *Göttinger Miszellen* 64, 35–52

Manley, D. and P. Rée 2001, *Henry Salt: Artist, Traveller, Diplomat, Egyptologist.* London: Libri

Manning, J. 1999, The Land-Tenure Regime in Ptolemaic Upper Egypt, in A. K. Bowman and E. Rogan (eds), *Agriculture in Egypt: from Pharaonic to Modern Times.* Proceedings of the British Academy 96, 83–105, Oxford: OUP

Manning, J. 2003, *Land and Power in Ptolemaic Egypt: the Structure of Land Tenure, 332–30 BCE.* Cambridge: CUP

Mansfield, P. 1969, *Nasser's Egypt.* Harmondsworth: Penguin

Manzanilla, L. 1995, La Zona del altiplano central en el clásico, in L. Manzanilla and L. López (eds), *Historia antigua de México* II, 139–173. Mexico: Instituto Nacional de Antropologia e Historia – Universidad Nacional Autónoma de México – Porrúa

Marchal, E. 1844, Notice sur les relations commerciales des Flamands avec le Port d'Alexandrie d'Egypte, avant la découverte du Cap de Bonne-Espérance. *Bulletin de l'Académie Royale des Sciences et Belles-Lettres* 11, 153–176

Marcone, A. 1993, Gli "Studi per la storia del colonato romano" di Michele Rostovtzeff. *Ostraka: Rivista di antichità* 2, 177–186

Marlowe, J. 1965, *Anglo-Egyptian Relations 1800–1956*. 2nd edition, London: Frank Cass

Marsot, A. L. A. 1985, *A Short History of Egypt*. Cambridge: CUP

Martins Sarmento, F. 1933, *Dispersos. Colectanea de artigos publicados desde 1867 a 1899, sobre arqueologia, etnologia, mitologia, epigrafia, e arte prehistorica*. Coimbra: Imprensa da Universidade

Massingham, H. J. 1926, *Downland Man*. London: Jonathan Cape

Massingham, H. J. 1927, *Pre-Roman Britain*. London: Benn

Massingham, H. J. 1942, *Remembrance: an Autobiography*. London: Batsford

Matless, D. 1998, *Landscape and Englishness*. London: Reaktion

**Matthews, R. and C. Roemer (eds) 2003, *Ancient Perspectives on Egypt*. London: UCL Press**

Maurice, J. F. 1887, *The Campaign of 1882 in Egypt*. London: Eyre and Spottiswoode

Mayes, S. 1959, *The Great Belzoni*. London: Putnam

McIntosh, R. J. 1999, Western Perceptions of Urbanism and Invisible African Towns, in S. K. McIntosh (ed.), *Beyond Chiefdoms: Pathways to Complexity in Africa*, 56–65. Cambridge: CUP

McNaught, L. 1978, Henry Salt: His Contribution to the Collections of Egyptian Sculpture in the British Museum. *Apollo* 108, 224–231

Medina-González, I. 1998, William Bullock's 'Ancient and Modern Mexico': Images and Messages on Display at the Beginning of the Nineteenth Century in London, unpublished MA dissertation, University of York

Medina-González, I. 2003, Nineteenth-Century Three-dimensional Representations of Mesoamerica. Interpretations of Mesoamerican cultures through British Displays 1824–1900. *Proceedings of the 50th International Congress of Americanistas*, Warsaw: International Congress of Americanists

Mélida, J. R. 1903–1905, Las Esculturas del Cerro de los Santos, cuestión de autenticidad. *Revista de Archivos, Bibliotecas y Museos* VIII–XIII

Menu, B. 1982, *Recherches sur l'histoire juridique, économique et sociale de l'ancienne Égypte*. Versailles: Menu

Meredith, J. (ed.) 1998, *Ombusman Diaries 1898*. Barnsley: Leo Cooper

Merrillees, R. 1990, *Living with Egypt's Past in Australia*. Melbourne: Museum of Victoria

Meskell, L. 1998, *Archaeology Under Fire: Nationalism, Politics and Heritage in the Eastern Mediterranean and the Middle East*. London: Routledge

Meskell, L. 1999, Review of Lustig J. (ed). 1997 Anthropology and Egyptology: a Developing Dialogue. *American Journal of Archaeology* 103, 127–129

Meskell, L. 2000, The Politics and Practice of Archaeology in Egypt, unpublished paper for New York Academy of Sciences meeting, 14 April 2000, on Ethical Dilemmas for Anthropology in the 21st Century. Columbia University, Department of Anthropology

Meskell, L. forthcoming, Sites of Violence: Terrorism, Tourism and Heritage in the Archaeological Present, in L. Meskell and P. Pels (eds), *Beyond Ethics: Anthropological Moralities on the Boundaries of the Public and the Professional*. Oxford: Berg

Michelet, J. [1879] 1967, *History of the French Revolution* (trans. G. Wright). Chicago: University of Chicago Press

Mikhail, K. 1911, *Copts and Moslems under British Control (Egypt). A collection of facts and a resumé of authoritative opinions on the Coptic question*. London: Smith, Elder and Co

Miller, O. 1972, *The Age of Charles I*. London: Tate Gallery

Milner, A. 1893, *England in Egypt*. London: Edward Arnold

Mitchell, T. 1990, The Invention and Reinvention of the Egyptian Peasant. *Journal of Middle East Studies* 22, 129–150

Mitchell, T. 1991, *Colonising Egypt*. Cambridge: CUP

Mohen, J-P. 1989, *The World of Megaliths*. London: Cassell

Momigliano, A. 1966, M. I. Rostovtzeff. *Studies in Historiography*, 91–104. London: Weidenfield and Nicolson (first published in *The Cambridge Journal* 7 (1954))

Momigliano, A. 1975, *Alien Wisdom: the Limits of Hellenization*. Cambridge: CUP

Momigliano, A. 1977, The Cult of the Greeks, in A. Momigliano, *Essays in Ancient and Modern Historiography*, 9–24. Oxford: Basil Blackwell

Momigliano, A. 1980, Foreword, in N. D. Fustel de Coulanges, *The Ancient City: a Study on the Religion, Laws and Institutions of Greece and Rome*, ix–xv. Baltimore: Johns Hopkins UP

Montelius, O. 1899, *Der Orient und Europa*. Stockholm: Königlich Akademie der schönen Wissenschaften, Geschichte und Alterthumskunde

Montero Blanco, T. 1986, *Eduardo Toda i Güell y el Antiguo Egipto*. Barcelona

Montserrat, D. 2000, *Akhenaten: History, Fantasy and Ancient Egypt*. London: Routledge

Moore-Colyer, R. J. 2001, Back to Basics: Rolf Gardiner, H. J. Massingham and 'A Kinship in Husbandry'. *Rural History* 12, 85–108

Morales Lezcano, V. 1992, *España y la Cuestión de Oriente*. Madrid: Biblioteca Diplomática Española, Sección Estudios 9

Morales-Moreno, L. 1994, History and Patriotism in the National Museum of Mexico, in F. Kaplan (ed.), *Museums and the Making of 'Ourselves'. The Role of Objects in National Identity*, 173–191. Leicester: Leicester UP

Moret, A. and G. Davy 1926, *From Tribe to Empire: Social Organization among Primitives and in the Ancient Near East*. London: Kegan Paul

**Morkot, R. G. 2003, On the Priestly Origin of the Napatan Kings: The Adaptation, Demise and Resurrection of Ideas in Writing Nubian History, in D. O'Connor and A. Reid (eds), *Ancient Egypt in Africa*, 151–168. London: UCL Press**

Morris, I. 1994, *Classical Greece: Ancient Histories and Modern Archaeologies*. Cambridge: CUP

Morris, S. P. 1989, Daidalos and Kadmos: Classicism and 'Orientalism'. *Arethusa* 39–54

Morris, S. P. 1992, *Daidalos and the Origins of Greek Art*. Princeton: Princeton UP

Moser, S. 1992, The Visual Language of Archaeology: a Case Study of the Neanderthals. *Antiquity* 66, 831–844

Moser, S. 1998, *Ancestral Images: the Iconography of Human Origins*. New York: Cornell UP

Moser, S. 2001, Archaeological Representation: the Visual Conventions for Constructing Knowledge about the Past, in I. Hodder (ed.), *Archaeological Theory Today*, 262–283. Cambridge: Polity

Mu-Chou Poo, 1998, Encountering the Strangers: a Comparative Study of Cultural Consciousness in Ancient Egypt, Mesopotamia, and China, in C. J. Eyre (ed.), *Proceedings of the Seventh International Congress of Egyptologists*, 885–892, Leuven: Peeters

Murray, M. 1963, *My First Hundred Years*. London: William Kimber

Murray, O. 1993, *Early Greece*. Cambridge, Mass: Harvard UP

Musa, S. 1961, *The Education of Salama Musa*. Leiden: Brill

Mustafa, A. R. 1968, The Hekekyan Papers, in P. M. Holt (ed.), *Political and Social Change in Modern Egypt*, 68–75. London: Curzon

Myres, J. L. 1911, *The Dawn of History*. London: Williams and Norgate

Naville, E. 1894, *The Temple of Deir el Bahri: its Plan, its Founders and its First Explorers*. London: Egypt Exploration Society

Naville, E. 1903, *The Stone-City of Pithom and the Route of the Exodus*. 4th edition, London: Egypt Exploration Fund

Neale, J. M. 1850, *A History of the Holy Eastern Church: General Introduction*. London: Joseph Masters

Nightingale, F. 1854, *Letters from Egypt*. London: A. and G. A. Spottiswoode

Noakes, A. 1962, *Cleopatra's Needles*. London: Witherby

Norman, B. 1843, *Rambles in Yucatan; or Notes of Travel Through the Peninsula. Including a Visit to the Remarkable Ruins of Chi-chen, Kabah, Zayi, and Uxmal*. New York: Langley, Thomas and Cowperthwait

**North, J. A. 2003, Attributing Colour to the Ancient Egyptians: Reflections on *Black Athena*, in D. O'Connor and A. Reid (eds), *Ancient Egypt in Africa*, 31–38. London: UCL Press**

O'Connor, D. 1993, Urbanism in Bronze Age Egypt and Northeast Africa, in T. Shaw, P. J. J. Sinclair, B. Andah and A. Okpoko (eds), *The Archaeology of Africa: Food, Metals and Towns*, 570–586. London: Routledge

**O'Connor, D. and S. Quirke (eds) 2003, *Mysterious Lands*. London: UCL Press**

**O'Connor, D. and A. Reid 2003a, Introduction — Locating Ancient Egypt in Africa: Modern Theories, Past Realities, in D. O'Connor and A. Reid (eds), *Ancient Egypt in Africa*, 1–22. London: UCL Press**

**O'Connor, D. and A. Reid (eds) 2003b, *Ancient Egypt in Africa*. London: UCL Press**

Oates, J. F., R. S. Bagnall, S. J. Clackson, A. A. O'Brien, J. D. Sosin, T. G. Wilfong and K.A. Worp (eds) n.d. *Checklist of Editions of Greek and Latin Papyri, Ostraca and Tablets*. http:// scriptorium.lib.duke.edu/papyrus/texts/clist.html

Oettermann, S. 1997, *The Panorama: History of a Mass Medium*. New York: Zone

d'Onofrio, C. 1967, *Gli Oblieschi di Roma*. Rome: Bulzoni

Ortega y Medina, J. 1962a, Monroismo arqueológico I. Un intento de compensación de Americanidad insuficiente, in *Ensayos, Tareas y Estudios Históricos*, 168–189. Mexico: Universidad Veracruzana

Ortega y Medina, J. 1962b, Monroismo arqueológico II. Un intento de compensación de Americanidad insuficiente, in *Ensayos, Tareas y Estudios Históricos*, 158–186. Mexico: Universidad Veracruzana

Ortega y Medina, J. 1987, *Zaguán abierto al México Republicano*. Mexico: Universidad Nacional Autónoma de México

Ozouf, M. 1988, *Festivals and the French Revolution*. Cambridge, Mass: Harvard UP

Pagdem, A. 1993, *European Encounters with the New World*. Yale: Yale UP

Parkinson, R. B. 1999, *Cracking Codes: the Rosetta Stone and Decipherment*. London: British Museum

Pascoe, C. F. 1901, *Two Hundred Years of the S. P. G.: An Historical Account of the Society for the Propagation of the Gospel in Foreign Parts, 1701–1900 (based on a digest of the Society's records)*. London: Society for the Propagation of the Gospel

Pascual González, J. 2001, Las jornadas en Siria y Palestina de Juan de Dios de la Rada y la expedición de la fragata de guerra Arapiles, in J. Córdoba Zoilo, R. Jiménez Zamudio and C. Sevilla Cueva (eds), *El Redescubrimiento del oriente próximo y Egipto antiguos*. Madrid: Centro Superior de Estudios de Asiriología y Egiptología

Paxton, M. 1986, Frederick Catherwood and the Maya. Reorientation of Nineteenth-Century Perceptions, in P. Briggs (ed.), *The Maya Image in the Western World*, 11–21. Albuquerque: University of New Mexico

Peacock, D. P. S. 1992, *Rome in the Desert: a Symbol of Power*. Southampton: University of Southampton Press

Pearce, S. 2000, Giovanni Battista Belzoni's Exhibition of the Reconstructed Tomb of Pharaoh Seti in 1821. *Journal of the History of Collections* 12, 109–125

Peet, T. E. 1912, *Rough Stone Monuments and their Builders.* London: Harper

Pennington, J. D. 1982, The Copts in Modern Egypt. *Middle Eastern Studies* 18, 158–179

Perpillou-Thomas, F. 1993, *Fêtes d'Egypte ptolémaïques et romaine d'après la documentation papyrologique grecque.* Studia Hellenistica 31, Leuven: Peeters

Perry, W. J. 1918, *The Megalithic Culture of Indonesia.* Manchester: Manchester UP

Perry, W. J. 1923, *The Children of the Sun: a Study in the Early History of Civilization.* London: Methuen

Perry, W. J. 1924, *The Growth of Civilization.* 1st edition, London: Methuen

Perry, W. J. 1926, *The Growth of Civilization.* 2nd edition, London: Methuen

Petrie, H. 1933, *Six Notes on the Bible from Flinders Petrie's Discoveries.* London: Search

Petrie, W. M. F. 1931, *Seventy Years in Archaeology.* London: Sampson Low, Marston and Co

Pfaffenberger, B. 1988, Fetishized Objects and Humanized Nature: Towards a Social Anthropology of Technology. *Man* 23, 236–252

Phelan, J. 1960, Neo Aztecism in the 18th Century and Genesis of Mexican Nationalism, in *Culture in History: Essays in Honor of Paul Rodin*, 760–770. New York: Columbia UP

Pococke, R. 1743–1745, *A Description of the East, and Some Other Countries.* London: W. Bowyer

Poethke, G. 1969, *Epimerismos: betrachtungen zur zwangspacht in Ägypten während der prinzipatzeit.* Brussels: Fondation Égyptologique Reine Elisabeth

Porter, J. R. 1977, Two Presidents of the Folklore Society: S. H. Hooke and E. O. James. *Folklore* 88, 131–145

Poulsen, F. 1912, *Der Orient und die frühgriechische kunst.* Leipzig: B.G. Teubner

Prakash, G. 1995, *After Colonialism: Imperial Histories and Postcolonial Displacements.* Princeton: Princeton UP

Pratt, M. 1992, *Imperial Eyes: Travel-Writing and Transculturation.* London: Routledge

Préaux, C. 1939, *L'Économie royale des lagides.* Brussels: Fondation Égyptologique Reine Elisabeth

Préaux, C. 1978, *Le Monde Hellénistique.* Nouvelle Clio 6, Paris: Presses Universitaires de France

**Price, C. and J-M. Humbert 2003, Introduction – An Architecture between Dream and Meaning, in J-M. Humbert and C. Price (eds), *Imhotep Today: Egyptianizing architecture*, 1–24. London: UCL Press**

Proudfoot, B. 1976, The Analysis and Interpretation of Soil Phosphorus in Archaeological Contexts, in D. A. Davidson and M. L. Shackley (eds), *Geoarchaeology: Earth Science and the Past*, 93–113. London: Duckworth

Quibell, A. A. 1925, *A Wayfarer in Egypt.* London: Methuen

Rada y Delgado, J. de D. de la 1875, *Antiguedades del Cerro de los Santos en el término de Montealegre (discurso leído ante la Real Academia de la Historia).* Madrid: T. Fortanet

Rada y Delgado, J. de D. de la 1876, *Viaje a oriente de la fragata de Guerra Arapiles y de la Comisión Científica que Llevó a Bordo.* Barcelona: Jaime Jepús Roviralta

Ramírez, F. 1982, La Visión Europea de la América tropical: los artistas viajeros, in *Historia del Arte Mexicano*, 138–163. México: Secretaría de Educación Pública, Instituto Nacional de Bellas Artes

Rashed, R. 1980, Science as a Western Phenomenon. *Fundamentae Scientiae* I, 7–21

Rathbone, D. W. 1991, *Economic Rationalism and Rural Society in Third-Century AD Egypt: the Heroninos Archive and the Appianus Estate.* Cambridge: CUP

Reeves, N. 1990, *The Complete Tutankhamun*. London: Thames and Hudson

Reghellini de Schio, M. 1825, *Esprit du dogme de la Franche-Maçonnerie. Recherche sur son origine et celle de ses différents rites, Compris Celui du Carbonarisme*. Brussels

Reghellini de Schio, M. 1833, *La Maçonnerie considérée comme le résultat des religions Égyptienne, Juive et Chrétienne*. Paris: Dondey-Dupré

**Reid, A. 2003, Ancient Egypt and the Source of the Nile, in D. O'Connor and A. Reid (eds), *Ancient Egypt in Africa*, 55–76. London: UCL Press**

Reid, D. M. 1985, Indigenous Egyptology: the Decolonization of a Profession? *Journal of the American Oriental Society* 105, 233–246

Reid, D. M. 1998, The 'Urabi Revolution and the British Conquest, 1879–1882, in M. W. Daly (ed.), *Cambridge History of Egypt. Volume 2: Modern Egypt from 1517 to the End of the Twentieth Century*, 217–238. Cambridge: CUP

Reid, D. M. 2002, *Whose Pharaohs? Archaeology, Museums, and Egyptian National Identity from Napoleon to World War I.* Berkeley: University of California Press

Reinach, S. 1893, *Le Mirage Oriental*. Paris: Masson

Renfrew C. and P. Bahn 1991, *Archaeology: Theories, Methods and Practice*. New York: Thames and Hudson

Renfrew, C. 1973, *Before Civilization: the Radiocarbon Revolution and Prehistoric Europe*. London: Jonathan Cape

Reparaz, G. de 1907, *Política de España en África*. Barcelona: Imprenta Barcelonesa

**Rice, M. and S. MacDonald, Introduction – Tea With A Mummy: The Consumer's View of Egypt's Immemorial Appeal, in S. MacDonald and M. Rice (eds), *Consuming Ancient Egypt*, 1–22. London: UCL Press**

Ridley, R. T. 1998, *Napoleon's Proconsul in Egypt: the Life and Times of Bernardino Drovetti*. London: Rubicon

Riegel, H. 1996, In the Heart of the Irony: Ethnographic Exhibitions and the Politics of Difference, in S. MacDonald and G. Fyfe (eds), *Theorising Museums*, 83–104. Oxford: Blackwell

Rivers, W. H. R. 1906, *The Todas*. London: Macmillan

Rivers, W. H. R. 1914, *The History of Melanesian Society.* Cambridge: CUP

Roberts, D. 1849, *Egypt and Nubia 3.* London: F. G. Moon

Rojas Garciadueñas, J. 1988, Carlos de Sirgueza y Góngora y el primer ejemplo de arte neo-prehispánico en América (1680), in D. Schavelzón, *La Polémica del arte nacional*, 47–51, Mexico: Fondo de Cultura Económica

Rostovtzeff, M. I. (Rostowzew) 1910, *Studien zur Geschichte des römischen Kolonates. Archiv.* Leipzig and Berlin: Beiheft I

Rostovtzeff, M. I. 1926, *Social and Economic History of the Roman Empire*. Oxford: OUP

Rostovtzeff, M. I. 1941, *Social and Economic History of the Hellenistic World*. Oxford: Clarendon

Roth, A. M. 1995, Building Bridges to Afrocentrism: a Letter to my Egyptological Colleagues. *Newsletter of the American Research Center in Egypt* 167, 14–17; 168, 885–892

Roth, A. M. 1998, Ancient Egypt in America: Claiming the Riches, in L. Meskell (ed.), *Archaeology Under Fire: Nationalism, Politics and Heritage in the Eastern Mediterranean and Middle East*, 217–229. London: Routledge

Rowlands, M. 1989, A Question of Complexity, in D. Miller, M. Rowlands and C. Y. Tilley (eds), *Domination and Resistance*, 29–40. London: Unwin Hyman

Rowlands, M. 1994, Childe and the Archaeology of Freedom, in D. Harris (ed.), *The Archaeology of V. Gordon Childe: Contemporary Perspectives*, 35–50. London: UCL Press

Rowlands, M. 1998, Ritual Killing and Historical Transformation in a West African Kingdom, in K. Kristiansen and M. Rowlands (eds), *Social Transformations in Archaeology: Global and Local Perspectives*, 397–409. London: Routledge

Rowlandson, J. 1996, *Landowners and Tenants in Roman Egypt: the Social Relations of Agriculture in the Oxyrhynchite Nome*. Oxford: OUP

Rudich, V. 2000, The Return of the Exile: Mikhail Rostovtsev in the Post-Soviet Russia. *Journal of Roman Archaeology* 13, 449–452

Ruiz Bremón, M. 1989, *Los Exvotos del santuario Ibérico del Cerro de los Santos*. Albacete: Instituto de Estudios Albacetenes

Russell, E. J. 1957, *The World of the Soil*. London: Collins

Russell, L. 1997, Focusing on the Past: Visual and Textual Images of Aboriginal Australia in Museums, in B. Molyneaux (ed.), *The Cultural Life of Images. Visual Representation in Archaeology*, 230–248. London: Routledge

Saad, Z. Y. 1937, Khazza Lawizza. *Annales du Service des Antiquités de l'Égypte* 37, 212–218

Sadat, A. El 1978, *In Search of Identity – An Autobiography*. New York: Harper and Row

Sahlins, M. 1985, *Islands of History*. Chicago: University of Chicago Press

Said, E. 1978, *Orientalism*. New York: Vintage

Said, E. 1993, *Culture and Imperialism*. London: Chatto and Windus

Salt, H. 1825, *Essay on Dr Young's and M. Champollion's Phonetic System of Hieroglyphics; with some Additional Discoveries by Which it may be Applied to Decipher the Names of the Ancient Kings of Egypt and Ethiopia*. London: Longman, Hurst, Rees, Orme, Brown and Green

Sasson, J. M. 1995, *Civilizations of the Ancient Near East, Vol. 1*. New York: Charles Scribner's Sons

Savirón, P. 1875, Noticia de varias excavaciones del Cerro de los Santos. *Revista de Archivos, Bibliotecas y Museos* 1875, nos. 8, 10, 12 and 14

Sayce, A. H. 1911, Preface, in K. Mikhail, *Copts and Moslems under British Control (Egypt). A Collection of Facts and a Resumé of Authoritative Opinions on the Coptic Question*, vii–xiv. London: Smith, Elder and Co

Scarre, C. 1994, The Meaning of Death: Funerary Beliefs and the Prehistorian, in C. Renfrew and E. Zubrow (eds), *The Ancient Mind: Elements of Cognitive Archaeology*, 75–82. Cambridge: CUP

**Schadla-Hall, R. T. and G. Morris 2003, Ancient Egypt on the Small Screen – From Fact to Faction in the UK, in S. MacDonald and M. Rice (eds), *Consuming Ancient Egypt*, 195–216. London: UCL Press**

Scham, S. 2001, The Archaeology of the Disenfranchised. *Journal of Archaeological Method and Theory* 8, 183–209

Schama, S. 1995, *Landscape and Memory*. London: Fontana

Schayes, A. G. B. 1854, *Catalogue et description du Musée Royal d'Armures, d'Antiquités et d'Artillerie*. Brussels: Jmar

Scheidel, W. 2001, *Death on the Nile: Disease and the Demography of Roman Egypt*. Leiden: Brill

Segal, R. 2002, *Islam's Black Slaves: a History of Africa's Other Diaspora*. London: Atlantic

Sergi, G. 1904, *The Mediterranean Race: a Study of the Origin of European Peoples*. London: Walter Scott

**Sevilla Cueva, C. 2003, Vicent Lleó's Operetta: *La Corte de Faraón*, in S. MacDonald and M. Rice (eds), *Consuming Ancient Egypt*, 63–76. London: UCL Press**

Shanks, M. and C. Tilley 1987, *Reconstructing Archaeology*. London: Routledge

Shaw, B. 1992, Under Russian Eyes. *Journal of Roman Studies* 82, 216–228

Shepherd, N. 1987, *The Zealous Intruders: the Western Rediscovery of Palestine*. London: Collins

Sherratt, A.G. 1997, *Economy and Society in Prehistoric Europe: Changing Perspectives*. Edinburgh: Edinburgh UP

Silberman, N. A. 1990, *Digging for God and Country. Exploration in the Holy Land 1799–1917*. New York: Knopf

Sladen, D. 1908, *Egypt and the English, Showing Public Opinion in Egypt upon the Egyptian Question: with Chapters on the Success of the Sudan and the Delights of Travel in Egypt and the Sudan*. London: Hurst and Blackett

Smith, A. D. 1986, *The Ethnic Origins of Nations*. Oxford: Blackwell

Smith, G. E. 1911, *The Ancient Egyptians and their Influence on the Civilization of Europe*. London: Harper

Smith, G. E. 1915, *The Migrations of Early Culture*. Manchester: Manchester UP

Smith, G. E. 1916, The Cranial Cast of the Piltdown Skull. *Man* 16, 131–132

Smith, G. E. 1919, *The Evolution of the Dragon*. Manchester: Manchester UP

Smith, G. E. 1923, *The Ancient Egyptians and the Origins of Civilization*. London: Harper

Smith, G. E. 1925, The London Skull. *Nature* 116, 678–680

Smith, G. E. 1927, Reports on the Human Remains in No. 5 Barrow at Dunstable. *Man* 27, 25–27

Smith, G. E. 1930, *Human History*. London: Cape

Smith, H. S. 1969, Animal Domestication and Animal Cult in Dynastic Egypt, in P. J. Ucko and G. W. Dimbleby (eds), *The Domestication and Exploitation of Plants and Animals*, 307–314. London: Duckworth

Solano Ortíz de Rozas, J. 1793, *Idea del Imperio Otomano. Parte histórica del diario de navegación, que en su viaje a Constantinopla en el año de 1778 Hizo el Capitán de fragata de la Real Armada Joseph Solano Ortíz de Rozas. En el que se da razón de otro viaje que ejecutó a Constantinopla en el anterior de 1786 y del que posteriormente hizo a Nápoles y Liorne en el de 1789*

Solé, R. and D. Valbelle 1999, *La Pierre de Rosette*. Paris: Edition du Seuil

Sowada, K. 1994, A Late Eighteenth Dynasty Statue in the Nicholson Museum, Sydney. *Journal of Egyptian Archaeology* 80, 137–143

Spencer, P. 1999, Egyptology, Past, Present and Future. *Egyptian Archaeology* 15, 1–5

Stavrianos, L. S. 1981, *Global Rift: The Third World Comes of Age*. New York: William Morrow

Steel, A. 1919, Shebin-el-Kanater, Evangelistic. *E. G. M. News, the Official Paper of the Egypt General Mission* 19, 57–59

Stephen, L. and S. Lee 1963, *Dictionary of National Biography – Dictionary of National Biography from the Earliest Times to 1900*. Oxford: OUP

Stephens, J. 1837, *Incidents of Travel in Egypt, Arabia, Petraea, and the Holy Land*. New York: Harper

Stephens, J. [1841] 1969, *Incidents of Travel in Central America, Chiapas and Yucatan*. London and New York: Dover

Stephens, J. 1843, *Incidents of Travel in Yucatan*. New York: Dover

Stocking, G. 1985, *Objects and Others: Essays on Museums and Material Culture*. Madison: University of Winconsin Press

Stocking, G. 1987, *Victorian Anthropology*. New York: Free Press

Stocking, G. 1996, *After Tylor: British Social Anthropology, 1888–1951*. London: Athlone

Storrs, R. [1937] 1943, *Orientations*. London: Nicholson and Watson

Suter, C. 2000, *Gudea's Temple Building: the Representation of an Early Mesopotamian Ruler in Text and Image*. Groningen: Styx

**Tait, J. 2003, The Wisdom of Egypt: Classical Views, in P. J. Ucko and T. C. Champion (eds), *The Wisdom of Egypt: changing visions through the ages*, 23–38. London: UCL Press**

*The Medal Yearbook*. Honiton: Token

*The Survey of London* 1897. London: Athlone

Thomas, N. 1995, *The American Discovery of Ancient Egypt: Essays*. Los Angeles: Los Angeles County Museum of Art

Thompson D. J. and W. Clarysse forthcoming, *Counting the People*. Cambridge: CUP

Thompson, J. 1992, *Sir Gardner Wilkinson and His Circle*. Austin: University of Texas Press

Tillett, S. 1984, *Egypt Itself*. London: SD Books

Toda, E. 1886, *Sesostris*. Madrid: Manuel Ginés Hernández

Toda, E. 1887, Son notém en tebas. *Boletín de la Real Academia de la Historia* 10, 91–148

Toda, E. 1920, La Découverte et l'inventaire du tombeau de Sen-Nezem. *Annales du Service des Antiquités de l'Egypte* 20, 145–160

Toledano, E. R. 1998, Social and Economic Change and the 'Long Nineteenth Century', in M. W. Daly (ed.), *Cambridge History of Egypt. Volume 2: Modern Egypt from 1517 to the End of the Twentieth Century*, 252–284. Cambridge: CUP

Tompkins, P. 1981, *The Magic of Obelisks*. New York: Harper

Trigger, B. G. 1979, Egypt and the Comparative Study of Early Civilizations, in K. Weeks (ed.), *Egypt and the Social Sciences: Five Studies*, 23–56. Cairo: American University in Cairo

Trigger, B. G. 1980, *Gordon Childe: Revolutions in Archaeology*. London: Thames and Hudson

Trigger, B. G. 1981, Akhenaten and Durkheim. *Bulletin de l'Institut Français d'Archéologie Oriental du Caire* 81 (supplement), 165–184

Trigger, B. G. 1984, Alternative Archaeologies: Nationalist, Colonialist, Imperialist. *Man* 19, 355–370

Trigger, B. G. 1985, The Past as Power: Anthropology and the American Indian, in I. MacBride (ed.), *Who Owns the Past?*, 11–40. Oxford: OUP

Trigger, B. G. 1989, *A History of Archaeological Thought*. Cambridge: CUP

Trigger, B. G. 1993, *Early Civilizations: Ancient Egypt in Context*. Cairo: American University in Cairo

Tritle, L. 1996, Chapel Hill Review of Not Out of Africa. *Bryn Mawr Classical Review* 96/5/7

Turner, E. G. 1984, Ptolemaic Egypt, in F. W. Walbank, A. E. Astin, M. W. Frederiksen and R. M. Ogilvie (eds), *The Cambridge Ancient History* 7, 118–174. Cambridge: CUP


Ucko, P. J. 1998, The Biography of a Collection: the Sir Flinders Petrie Palestinian Collection and the Role of University Museums. *Museum Management and Curatorship* 17, 4, 351–399

Ucko, P. J. 2001, Unprovenanced Material Culture and Freud's Collection of Antiquities. *Journal of Material Culture* 6, 269–322

**Ucko, P. J. and T. C. Champion (eds) 2003, *The Wisdom of Egypt: changing visions through the ages*. London: UCL Press**

Usick, P. 2002, *Adventures in Egypt and Nubia: The Travels of William John Bankes (1786–1855)*. London: British Museum Press


Van Dommelen, P. 1998, *On Colonial Grounds: a Comparative Study of Colonialism and Rural Settlement in First Millennium BC West Central Sardinia*. Faculty of Archaeology, University of Leiden

Vázquez, J. 1976, Los primeros tropiezos, in D. Cosío Villegas (ed.), *Historia General de México*, 3–60, México: Colegio de Mexico

Vico, G. B. [1725] 1968, *The New Science of Giambattista Vico* (trans. of the 3rd edition of *La Scienza Nuova* (1744) by Thomas Goddard Bergin and Max Harold Fisch). Ithaca: Cornell UP

Vidal-Naquet, P. 1967, *Le Bordereau d'ensemencement dans l'Egypte ptolémaique*. Brussels: Fondation Égyptologique Reine Elisabeth


Walzer, M. 1974, *Regicide and Revolution: Speeches at the Trial of Louis XVI*. Cambridge: CUP

Watson, C. M. 1909, *The Life of Major-General Sir Charles William Wilson*. London: John Murray

Weeks, K. 1979, *Egyptology and the Social Sciences*. Cairo: American University in Cairo

Weigall, A. E. P. B. 1915, *A History of Events in Egypt from 1798 to 1914*, Edinburgh and London: William Blackwood

Weiner, J. 2001, 'An Artist of Strong Jewish Feeling': Simeon Solomon's Depictions of Jewish Ceremonies, in *From Prodigy to Outcast, Simeon Solomon: Pre-Raphaelite Artist*, 14–22. London: Jewish Museum

Wengrow, D. 1998, The Changing Face of Clay: Continuity and Change in the Transition from Village to Urban Life in the Near East. *Antiquity* 72, 783–795

Wengrow, D. 1999, The Intellectual Adventure of Henri Frankfort: a Missing Chapter in the History of Archaeological Thought. *American Journal of Archaeology* 103, 597–613

Wengrow, D. 2001, Rethinking 'Cattle Cults' in Early Egypt: Towards a Prehistoric Perspective on the Narmer Palette. *Cambridge Archaeology Journal* 11, 91–104

**Werner, A. 2003, Egypt in London – Public and Private Displays in the 19th Century Metropolis, in J-M. Humbert and C. Price (eds), *Imhotep Today: Egyptianizing architecture*, 75–104. London: UCL Press**

Wes, M. A. 1990 *Michael Rostovtzeff, Historian in Exile: Russian Roots in an American Context*. Stuttgart: Historia Einzelschr. LXV

Whateley, M. 1870, *Ragged Life in Egypt, and More about Ragged Life in Egypt*. London: Seeley, Jackson and Halliday

**Wheatcroft, A. 2003, 'Wonderful Things': Publishing Egypt in Word and Image, in S. MacDonald and M. Rice (eds), *Consuming Ancient Egypt*, 151–164. London: UCL Press**

Wheeler, R. E. M. 1925, *Prehistoric and Roman Wales*. Oxford: Clarendon

Whitehouse, H. 1995, Egypt in European Thought, in J. M. Sasson (ed.), *Civilizations of the Ancient Near East 1*, 15–32. New York: Charles Scribner's Sons

Wilkinson, J. Gardner 1836, *Manners and Customs of the Ancient Egyptians*. London: John Murray

Wilkinson, J. Gardner 1878, *Manners and Customs of the Ancient Egyptians*. New edition, revised and corrected by Samuel Birch, London: John Murray

Willey, G. and J. Sabloff 1974, *A History of American Archaeology*. San Francisco: Freeman

Wilson, E. 1972, *To the Finland Station: a Study in the Writing and Acting of History*. London: Fontana/Collins

Wilson, J. A. 1964, *Signs and Wonders upon Pharaoh: a History of American Egyptology*. Chicago: Chicago UP

Winlock, H. and W. Crum 1926, *The Monastery of Epiphanius at Thebes: Part I*. New York: Metropolitan Museum of Art

Wissa, H. F. 1994, *Assiout, the Saga of an Egyptian Family*. Sussex: Book Guild

Wolf, E. 1982, *Europe and the People without History*. Berkeley: University of California Press

Wood, A. and F. Oldham 1954, *Thomas Young, Natural Philosopher 1773–1829*. Cambridge: CUP

Wood, M. 1998, The Use of the Pharaonic Past in Modern Egyptian Nationalism. *Journal of the American Research Center in Egypt* 35, 179–196

Wood-Martin, W. G. 1888, *The Rude Stone Monuments of Ireland*. Dublin: Hodges, Figgis

Woodward, A. S. and G. E. Smith 1917, Fourth Note on the Piltdown Gravel, with Evidence of a Second Skull of Eanthropus Dawsoni. *Journal of the Geological Society* 73, 1–10

Yoffee, N. 1993, Too Many Chiefs? (or, Safe Texts for the '90s), in N. Yoffee and A. Sherratt (eds), *Archaeological Theory: Who Sets the Agenda?*, 60–78. Cambridge: CUP

Young, R. 1990, *White Mythologies: Writing History and the West*. London: Routledge

# Index

**Note: figure numbers are denoted in bold type.**